THE POLITICAL ECONOMY
OF THE FAMILY FARM

PRAEGER SERIES IN POLITICAL ECONOMY

Rodney Green, *Series Editor*

Production, Distribution, and Growth in Transitional Economies
M. Katherine Perkins
1988

The Social and Political Implications of the 1984 Jesse Jackson
Presidential Campaign
Edited by Lorenzo Morris
1990

A Classical Approach to Occupational Wage Rates
David Gleicher and Lonnie Stevans
1991

THE POLITICAL ECONOMY OF THE FAMILY FARM

The Agrarian Roots of American Capitalism

Sue Headlee

Praeger Series in Political Economy

New York
Westport, Connecticut
London

The data utilized in this book were made available by the Inter-University Consortium for Political and Social Research. The agricultural and demographic records for rural households in the North, 1860, were originally collected by Fred Bateman and James D. Foust under a grant from the National Science Foundation. Neither the original collectors of the data nor the Consortium bear any responsibility for the analyses or interpretations present here.

Library of Congress Cataloging-in-Publication Data

Headlee, Sue E. (Sue Eleanor)
    The political economy of the family farm : the agrarian roots of
American capitalism / Sue Headlee.
        p.   cm. — (Praeger series in political economy)
    Includes bibliographical references and index.
    ISBN 0-275-93806-9 (alk. paper)
    1. Family farms—United States—History—19th century.
2. Capitalism—United States—History—19th century. 3. United
States—Industries—History—19th century. 4. Social classes—
United States—History—19th century. 5. United States—Economic
conditions—To 1865. 6. United States—Economic
conditions—1865-1918.   I. Title.   II. Series.
HD1476.U5H43   1991
338.1'6—dc20   91-19354

British Library Cataloguing in Publication Data is available.

Library of Congress Catalog Card Number: 91-19354
ISBN: 0-275-93806-9

First published in 1991

Praeger Publishers, One Madison Avenue, New York, NY 10010
An imprint of Greenwood Publishing Group, Inc.

Printed in the United States of America

The paper used in this book complies with the
Permanent Paper Standard issued by the National
Information Standards Organization (Z39.48-1984).

10 9 8 7 6 5 4 3 2 1

To my parents

Eleanor and Raymond Headlee

CONTENTS

TABLES

ACKNOWLEDGMENTS

This book grew out of my Ph.D. dissertation on the same topic, and I would like to thank Cynthia Taft Morris, the chair of my dissertation committee, for teaching me how to do cliometrics and how to measure institutional variables. I am also grateful to Wayne Rasmussen, recently retired historian of the U.S. Department of Agriculture, for teaching me about nineteenth century U.S. agriculture and life on a family farm.

I appreciate the help that Subodh Mathur gave me on developing my econometric models. Thanks are also due to Judith Klein for informing me about the computerized data sample which is the basis of my statistical and econometric analyses and for talking nineteenth-century agriculture with me. The data utilized in this book were made available by the Inter-University Consortium for Political and Social Research. The agricultural and demographic records for rural households in the North, 1860, were originally collected by Fred Bateman and James D. Foust under a grant from the National Science Foundation. Neither the original collectors of the data nor the Consortium bear any responsibility for the analyses or interpretations presented here.

Rodney Green, editor of this Series in Political Economy, was extremely helpful to me in writing the introduction to the book and locating it in the larger body of political economy literature. I also want to thank John Weeks who first taught me the theory of political economy.

I am grateful to Phillip Scribner for teaching me about the philosophy of social science.

Finally, I thank Jeffrey Reiman for teaching me about political philosophy and reflection in general. I am thrilled to be married to him.

This book is dedicated to my parents, Eleanor and Raymond Headlee.

THE POLITICAL ECONOMY
OF THE FAMILY FARM

INTRODUCTION:
DEBATES ON THE TRANSITION
TO CAPITALISM

This book is a study of the transition to capitalism in the United States in the mid-nineteenth century, especially the role of agriculture in that transition. My thesis is that the family farm system—with its progressive and egalitarian class structure—caused agriculture to play a revolutionary role in the transition to capitalism in the United States. By *progressive* I mean encouraging the development of productivity in the economy, and by *egalitarian* I mean no exploitation of one class by another. We shall see that the role of the family farm had economic and political aspects. To support this account, I present research on the economic relationships between family farming and fledgling industrial capitalism in the mid-nineteenth century. These economic relationships promoted the transition to capitalism by fostering simultaneous industrial and agricultural revolutions that resulted in the creation of an agro-industrial complex. At the same time, these economic relationships were the basis of a political alliance between family farmers and industrial capitalists in the form of the Republican Party, which enabled the industrial capitalists to take control of the state from the Democratic Party of the southern plantation owners. They were thus positioned to implement their economic policy program, which accelerated the transition to capitalism that was being constrained by the power of the slaveowners in the South.

In this introduction, I summarize the family farm thesis on the agrarian roots of American capitalism and then I relate my research to three important debates. First, I show that my findings support Maurice Dobb's position in his debate with Paul Sweezy on the transition from feudalism to capitalism in Western Europe.[1] Second, I explain how my research confirms Robert Brenner's view in his debate with British economic historians on the role of agrarian class structure in the economic development of pre-industrial Europe.[2] Third, I use my results to argue for the Beards-Hacker thesis on the role of the Civil War in the transition to capitalism in the United States.[3] It should be clear that these three debates are not about three isolated topics. Taken together, they provide the historical and theoretical context for understanding the role of agriculture in the transition to capitalism in general and in the particular case of the United States. The debates move from the very general level of analysis of the transition in Western Europe, through discussion of the role of agrarian class structure in that transition, to the specific consideration of this development in the mid-nineteenth-century United States. By relating my research to these three debates, I shall be able to show how U.S. development is linked to the European developments, of which it is an offshoot, and how all of these phenomena can be integrated into a single coherent theoretical framework.

THE AGRARIAN ROOTS OF AMERICAN CAPITALISM: THE FAMILY FARM THESIS

The family farm system in the nineteenth-century United States provided the agrarian roots of American capitalism. Marxist historians of European capitalism have argued that "the decisive part of the transition from feudalism to capitalism is played out in the countryside . . . , [a fact] not readily perceived when one is obsessed by the commercial and industrial manifestation of nascent capitalism."[4] I make this claim about American capitalism.

In the United States, capitalism's agrarian roots were of a specific nature which I call the family farm system. By *family farm*, I mean a family-owned farm with enough land to support the family and no more land than could be farmed by the labor force of the family. This implies that the family had no need to hire out family labor to supplement their income. If a family had less land than it needed to support itself, I call that a *family plot*, rather than a family farm. A family owning a family plot would have to supplement its income by performing wage labor off the family plot. This was rare in the nineteenth-century United States. That farm families did not have more land than could be farmed by the labor force of the family implies that they had no need to hire non-family labor. If a family had more land than they could operate and they did hire wage labor, I call that a *capitalist farm*, not a family farm. Again this was rare in the nineteenth-century United States.

Land policy in the United States made the ownership of a family farm possible for many families. The primary goal of farm families was to own their own farms. The primacy of this goal was due to the families' desire for political independence, liberty, and the rights secured by private property[5] and their desire for the material security that farm ownership provided. To achieve this goal of farm ownership, it was necessary to buy land and gain a legal, written title to the land. This in turn required credit and then cash. The need for cash provided the family farmer with the incentive to produce for the market. This incentive existed because of the unique opportunity for the common person in the United States to own private property. Tillers of the soil in modern world history have frequently desired to own land, once land was being appropriated; in the United States, this was at last a realistic desire for large numbers of people. The United States was known in common parlance as "the poor man's best country."

Land policy made ownership of a relatively large amount of land possible for the common person in the United States. This was due to several factors. First, there was a relative abundance of agricultural resources in the United States. Some of the best soil and climate on the globe for agriculture had not been cultivated by the native Americans and thus virgin land was there in abundance, unlike soil in Europe which had been cultivated for a thousand years. Unowned land in the public domain expanded greatly over time: from 1785, land west of the Allegheny Mountains was available; after 1803, land west of the Mississippi River became available; and as a result of the war with Mexico, even more land was added after 1845. Second, and more important, this abundant land was distributed in a relatively equal manner. Due to its political solidarity, the family farm community was able to win the struggle in Congress to continually liberalize land policy. Initially, the minimum-size parcel of land was too large to be afforded by common people. Under Jefferson and later under Jackson, the minimum size parcel was reduced so that a cultivator could afford to buy enough farm land to support his family and even a surplus of land beyond that. This, then, is why the family farmers had a potential surplus beyond the needs of the family to sell on the market. The farmers had an incentive to work hard and produce a surplus because they received the full product of that effort. There was no absolutist state demanding heavy taxes, as there was in Europe. There was no aristocratic land-owning class demanding heavy rent, as there was in Europe. This policy of a wide distribution of ample land produced many farmers with sufficient surplus and incentive to purchase capital goods and produce for the market.

In the early nineteenth century, family farms were mostly subsistence farms, not as much out of desire as out of necessity. The transportation system was not developed, and there was not much of a market for surplus production. Thus they did not produce much of a surplus. In this pioneer stage, family farmers were engaged in clearing the land of trees and in farm-making activities in general. They were also engaged in general farming: they produced a large variety of crops and livestock to meet the varied needs of the family. Under these conditions, the farm family could operate a large amount of land with family labor. Some surplus of several of their outputs was sold on local markets to give farm families the small amount of cash they needed to buy commodities that they could not make themselves, such as salt and guns. They also sold timber from clearing the forests for farm land. Uncleared land was used for livestock to forage in.

The family farm system was changed by the industrialization of the East Coast. After recovering from the depression of 1837 to 1843, the East began to industrialize rapidly. In the 1830s, the Erie Canal was built connecting the East and West. Railroads connecting the East and West were built in the 1850s. This provided the opportunity to produce for the eastern market, for which the western farmers were waiting. But the new commercial farming was specialized and had different labor requirements than their prior farm making and general farming. This posed a problem for the family farmers. To plant a large field of wheat in response to its high price would require a large labor force to harvest it, probably more than a farm family could provide. Commercial production of livestock would also require a large amount of corn to feed the livestock. To cultivate a large amount of corn would require more labor than the farm family had, but it would have been risky for a family farmer to hire a permanent wage-labor force.

Farmers were not risk takers, as capitalist entrepreneurs are. The most important implication of this is that the family farm was overwhelmingly dependent on family labor. The incentive to own a farm did not lead the farm family to hire labor and expand output to earn cash to finance the farm, because this would be a threat to the long-term goal of farm ownership. If a farm family hired labor and increased production with it on more land, leased or bought, and there were an economic downturn, they might have had to default on loans they had on land or farm equipment. On the demand side, the possibility of losing farm ownership led the farm families to use only family labor, which could be sustained with minimal cash outlays, and not depend upon a permanent wage-labor force. On the supply side, because farm family had enough land to support themselves, they were not likely to hire out any family members. Thus, the nature of the family farm system prevented the development of a market (both demand- and supply-side) for wage labor.

Due to risk aversion, the option to hire labor was rejected. While it is true that there was little labor available for hire, it is also true that industry and construction were finding wage labor. If the family farmers had been risk-taking capitalists they would have paid a higher wage and would have obtained the wage labor they needed. Moreover, immigration could have been encouraged to provide a labor force.

Unwilling and unable (because little was available) to hire labor, the family farm had to mechanize to increase its output. Therefore, the decision to specialize and commercialize had to be simultaneous with the decision to mechanize. With farm machinery, the farm family was able to spread limited family labor over abundant family land. Because of the goal of farm ownership, the farmer went into debt; to pay off the debt he had to produce for the market. When the farmer's debt or desire for cash reached a certain magnitude representing the need to produce a given amount for the market, the capacity of the farm family's labor was stretched to the limit and the pressure to mechanize began. Thus the family farm system was to be the form of the agricultural sector in the United States.

Turning now from the micro-economics of the family farm to the macro-economics of industrialization, we see that the family farm system served many of the essential needs of an industrializing country. When it commercialized and mechanized, the family farm system increased its production dramatically. It provided cheap food for industrial workers, thus creating downward pressure on labor costs and making room for substantial profits for all industrial capitalists. In the mid-nineteenth century much of the GNP was raw materials produced on the farm and processed in factories: wheat milling, corn grinding, liquor, leather and lumber processing. The family farm system provided all these raw materials in abundance and cheaply. Industrial capitalism also needs a home market for what it produces: consumer goods and producer goods. Because of the equal distribution of abundant land to farm families, there was a massive and prosperous land-owning population to be that market. In addition, in the early stages of capitalist development, most of the population was rural and thus the market for consumer goods had to be rural. The prosperous family farm system provided a mass market for capitalist industry that produced cotton and woolen goods, men's clothing, boots and shoes, and so on.

The family farm system was a very important market for producer goods. What follows documents this key transaction in the transition to capitalism in the United States: the production of horse-drawn farm machinery for purchase by the family farmers in the 1850s. This machinery was invented and then mass-produced for this family farm market. This was a tremendous stimulus to the capitalist manufacture of machinery. The backward link from agricultural development to the growth in the sector of the capitalist manufacture of farm machinery was crucial. Without the farm machinery, the food needs of the U.S. industrialization probably would not have been met. But without the family farm system, the mass production of that machinery probably would not have been taken on by American entrepreneurial capitalists. The horse-drawn mechanical reaper to harvest the wheat crop was the first (and most important) of a set of horse-drawn machinery that was invented and diffused over the remaining decades of the nineteenth century until World War I.

A major factor that held back the transition to industrial capitalism was the slave oligarchy's control of the federal government, the Presidency, the Congress, and the Supreme Court. The economic links described above between the family farmers and the industrial capitalists were the economic basis of the formation of the Republican Party and subsequent election of Lincoln, followed by the Civil War and the abandonment of Congress by southern senators and representatives. The industrial capitalists probably would not have achieved this political victory without the support of the family farmers.[6] The farmers' desertion of the agrarian Democratic Party and their alliance with the industrial capitalists in the Republican Party did lead to a social revolution at the state level where a new class took political power. After the Civil War, conservative Republicans reconstructed the North with their economic policy package. This made way for the triumph of U.S. industrial capitalism—this is the Beards-Hacker thesis.

The economic policy package of the Civil War Congresses removed the constraints on capitalism and added spurs to its development. In 1862, the Republican Congress prohibited slavery in the territories. Slavery in the territories would have inhibited the advance of industrial capitalism in two ways. Politically, if slave states were created out of the territories, the federal government would remain under the domination of the slaveowners in the South. Economically, the slave system provided no market for industrial capitalism. The slave plantations used few complex capital goods, due to the coercive nature of the master-slave relation, and thus there was no market for producer goods. Slave plantations were self-sufficient and thus no market for consumer goods, or even marketed food.

In addition to eliminating the constraint on capitalist development represented by slavery, the Civil War Congresses provided five spurs to industrial capitalism. In 1862, Congress granted the charters for the first transcontinental railroads connecting the East and West Coasts of the North American continent, thus creating the largest market in the world capitalist economy. The Homestead Act of 1862 and the sale of railroad land ensured that this vast territory would be filled with family farms, which constituted a market for industrial goods. This enormous market was then protected by a tariff enacted in 1861 and kept high throughout the entire process of industrialization of the United States in the rest of the nineteenth century. Industrial capitalism needs more than a market, however; it needs capital and labor. To help with capital formation, a national currency and a system of national banks were set up in 1863 and 1864. And in order to provide labor, it was necessary to liberalize procedures for immigration, which the Congress did in 1864.

With this social revolution in the class in power in the United States and the economic policy package in place, the transition to capitalism was rapidly achieved by the "robber barons" of the post-Civil War era[7] and culminated in the Gilded Age of the turn of the century. The Civil War was a social revolution because it removed from power the pre-capitalist ruling class of slaveowners and related northern merchants and replaced them with a ruling class made up of industrial capitalists and their allies, the family farmers. The economy had been struggling through the transition to capitalism but was held back by the pre-capitalist political power. With that removed, capitalism could speed ahead and triumph.

The transition to capitalism in the United States begins and ends with economic policy. Egalitarian land policy created the family farm system. The family farmers' alliance with industrial capitalists under the Republican Party made possible the economic policy package described above. This has implications for Third World development policy and even for U.S. economic policy today.[8] My study suggests that equal income and wealth distribution is good, not bad, for capitalist development. It presents an alternative to the view that inequality is needed for modern economic growth.

The view of the family farm developed here is an alternative to the neoclassical economic theory of the profit-maximizing farm. The family farm is quite different from a neoclassical firm: while the output is commercialized, the inputs, such as labor, are not commercialized. In Chapter 2 I do use neoclassical theory to see how far it can be stretched to accommodate the family farm. One can make the family farmer a utility maximizer instead of a profit maximizer. Then one can insert the desire for homeownership into the utility function. One can make the family farmer risk-averse. But one cannot place the desire for political independence, for liberty, and for the rights secured by private property into the neoclassical utility function. This is what drove the American family farmer. One must also appreciate the lack of exploitation in the family farm system. This is what made the American family farm system different from the English capitalist farm system that did exploit wage labor. This is why one needs to add politics to economics in one's analysis of the family farm and why one needs to look at the class structure of all agrarian systems.

The explanation of the adoption of agricultural improvements by the family farm system developed here is likewise an alternative to the neoclassical economic theory that market forces are the most important factor in explaining economic change. More precisely, what is at issue between neoclassical economists on the one hand, and Marxists and other institutionalists on the other hand, is the relative importance of market forces and institutional change in causing development. This difference is especially important in the case of explaining the transition to capitalism when institutions are changing. Neoclassical economists assume that there is no change in institutions, whereas Marxian analysts focus on the change in institutions in the transition to capitalism. Thus the latter has more explanatory power.

The rise of markets, especially the market for grain, appears to have caused great agricultural improvements in the North of the United States in the nineteenth century. American economic historians put too much emphasis on these market forces. They say that the high price of wheat caused American farmers to supply great quantities of wheat which they were able to produce by specializing, commercializing, and mechanizing farm production. The model accepted by American economic historians, such as the one devised by Paul David, is incomplete.[9] The major problem in this model is that it treats the family farm as a neoclassical profit-maximizing firm. The family farm system is characterized here by its use of family labor, whereas neoclassical profit-maximizing firms use wage labor. To confound the two prevents us from understanding the difference between the English road to capitalism (based on wage labor) and the American road (based on family labor). In the family farm system there is no exploitation of class by class. Everyone was in the same class. Moreover, the farm family had a hierarchy of economic objectives. At the top of the hierarchy, it sought utility in farm ownership. Next, it sought to secure present and future consumption. Instead of seeking to maximize consumption, it sought a level and a stability of consumption consistent with the higher goal of farm ownership. Family farmers were risk-averse, unlike capitalist entrepreneurs. In capitalist agriculture, the capitalist farmer exploits the agricultural wage laborer.[10] Neoclassical profit-maximizing firms would own farm land only if it would maximize profits and they do not pursue utility as family households do. As we will see, its unique features led the family farm to adopt agricultural improvements before a profit-maximizing firm would have done so in response to the dictates of the market.

The relative scarcity of labor in the United States appears to have caused agricultural improvements in the North, especially the substitution of capital for labor in the form of farm machinery. Again, American economic historians put too much emphasis on market forces. They say that the relative rise in the price of labor—David's view, or the relative scarcity of labor, the view of Heywood Fleisig[11]—caused American farmers to mechanize their farm operations. But it was not market forces alone, or even primarily, that kept the family farm overwhelmingly dependent on family labor. On the supply side, the ability of the farm family to own enough land to support their family meant that they did not have to sell their labor on the market. On the demand side, the goal of farm ownership prevented them from taking the risk of hiring a permanent wage-labor force on the market. Moreover, because the family farm did not depend on the market for labor, it was not subject to the dictates of the market. Market forces alone cannot explain the behavior of the family farm.

Finally, neoclassical economics and supply-side economics of the 1980s argue for more income and wealth inequality to spur savings, investment, and growth. My research suggests the opposite: that income and wealth equality, given the abundance of resources in the United States, led to a mass market for mass production which led to unprecedented economic growth and improved standards of living.

In the next three sections I will show how my study sheds light on three debates on the relative importance of market forces and institutions in the transition to capitalism. In the transition to capitalism, class relations and institutions are changing. Neoclassical economic theory holds institutions constant and thus is not well equipped to explain such revolutionary change. Marxian social scientists and other institutionalists are in a much better position to explain the transition of a society from one mode of production to another.

THE TRANSITION FROM FEUDALISM TO CAPITALISM IN EUROPE

In the 1950s, an international debate on the transition from feudalism to capitalism in Western Europe took place in the pages of the American periodical *Science and Society*. It began with Sweezy's 1950 review of Dobb's 1946 book *Studies in the Development of Capitalism*.[12] The debate between Sweezy and Dobb centers on the causes of the decline of feudalism and the nature of the transition period which lasted more than 200 years.

One reason that it is worth while to look at this debate on the European transition is that it will demonstrate how the European and American phenomena can be integrated into a single coherent theoretical framework and to demonstrate the similarities of capitalist development despite superficial differences. That framework is the Marxian theory of the transition to capitalism, based on historical materialism. This is "a view of history as a succession of class systems, with social revolution (in the sense of the transfer of power from one class to another) as the crucial mechanism of historical transformation."[13] Historical materialism holds further that societies are normally dominated by one mode of production, such as the capitalist mode of production, although other forms of production, such as the family farm system, may coexist alongside the dominant one. In the transition from one mode to another, old classes and social relations decay and new classes and new social relations are formed through struggle. The major class systems in Western civilization have been based on slavery, serfdom, and free wage labor. The social revolution in England took place in the seventeenth century when power was transferred from the feudal ruling class to the capitalist ruling class in the English Civil War. The French Revolution in the eighteenth century was such a social revolution. Charles and Mary Beard, Louis Hacker, and Barrington Moore[14] argue that the American Civil War was the comparable American social revolution in that it replaced the pre-capitalist ruling class with an industrial capitalist ruling class.

Another reason to investigate the European transition is that American development is linked to European developments of which it is an offshoot. Most obvious is that English mercantile capitalism established the American colonies in the seventeenth century. Less obvious is the fact that struggles of European serfs and peasants in the transition from feudalism to capitalism led to various forms of cultivator independence, of cultivator possession and ownership of land, which culminated in the family farm system in the United States.

Finally, the family farm thesis on the agrarian roots of U.S. capitalism and the evidence for it to be presented in the body of this book lends support to Dobb's position in the debate and thus further illuminates the role of agriculture and agrarian society in the transition to capitalism. As we will see, Dobb argued that social differentiation among the feudal peasantry led to the development of the two classes of capitalism, capitalists and wage laborers. Sweezy argued that it was the rise of trade, markets, and towns that caused the transition to capitalism.

The transition has two phases: the decline of feudalism and the rise of capitalism. In the rest of this section, we first look at the nature of feudalism and the debate on the causes of its decline. Second, we look at the nature of capitalism and its rise.

The Nature of Feudalism and Its Decline

Rodney Hilton, British historian and author of the introduction to a 1976 book on the Dobb-Sweezy debate, offered a good description of the *feudal mode of production*: "a whole social order whose principal feature was the domination of the rest of society, mainly peasants, by a military, landowning aristocracy."[15] For Dobb, the crucial characteristic of feudalism lay in the relations of production, the relationship between the cultivators and their lords. The key point is that feudalism was the exploitation of the cultivator by means of direct politico-legal compulsion, classically, the enforced performance by the cultivator of obligatory labor services on the lord's estate. This was an openly coercive relationship in which the ruling class directly extracted the surplus labor (labor beyond that necessary for the support of the cultivator family) from the producers on threat of physical violence. This extraction took various forms: labor services on the lord's demesne, rent-in-kind, money rent for the use of the cultivators' plots, and *banalités* (forcing the cultivator to use and pay for the use of the lord's mill, press, and so on).[16]

As for their own subsistence, the cultivator and his family possessed enough land to support themselves. This arrangement in which cultivators possess enough for their own subsistence is called the *petty mode of production*.[17] It accounts for why the rulers had to use force to obtain the surplus: Because the cultivator possessed the means for his own support, he did not have to work for the lord to earn a living. This petty mode of production is the origin of the family farm system that we find in the United States many centuries later. Its essential feature is the possession of enough land to support a family. This is not found in many places in Latin America and Asia.[18]

In European feudalism, the cultivators did not spend all their time on their plots. The lord had power over the work time of the cultivators, leaving them only barely enough time to work their own land to eke out their material living. In the United States, the petty mode of production became the *medium-sized mode of production* in that the farmer owned enough land to support the family and enough additional land to occupy the family full time, which the farm family was free to do.[19] The essential feature of the medium-sized mode of production is the possession of enough land to occupy the labor force of a family, where this is substantially greater than the amount of land needed to support the family.

The feudal economy of Europe underwent a severe crisis in the fourteenth century. The feudal system based on serfdom had led to the expansion of European society, economy, and population. But in time it ran up against limits and the serf-based feudalism could no longer support the large population it had spawned. The result was a crisis of productivity. The outcome of the crisis was that cultivators won their freedom in Western Europe. In some important cases this coincided with the commutation of labor services on the lords' demesnes and its replacement by the requirement for rent-in-kind and/or money rent from the cultivators for the use of the cultivators' plots. The essential point was the change in the cultivators' status from unfree to free. In the debate, this change is called "the demise of feudalism." I would call it the demise of serfdom. A serf is an unfree person who is forced to give his surplus to the lord in the form of labor services, rent-in-kind, money rent, or *banalités*. A peasant is a free person who is forced to give his surplus labor in the form of rent (in-kind or money rent). The difference between the unfree and the free here is that the free are free from arbitrary taxation by the landlords, from arbitrary extractions of the cultivator's labor, time, product, and so forth, and free from demeaning personal dependence upon the lord. Thus, these events amount to a change of serfs into peasants *within* the feudal system. These events could also be called "the demise of the manorial system" in that agricultural production was greatly reduced on the large-scale demesnes, and replaced by small-scale production on leased pieces of the demesnes and on the peasants' plots. What makes both serf and peasant feudal statuses was that they were still subject to exploitation by direct (extra-economic or political) force.

The farmer does not have a feudal status at all because he is free of feudal (extra-economic or political) exploitation. The American farmer was a cultivator of the soil like the serf and peasant in feudal Europe, but he was independent of feudal exploitation and of capitalist exploitation. The English farmer was not a cultivator of the soil. Rather he hired wage labor to cultivate the soil that he rented from the land-owning class in England. The agricultural wage laborer in England was the cultivator and he was exploited by capitalist methods.

Sweezy argued that it was the rise of trade that led to the disintegration of feudalism as described in the previous paragraphs. Basing his account on the work of the Belgian historian Henri Pirenne, Sweezy located the stimulus to feudalism's decline in the development of trade by Scandinavians (in the North Sea and the Baltic via Russia to the Black Sea) in the tenth century and the reopening of Mediterranean shipping (in the western half of the Mediterranean) in the eleventh century.[20] This long-distance trade, primarily in luxury goods, generated towns as trading centers. In the twelfth and thirteenth centuries, there was a great growth of such towns in Western Europe. Sweezy argued that the rise of trade and trading centers caused the rise of production for markets. The people living in the towns needed provisions from the surrounding countryside and this caused production for the market on the lord's estates and on peasant plots. People in the towns produced handicrafts for the townspeople and for the rural population to purchase in the town market in exchange for food.[21]

According to Sweezy, the rise of this exchange economy had several effects. First, it showed feudal lords and peasants how inefficient the old system of production was. Previously, serfs in workshops on the estates produced textiles and farming tools. In the course of the twelfth century, this serf production was replaced by urban handicraft production for sale in the markets. It was cheaper to buy textiles and farming tools from these artisans than to make them on the estate. A second effect of the new money economy was that the feudal ruling class developed a desire to accumulate wealth in the form of money rather than in the form of luxuries and armaments. Third, the feudal ruling class developed new tastes in food, clothing, household furnishing, and arms. These articles changed dramatically in quality and variety between the eleventh and twelfth centuries, causing the feudal ruling class to have increased need for revenue. Finally, the rise of the market towns gave the serfs of the countryside a view of a freer and better life.[22]

By linking the growth of trade to the growth of trading towns, Sweezy could offer an explanation of the causal relationship between the rise of the exchange economy and the decline of serfdom. The rise of the towns not only exerted a pull on the serfs, but had an effect on the serfs who stayed on the estates. The higher standard of living in the town resulted in pressure on the lords to increase the standard of living on the estates. This meant a shift in bargaining power, a real shift in power. Concessions had to be made. This explains the commutation of labor services described above. Second, although the manor was turned to production for the market, it was inefficient and unsuited to this purpose. Techniques were primitive. There was little development of the division of labor and specialization. Production was regulated by custom and tradition. This was a second pressure to commute labor services on the demesne and to lease the land to cultivators for money rent.[23]

In his book and in his reply to Sweezy's review, Dobb argued that the most important cause of the demise of serfdom was the class struggle of the serfs themselves in reaction to the increased exploitation by the lords. For Dobb, there was continuous class struggle between the cultivators and the lords throughout the centuries of feudalism, over the surplus production beyond the needs of the cultivator families. In the classical form of feudalism in which labor services were extracted from serfs, the struggle was over how many days the serf worked on the lord's land (the demesne) and how many days on his own plot. Later, in the High Middle Ages, according to Dobb, the feudal ruling class came to need more revenue (he concedes that on this, Sweezy is right) and the easiest way to obtain this was to squeeze the serfs more, to make them work more intensely. This exhausted the labor force and in many cases led to its disappearance. Many serfs ran away to the towns.[24] Those who stayed on the manor could wring concessions from the lords. They won some freedom and no longer had to provide labor services on the lord's demesne. The lords demanded rent-in-kind or money rent for peasant plots in return for commuting their labor services. The landowners rented the demesne in subdivided pieces or farmed it with wage labor if any was available.[25]

This may sound similar to what Sweezy said. The difference is that for Sweezy the rise of the market economy directly resulted in the demise of serfdom by showing the manor system to be less efficient than free peasant plots, whereas for Dobb, it was the successful struggle of the serfs to become free peasants that led to these results. This is the classic "class struggle" versus "forces of production" theory. Peasants fought to make their petty mode of production less dependent on feudal overlordship. Among other things, they fought for and won freedom from supervision. There was no supervision by the lord's agents on the peasant plot or on the leased holdings, whereas on the estate there had been. The French historian Georges Lefebvre points out that "when production is based on the exploitation of a labourer who is coercively held in a condition of servitude, the difficulty for the master is to supervise his work to assure its efficiency."[26] Part of freedom is freedom from such supervision.[27]

As evidence for his case against Sweezy, Dobb presented two counter-examples in which the rise of markets was accompanied by the intensification rather than demise of serfdom. First, in the backward north and west of England, serfdom disappeared relatively early, whereas in the advanced south and east of England, near the market towns and trade routes, serfdom survived longer. Second, just as serfs were winning their freedom in Western Europe, free peasants in Eastern Europe were being enserfed. Pirenne writes that in the thirteenth century, colonist peasants east of the Elbe River were free. By the fifteenth and sixteenth centuries they were systematically deprived of land and reduced to serfs as Eastern Europe became grain exporters to the west. These two counterexamples show that there had to be other forces at work in addition to the rise of trade to explain the demise of serfdom in Western Europe. Dobb presents additional counterexamples from different centuries in England and in other parts of Europe.

Dobb's case can be supplemented with other examples of civilizations with highly developed trade and commodity production, such as ancient Greece, ancient Rome, even capitalist production in Italian city-states and in Flemish towns. In none of these cases did highly developed trade and commodity production lead to the transition to capitalism.

Dobb cautions against confusing a change in the form of feudal exploitation with a change in the rate of feudal exploitation. In some of the counterexamples he cites, the change in form from labor services to tribute in money rent did not necessarily mean less exploitation. The lord might be able to extract more in the form of money rent than in labor services. In the fourteenth century in Western Europe, however, the commutation of labor service did mean less exploitation. The difference results from the different sources of pressure to commute, whether it came from the lord in search of money revenue or from the peasants in search of freedom—that is, market pressure or class struggle. In short, Dobb argues that the unique feature of the demise of Western European serfdom, including the reduction in exploitation that accompanied it, can only be explained by class struggle.

Dobb does not deny that the rise of trade played a role in the transition. He argues that it was the interaction between the rise of trade and class struggle that caused the fall of serfdom, not trade alone. According to historical materialism, there are interactions in a society between internal conflicts and external forces, with the internal conflicts being primary. This is because the "internal conflicts would operate in any case, if on a different time scale."[28] The internal conflicts determine the form and direction of the effects which external influences can have. Dobb argued that trade—an external force—accentuated the internal conflicts within the old feudal mode of production. Trade accelerated the social differentiation among the cultivators and artisans, which, we will see below, hastened to the development of the two classes of capitalism. Trade also increased conflict between the lords and the cultivators. Trade meant that both lords and cultivators had reason to produce more, the lords for conspicuous consumption and warfare, the cultivators for a higher standard of living via leasing more land to add to their subsistence plots. This extra product stimulated by trade then was the source of conflict between cultivator and lord over who would reap the rewards of the extra effort stimulated by trade. Finally, by stimulating the desire for money wealth among the lords, trade increased inter-lord rivalry. In addition to increasing the rate of exploitation of the serfs, a feudal lord could increase his money income by increasing the amount of land and the number of serfs he controlled. This was achieved though warfare with other lords.[29]

The Nature of Capitalism and Its Rise

Since our goal is to explain the rise of capitalism in the United States, we turn now to the rise of capitalism in Europe, as the development of capitalism has certain essential features, regardless of where it arises. In addition, American development is an offshoot of European development and thus some of the explanation of the rise of capitalism in the United States has to be traced back to Europe. Finally, by looking at class struggle in the rise of capitalism in Europe, we see an argument for how class struggle led to the transition to capitalism in the United States. Before examining the transition period which follows this demise of serfdom, some general remarks about the *capitalist mode of production* and its rise are in order. The capitalist mode of production was the object of study of Marx's three-volume work *Capital*. Dobb described capitalism as "a particular form of the appropriation of surplus labor by a class possessing economic power and privilege."[30] The particular form is as follows. The bourgeoisie or capitalists own the means of production. The working class is forced to sell its labor power in order to support itself because it does not own means of production or means of subsistence, as feudal cultivators had. The capitalists exploit the wage laborers through the economic forces that make it necessary for the latter to work for the former, rather than by the direct force or political-military coercion used against the serfs and peasants. The exploitation takes the form of the workers producing more value than they receive back in wages.[31] Furthermore, competition between capitalists generates continual revolution in the instruments of production which in turn causes dramatic decline in the cost of production and growth in the productivity of labor. This makes possible the increase in the standard of living of the working people, if they win the class struggle to take part of the productivity gain in real wage increases instead of letting the capitalists take it all in profits.

Moving from an abstract analysis of the capitalist mode of production to the concrete history of Western Europe, Marx dates the first sporadic beginnings of capitalist production in the fourteenth and fifteenth century in a few towns on the Mediterranean.[32] However, the capitalistic era as such dates from the sixteenth century with the rise of world trade and a world market, which had been made possible by the great territorial discoveries of the late fifteenth century.

Dobb's argument assumes that the cause of the demise of serfdom was internal to feudalism (class struggle), whereas Sweezy's argument assumes that the cause of the demise was external to feudalism (the impact of trade). According to Giuliano Procacci, an Italian historian, "the precondition of the flowering of mercantile activity and commodity production was the development of the agrarian sector of the economy."[33] This was a development internal to the feudal mode of production. It was not trade that created capitalism; rather it was the development of feudal agriculture toward capitalist agriculture that made trade and commodity production possible. Thus when Dobb says trade produces the transition, but via class struggle rather than directly, as Sweezy thought, trade becomes internal to the evolution of feudalism, not external as Sweezy would have it.

Dobb argues that capitalism was born from the petty mode of production as it broke free of feudal domination and as social differentiation took place within it. Social differentiation means that, in the struggle over feudal rent and in the competition of the marketplace, some people won and some people lost. Some peasants were more successful than others in their struggle with the lords and in their participation in the new market economy. By the fifteenth century, the stimulus of rent struggle was replaced by the stimulus of market struggle as the factor promoting social differentiation. The successful farmers, Dobb's *kulaks*, or, as I prefer to call them, the yeomen or freehold farmers, were important at the dawn of capitalism. They hired the poorer, landless peasants for their village enterprises.

In the sixteenth century, the yeomen pioneered the new and improved methods of enclosed farming. In England, they, along with the gentry, organized the country cloth industry, and were an important driving force in the bourgeois revolution, making up much of Cromwell's New Model Army. The less successful peasants lost their land and had to work for wages. For Dobb, this was crucial for the rise of capitalism, because "the transition from coercive extraction of surplus labor by the estate owners to the use of free labor depends on the existence of cheap labor for hire."[34] If there is no class of people who must work for a wage to live, then the old social system will survive. If there is a class of wage laborers, then the old system will dissolve. This is the classic English case of capitalist farmers renting from aristocratic landowners and exploiting agricultural wage laborers.

Marx called this emergence of industrial capitalism from within the petty mode of production, "the revolutionary way." This is in contrast to the view that it was the merchant capitalists who became the industrialists. Merchant capitalists were allied with the feudal ruling class and thus could not be a revolutionary force propelling capitalism to the position of the dominant mode of production. But direct producers, such as craftsmen, artisans, and mechanics, because they were involved in production, could revolutionize the methods of production, which occurs in capitalism. Moreover, they had little vested interest in the pre-capitalist system and thus were a new political, as well as economic, power.

The family farmers in the nineteenth-century United States fit the model of Marx's revolutionary way: They invented much of the new farm machinery. They were petty producers who purchased fixed capital on the market in the form of farm machinery, propelling the transition to capitalism in the United States (although they were unique in that they hired no wage labor). Furthermore, the farmers were revolutionary in that they allied with industrial capitalists in the Civil War, our bourgeois revolution. Japanese historian Kohachiro Takahashi[35] contrasts England, the United States, and France, which had bourgeois revolutions and industrial capitalists rising in the revolutionary way, with Prussia and Japan, where merchant capitalists became industrialists and capitalism prevailed without bourgeois revolutions. This latter way was not associated with democracy.[36]

The civil war in seventeenth-century England was a social revolution that brought to power a new bourgeoisie which then could hasten the process of transforming the feudal mode of production into the capitalist mode of production. Feudal rent was abolished by this revolution. I agree with Dobb that the ruling class which was deposed in this revolution was feudal. However, it was a unique kind of feudal ruling class in that it existed over 200 years alongside centralized state power, whereas in classical feudalism, political power was decentralized. This ruling class was feudal because it depended for its income on feudal methods of exploiting the petty mode of production. They collected rent from a dependent peasantry. Dobb grants that trade was very important in this period and the feudal ruling class made economic and political alliances with the merchant bourgeoisie.

In the transition period there were many transitional forms: merchant bourgeoisie, urban artisans, "well-to-do and middling well-to-do" freehold farmers, and hired labor farming estates.[37] Dobb considers all these to be free of feudal exploitation. However, the major form in the period, namely, small tenants paying money rent, was still characterized by feudal dependence. Dobb argues that feudal dependence exists insofar as the peasant was restricted in his movements and remained dependent on the landlord in many ways. Political constraints and pressures of manorial custom continued to rule economic relationships between the peasant and the estate owner. There was neither a free market in land nor free labor mobility. The direct producers, the peasants, possessed enough land to support their families, and yet they still had to perform for their landlord.

They were forced to give their surplus labor as tribute to him. Instead of giving the surplus labor directly on the demesne, they gave it in the form of money obtained from the sale of the surplus product from their customary plots and/or their leased land on the demesne.

This feudal rent contrasted with the case of capitalist money rent wherein the farmer was an independent tenant paying contractual rent, hiring wage labor, and merely sharing the surplus with the landowner. Hilton adds that "ground rent under capitalism is not the main source of the income of the ruling class. It is merely a 'super-profit' derived by the landlords from the capitalist farmer by virtue of his monopoly of a force of nature, the land."[38]

In contrast to Dobb, Sweezy did not consider this transitional period to be feudal in nature. He called the transition system *pre-capitalist commodity production*. He called it commodity production to emphasize that it was production for the market, as opposed to production for use, that undermined serfdom. It was pre-capitalist because it prepared the way for capitalism. It was not capitalist in that it did not use wage labor. Sweezy's pre-capitalist commodity production does not include ownership of the means of production by producers. Thus it should not be confused with *simple commodity production*, the concept that Marx used to explain how the law of value comes to regulate capitalist production. In Marx's simple commodity production, the independent producers owned their means of production and satisfied their wants by means of mutual exchange; whereas in Sweezy's pre-capitalist commodity production, the major means of production, land, was owned by a non-producing class. Sweezy's pre-capitalist commodity production was neither feudal nor capitalist. It was not on a par with the two major modes of production. Sweezy argues that pre-capitalist commodity production was strong enough to destroy feudalism, but not strong enough to develop into an independent "structure" of its own. Relating this to the American family farm when it began producing substantially for the market, it was a form of simple commodity production because the farmers owned their land, and not pre-capitalist commodity production, in Sweezy's sense.

Sweezy is correct to point out that as money rent developed in the transition period, two new forms emerged: the case where land was transformed into independent peasant property and the case where it was rented for money by a capitalist tenant. As we will see, money rent developed into independent peasant property in France and into capitalist rent in England. The petty mode of production in England became the independent farmer owning property in the United States, or as I have called it medium-sized mode of production. In the transition to capitalism in America, it became simple commodity production.[39]

In sum, in Europe there was a petty mode of production and in the United States it was a medium-sized mode of production. This size difference can be operationalized by saying that in the petty mode, the cultivator possessed enough land to support his family and in the medium-sized mode, the cultivator had enough land to occupy the family which was substantially more land than needed to support the family. In Europe there developed a pre-capitalist commodity production involving cultivators who did not own farm land. In the United States there developed a simple commodity production in which the cultivators did own farm land. Finally, there is Marx's analytic concept of simple commodity production, where the direct producer owns the means of production, leading to the law of value regulating production and hence evolving into the capitalist mode of production. The nineteenth century American family farm developed into simple commodity production , but not into a capitalist mode of production, and was not regulated by the law of value.[40]

Early settlers in the United States represented all sorts of fragments of decaying feudalism, results of various stages of social differentiation of the petty mode of production. Before the English Civil War, yeoman farmers left England for the American colonies. Also from the seventeenth century on, those who did not win in the social differentiation process in the transition from feudalism to capitalism in Western Europe migrated to the American colonies and won the struggle in the United States to become independent land owners and freehold farmers. Later settlers were northern European peasants fleeing decaying feudalism.

The reason that I claim that my research supports Dobb rather than Sweezy is that American economic historians argue, in a way similar to Sweezy, that trade and market forces explain modern economic growth in the nineteenth-century United States. Douglass North makes this broad argument.[41] David and Fleisig argue that farmers were profit maximizers and that market forces caused the farmers to pioneer the new and improved methods of mechanized agriculture in the nineteenth century. I argue that market forces alone cannot explain this mechanization, which was crucial in the rise of capitalism in the United States. Rather, it is necessary to look at the class structure of the family farm system, initially a form of petty mode of production and eventually transformed into simple commodity production. Without this, we cannot account for the fact that most farmers adopted the reaper *before* it would have been rational to do so strictly on profit-maximizing terms. I show in Chapter 2 that if family farmers had been profit maximizers they would *not* have adopted the horse-drawn mechanical reaper in the 1850s. However, in fact, they did adopt the reaper in the 1850s, so it must have been for reasons other than to maximize profits. Moreover, without looking at class structure, we cannot account for the fact that family farmers were overwhelmingly dependent on family labor. I discuss in Chapter 3 that family farmers had reasons for limiting their use of labor to that of the farm family's, that is beyond the reason that labor was scarce in the market. In Chapter 4 I show how the family farm system, due to its internal class structure, improved agricultural productivity in the northern United States in response to its own needs as well as in response to market signals. *Market forces do not work in or transform all agrarian class structures.* We want to see how it is that some agrarian class structures help the transition to capitalism and others impede the transition. This brings us to the Brenner debate.

THE ROLE OF AGRARIAN CLASS STRUCTURE IN THE EUROPEAN TRANSITION

The Marxian debate on the transition from feudalism to capitalism broke onto the non-Marxian scene in 1976 when Brenner criticized both a market forces explanation and a demographic explanation of European economic development from the medieval to the early modern period. In "Agrarian Class Structure and Economic Development in Pre-Industrial Europe," published in *Past and Present*, Brenner presented his agrarian class structure explanation of the key events in the transition.

Two False Trails—Market and Population Models

First we look at the market model and Brenner's critique of it. Like Sweezy, Douglass North and Robert Thomas explained the demise of serfdom in medieval Western Europe as caused by the rise of markets.[42] Unlike Sweezy, however, they defined serfdom as the exchange of labor services by the serf to the lord in return for his protection and administration of justice. Serfdom was seen as a contract between equals who happened to own different resources. Brenner cites two counterexamples of Postan's and adds one of his own to criticize the rise of the market view. Postan, the dean of English medieval studies, had already criticized this market view by pointing out that London was a counterexample.[43] In the thirteenth century, one found an intensification of serfdom around the London market in the face of market forces, not its demise, as North and Thomas would have it. Postan further pointed out that in the twelfth century, the lords had commuted labor services of the peasants and demanded money rent instead. Then in the thirteenth century, under more market pressure, labor services were demanded and obtained again. In sum, as we saw in discussing Sweezy, there is no automatic causal relation between the rise of markets and the fall of serfdom. Postan had a second counterexample to use against the market model. He pointed out that market forces, in the form of the development of a world grain market, led to the rise of serfdom in Eastern Europe at the same time as serfdom was being destroyed in the west. Brenner adds another counterexample, namely, the area around Paris. Around the Paris market, one could find regions with serfs, regions with free peasants, and regions where the direct producers were halfway between serf and free peasants. Thus the rise of the Paris market did not uniquely cause the demise of serfdom, as North and Thomas would have it.

Brenner's criticism of the market model went deeper than Postan's, who had gone so far as to defend feudalism from the charge of exploitation. Brenner sees the exploitation of serfs by lords in classic feudalism. Like North and Thomas, Postan saw feudalism as protecting serfs in return for their labor. But, instead of protecting serfs from violence, Postan saw feudalism protecting them from the vagaries of the market, particularly in face of rising inflation and land hunger. Brenner argued that the market model's very definition of serfdom is wrong. The major error was to think of serfdom as merely a matter of labor services due the lord from the cultivator. Serfdom is characterized, continues Brenner, by cultivator unfreedom and by arbitrary extractions by the lord of the cultivators' surpluses, whatever its form: labor services, rent-in-kind, money rent, and *banalités*. The lords controlled the mobility of the serf. Thus even when labor services were commuted into money rent, the cultivator was still unfree, unable to move, and still subject to arbitrary fines. And as Postan pointed out, labor services were reinstated in England after being commuted. This shows the extra-economic power of lords over cultivators in feudalism, required because of the fact that cultivators possessed enough land to live.[44] The cultivator had no economic reason to work for the lords. The lords played no entrepreneurial function. Cultivators had to be forced to work for the lord.[45]

In sum, then, one cannot say that market forces inevitably led to the decline of serfdom or to the rise of capitalist agriculture. As we saw above, American economic historians make a similar error when they take market forces alone to have caused the family farm system to mechanize in the nineteenth century.

Neoclassical economics often used relative factor scarcities to supplement the causal role of market forces. But even this is not enough to explain the rise of capitalism in Europe or the United States. Postan developed a demographic model to replace the market model, which he had criticized. He argued that the population increase in the twelfth and thirteenth centuries, and the consequent low land-labor ratio, weakened the position of the cultivator vis-à-vis the lords, resulting in high rents for the lords and low real income for the cultivators. Here too, Brenner points to France as a counterexample. Brenner points out that French lords were not able to raise rents in response to population pressure in the thirteenth century, as English lords were able to do in Postan's example. More fundamentally, Brenner argues that the level of rent, the key income category of feudalism, was not determined solely by the relative scarcity of land and labor, but rather by the prior distribution of land, prior distribution of the product of

land, and by the direct use of force, that is, feudal power. Brenner accounts
for the difference between England and France on this score by reference
to conditions relevant to class struggle, namely, the relatively strong self-
organization of the English lords and the relatively weak and decentralized
French aristocracy, which in turn was relative to earlier class struggle in the
two countries (see below).[46]

Postan had argued for a second demographic phase in the fourteenth and
fifteenth centuries when population fell and caused the land-labor relation
to improve for the cultivator. This caused a decline in rent and a rise in
cultivator real income, and was ultimately manifested in the demise of
serfdom. Population decline, then, caused the decline of serfdom. Enter
Brenner with Postan's own Eastern European counterexample. The decline
of population in Eastern Europe was associated with the rise of serfdom,
not its fall. According to Brenner, this is one of the great divides in
European history and it cannot be explained by the demographic model,
any more than it can be by the market model.

Emmanuel Le Roy Ladurie carried the demographic model on through
two more phases.[47] In the "long sixteenth century," the rise of population
caused a real problem for peasants who had access to relatively less land.
In Malthusian style, this led to the crisis of the seventeenth century and
population decline. For Le Roy Ladurie, the fall in population was the
cause of an income distribution favoring the peasants over the lords.
Brenner criticizes Le Roy Ladurie by pointing out that, in the face of rising
population pressure in England in the long sixteenth century, we do not see
a crisis generated in the seventeenth century, but rather the rise of capitalist
agriculture. England was free of the crisis of the seventeenth century, unlike
France and much of continental Europe. Brenner argues that this is another
great divide in European history that cannot be explained by the demographic model.

American economic historians have not developed as complete a
demographic model as the Europeans, but they integrate population into
the relative-factor-scarcity part of their market model. David and Fleisig
argue that the relative scarcity of labor in the American system caused the
adoption of farm machinery in the nineteenth century. But we have seen
that labor scarcity can lead to divergent outcomes. Labor scarcity in the
fourteenth century led to the fall of serfdom in Western Europe and its rise
in Eastern Europe. Labor scarcity in seventeenth-century France caused no
agricultural improvement. In seventeenth-century England, there was no
labor scarcity and yet there was massive agricultural improvement. In sum,
there is no automatic, causal relation between scarcity of labor and
agricultural improvement.

Agrarian Class Structure Model

In face of the failure of both the market and the demographic models to explain what Brenner referred to as the two divides in European history, Brenner offered his agrarian class structure model. He argued that there were two key events in European history that were crucial to the transition from feudalism to capitalism: the demise of serfdom and the demise of small peasant property. The one region of Europe that did see the demise of serfdom and of small peasant property was England, the home of capitalism, the first industrial revolution, and of uniquely successful economic development. Eastern Europe was condemned to backwardness for centuries by the persistence of serfdom there. And France, though freed of serfdom, was kept from rapid development by the persistence of peasant property.

Brenner explained these contrasting economic developments by reference to agrarian class structures. First, let us look at his interpretation of the decline of serfdom in Western Europe. Inherent in the feudal mode of production was a conflict between the development of cultivator production and the exploitative relationship between the lord and the cultivator. The tendency to crisis of agricultural production was not just a natural fact, as Postan would have it, but rather a social fact. The lords had the power to extract 50 percent of the cultivator's production. Not only could the cultivator not invest, he could hardly maintain production. Thus there was always downward pressure on the productivity of the soil and on the cultivator's ability to obtain anything from that soil. This inherent tendency manifested itself in the crisis of fourteenth-century Europe. In face of this agricultural crisis and population decline, there was great class conflict between the lords and the cultivators. The cultivators struggled to get free and survive as they could. The lords struggled to increase their diminished revenues by squeezing a larger share of the cultivators' product from them. Brenner argues that the cultivators in the west won this conflict and their freedom from serfdom and that the cultivators in the east lost the conflict and their freedom by being enserfed.

Why did the peasants in the west win and those in the east lose the class conflict? Brenner seeks an answer in the agrarian class structures of the two halves of Europe. He argues that in the west there was a greater development of cultivator solidarity and strength at the village institutional level, or what he calls a superior institutionalization of cultivators' class power. For empirical evidence, he contrasts west and east Elbian Germany in the fourteenth century. In the west, village by village, cultivators won the right to economic self-regulation and political self-governance. The agriculture of the cultivators was semicommunal. Common lands were used for grazing, and fuel, and had to be regulated. The common field rotation system had to be coordinated. Cultivators organized to establish fixed rent and heritability. In contrast to this, in east Elbian Germany there were few independent political institutions and cultivators had few rights. And why was this? Brenner argues that the east was colonized and thus somewhat artificially implanted. Colonization was led by the lords. Rather large fields were set up from the beginning, in counterdistinction to the western evolution of feudalism which contained scattered cultivator parcels across open and common fields. There were few commons in the east. Thus there was less, or lack of any, communal nature to the agriculture practiced by the eastern cultivators. Moreover, in the east each village was subject to one lord; in the west, a village might have several lords and thus could play them off each other. Thus in the west, the cultivator was more likely to win his freedom.

What were the effects of the divergent class structures that resulted from the class conflicts of the late medieval period? In the east, the newly established serfdom came under the impact of the world market. The stimulus of the rise of the market and the rise of the price of food grains did not lead to improvements in the productivity of grain production and did not lead to industrialization. Brenner explains the mechanisms at work here. First, with unfree cultivators to squeeze, the lords had no incentive to bother with the hard work and risk of making improvements. Second, the squeezing of the cultivators prevented the development of a home market among the cultivators, which would have been a stimulus to industrial production. Third, the control lords had over the mobility of the cultivators prevented the creation of a labor force for industry. Consequently, Eastern Europe remained a backward rural society for centuries.[48]

On the other hand, the decline of serfdom opened up new possibilities for the western part of Europe under the impact of the world market. Since serf labor had been forced labor, "careful application of fixed capital or high skill without high supervisory costs" was not possible.[49] With the decline of serfdom, application of fixed capital and high skill became possible. This is not to say that capitalism automatically arose out of the ashes of serfdom. It would take a few centuries of additional struggle between lord and cultivator over ownership of land for that to occur. This struggle was played out in Western Europe. This is the key conflict, because if the peasants lose and become "free" labor, then there is labor for capitalists to hire and capitalism can become the dominant mode of production. Commodity production in the past—ancient Greece and Rome and medieval Flanders and Italy—did not become capitalist because there was not a large class of free labor. Part of the conflict between rising capitalists and lords was over access to labor.

This leads us to the second step toward capitalism, the demise of peasant property. This occurred in England and not in France. Brenner argues that in both countries, lords and free peasants engaged in class conflict over whether peasants would have freehold rights to their land after the demise of serfdom. The English peasants had lost this struggle. By the end of the seventeenth century, the landlords controlled 70 to 75 percent of the land in England.[50] This led to the rise of new class relations, especially between landlords and the surviving large tenant farmers. The demise of small peasant property led both to larger farms and to abundant wage labor (from the ranks of the recently dispossessed peasants). The result was a transformation of English agriculture, great gains in productivity of agriculture, and the rise of agrarian capitalism. On the other hand, the French peasants won the class conflict to control the land as essentially freehold tenure. At the end of the seventeenth century, the French peasants controlled 45 to 50 percent of the farm land.[51] Thus in the French countryside we see the emergence and predominance of secure small peasant property. The result was France fell into another crisis of agricultural production and population, the general crisis of the seventeenth century, which England escaped.

Why did the French peasants win and the English peasants lose? Brenner explains the differential balance of class forces in early modern Europe in relation to the development of the monarchial state. Why did the French peasants win the proprietorship of their land? After the demise of serfdom, the French monarchical state strove to assert an arbitrary power to tax the land. If all of the peasants' surplus went to the landlord, there would be nothing left for the monarchical state. Thus the state had an interest in protecting peasant property and production. As early as the thirteenth century in the Paris region, the state intervened to help the cultivators in their struggle against the lords who were trying to increase their arbitrary power to tax the peasants at will. This intervention signified that the cultivators were free in legal status and could not be treated arbitrarily. This opened up the way for fixed rents and essentially freehold property. In the fifteenth century, the French monarchy confirmed the peasants' hereditary tenure. This prevented the lords from adding land abandoned as a result of the fourteenth- and fifteenth-century population decline (and wars) to their demesnes, leaving it instead for peasant proprietorship. Furthermore, the monarchy organized elected village assemblies to help collect state taxes. The French state was based on peasant property and not on an alliance with the lords, and thus there was a decay of parliamentary institutions for the nobles in France, and the rise of an absolutist state, with an implicit alliance of peasants.[52]

The class alliances in England were quite different. There the monarchy and the landlords allied against the peasants. The English monarchy was not absolutist; it had strong parliamentary institutions for the nobles. The monarchy had relied on the landlord class in its drive toward centralization in the late fifteenth and early sixteenth century. The landlords were threatened by the disruption due to warlord activity at this time, and that is why they supported the monarchy. These same lords wanted to remove the peasants from their land so that they could consolidate their holdings, engross, and enclose them. The monarchy was indebted to the landlords and sided with them in their struggle with the peasants. The English landlords had two means to undermine peasant property that were not available to the French landlords. First, the English lords were able to add to their demesnes land that was abandoned as a result of the population collapse of the fourteenth and fifteenth century. This took land out of the stock that peasants could claim for themselves. Second, the lords were able to assert their power to charge an entry fee whenever a peasant sold land or inherited it. The fee could be so large that the peasant would have to give up his inheritance. Initially, the peasants refused to pay these fines and succeeded in their resistance in the fifteenth and even in the sixteenth century when the population pressure was against the peasants. The second half of the sixteenth century saw a large number of peasant uprisings in England. These struggles were over the security of peasant property and arbitrary fines. The peasants lost these struggles because the state allied with the landlords. Unlike France, peasants in England were not recognized as citizens by the royal courts. They were thus subject to the "justice" of their lords in the manorial court, without the royal court to protect them.

Now we turn to the different effects of the two agrarian class structures that came out of the class conflicts of the seventeenth century. In the case of France, agriculture on the lord's demesne or on the peasant's plot was incapable of sustaining the population, and the country fell into depression. The French peasants kept their land, avoided class differentiation into rich and poor peasants, but were uniformly depressed into poverty. Copyholders did not buy each other out. No class of yeomen arose. The peasant proprietor was under no pressure to improve his production. All he cared about was providing for his family and paying his money rent and his taxes. He held on to his land for his living and for his heirs. If his plot was extremely small, he could supplement his production with wage labor to earn cash for the rent and taxes. His plot, while owned, was small, due to population pressure and to his own custom of partible inheritance, that is, subdivision among heirs at death. The lord rented parts of his demesne to small tenants. When he needed more revenue, he tried to squeeze more rent out of these tenants. There was no yeoman class of large and rich peasants to whom to rent. Neither lord nor peasant could improve production. If there was any surplus left after the landlord's share, the monarchical state took it in taxes. This condemned France to a dismal record of economic development. There was no development of productivity in agriculture and little development of a home market for manufactures.

On the other hand, in England, the new class structure was a spur to agrarian capitalism. The new class structure was a unique alliance between the landowners and large capitalist tenants.[53] Brenner does not explain where these large tenants came from. But we know from the Sweezy-Dobb debate that social differentiation of the peasantry means, on one hand, poor peasants or even landless peasants, and on the other hand, rich peasants who hired the poor and/or landless peasants. The new class alliance of lords and large tenants removed the antagonism of the old landlord-tenant relation. Instead of squeezing the tenant, the landlord now promised that if the tenant improved the holding then he (the landlord) would not take it all away by increasing the rent.[54] The increase in output possible from agricultural improvement would thus be shared by the landowner and the capitalist tenant who farmed the land on the basis of improvements and wage labor. This new agrarian class structure was so successful in promoting productivity growth in agriculture that by the end of seventeenth century 40 percent of the English population was released from the agricultural labor force into the industrial labor force.[55] Agricultural output was no longer a constraint on industrial development. A large home market for industrial products developed based on the prosperous tenant farmers and landlords. Cheap food kept wages down and thus helped industry's profits. Cheap food also meant more income to be spent on non-food, so the middle class and even the lower class was a home market for industrially produced goods. This agricultural revolution and the rise of capitalist relations in the countryside caused England to be the first country to have a modern industrial revolution. Brenner called this "the agrarian roots of European capitalism."[56]

I shall consider the American experience in light of Brenner's counter-examples of market development. The rise of markets in fourteenth-century Europe did not lead to such agricultural improvements, except for the case of Western Europe. The rise of markets in the seventeenth century did not lead to agricultural advances in Europe, except for the case of England. The rise of markets in the nineteenth-century United States did not lead to agricultural development except for the case of the North. Brenner explained how England did it based on their capitalist agrarian class structure. My research explains how the northern United States did it as a result of the family farm agrarian class structure and thus not simply as a response to high wheat prices. I will also show how the American family farm system differed profoundly from the English capitalist system.

I will also consider the American experience in the light of Brenner's counterexamples of labor scarcity. The relative scarcity of labor in fourteenth- and fifteenth-century Eastern Europe did not cause improvements in agricultural technique. The relative scarcity of labor in seventeenth-century France did not lead to agricultural advance. The relative scarcity of labor in the nineteenth-century United States did not lead to agricultural development except in the north. As Brenner showed us, the rise of capitalist relations in agriculture in England caused improvements there—a country without a labor scarcity. My study shows how the family farm system did improve without wage labor, not because of a labor constraint (labor scarcity) caused by market forces, but rather because the structure of the family farm system caused the system to rely on family labor which incidentally resulted in the lack of labor in the market. The family farm system prevented the development of labor markets in rural areas.

THE ROLE OF THE FAMILY FARM IN THE AMERICAN TRANSITION

Having analyzed the transition to capitalism in Europe and the role of agrarian class structures in that transition, we turn now to the transition to capitalism in America and the role of the agrarian class structure, known as the family farm system, in that transition. The transition to capitalism in America was initially analyzed by the Beards in *The Rise of American Civilization* (1927). It was modernized by Hacker in *The Triumph of American Capitalism* (1940). The thesis can be seen, translated into contemporary Marxian language of modes of production analysis, in Charles Post's "The American Road to Capitalism," published in the *New Left Review* in 1982.[57] In the latter's language, the transition to capitalism was effected by the expansion, transformation, and interaction among three forms of production in antebellum America: slavery, family farms, and capitalist manufacturing. The Civil War and Reconstruction of both North and South completed the transition to capitalism in America. In the rest of this section we will examine each of the three forms of production and the Civil War and their roles in the transition to capitalism in America.

Three Forms of Production in Pre-Capitalist America

The first form of production in the antebellum United States was slavery. Historians of slavery in the American South were shocked by the publication of Eugene Genovese's Marxian analysis of slavery in *The Political Economy of Slavery* (1965).[58] He argued that slavery was profoundly different from capitalism. The slave master was unable to adjust the size of his labor force with changes in the business cycle, whereas in capitalism, the wage laborers can be fired. The capital outlay for the slave labor was greater and more risky than for wage labor. The planter class was more likely than laissez-faire capitalists to interfere politically with the market. The supply of cheap labor in the form of slaves tended over time to shrink, making slaves more costly.[59] The planters used the surplus produced by slaves for conspicuous consumption, not unlike European feudal lords. In order to increase production, slave masters would buy more land and more slaves and move to more fertile soil, rather than innovate the production process. This again was not unlike the feudal lords, who expanded by taking more land and serfs by force or colonizing new land. Genovese argued that slavery held back the development of capitalism because it provided no home market for it. Due to the use of force with slaves in large gangs to produce cotton, planters could not introduce any but the most simple tools. Like the serfs, the slaves had no incentive to work carefully, and thus they had to be supervised when they worked. Thus there was no market for industries producing advanced forms of production tools. Second, the plantations were self-sufficient and thus were no market for consumer goods.

Some economists came to the rescue of historians. In 1974 the famous (or infamous) book by Robert Fogel and Stanley Engerman, *Time on the Cross*, indirectly refuted Genovese by arguing that the slave plantation behaved like a neoclassical firm and was profit maximizing and profitable and that the whole slavery system was allocating resources efficiently.[60] All this was supported with neoclassical economic theory and statistical evidence. This generated great debate among economic historians who preferred the traditional pre-Genovese version. Taking a middle ground, in *The Political Economy of the Cotton South* Gavin Wright argued against assuming that profit maximization was the principle followed by economic agents in the nineteenth-century South.[61] Rodney Green took Genovese's insights and incorporated them into a mode of production analysis.[62] As modes of production, slavery and capitalism are profoundly different.

Post argues that slavery was initially a spur to development in the United States but that it was transformed into an obstacle.[63] Under American merchant capitalism (which I would date from 1776—when English merchant capitalism ends—to 1843—when the economy emerged from a recession and took off),[64] the expansion of plantation slavery helped American development. Northeastern merchants made fortunes facilitating the cotton trade. Cotton was the major export in antebellum America. It created a favorable balance of trade for the United States and ensured "sound international credit for American merchants and bankers."[65] Finally, it stimulated mercantile capitalist activity in land speculation and construction of transportation projects, financed by European capital.

Ironically, these very developments would undermine the slavery system. Land speculation and transportation development stimulated the family farmers in the North to produce for the market, as we saw above. This, in turn, caused the family farm system to develop into a home market for industrial capitalism. On the basis of the family farm home market, industrial capitalism emerged and rose to dominance in the United States. To industrial capitalism, the geographical expansion of slavery was an obstacle, interfering with the expansion of wage labor and domestic market development. Slaveowners were hostile to wage labor and bought neither instruments of production nor the means of subsistence for the slaves on the market.[66]

At about the same time (1845), the United States conquered territories from Mexico.[67] If this land had been filled in with slave plantations rather than by family farms, there would have been no home market for the capitalist production of the means of production or the means of consumption. And politically, the planters would have had more power in the federal government and could have blocked the industrial capitalists from legislating their economic policy package.

The transition to capitalism was marked by the conflict between slavery and free labor in the form of the family farm. James O'Connor described the antebellum American family farm as a subsistence unit of production.[68] It was governed, he argued, by the "logic of subsistence." That meant that the farm family marketed only the surplus which they produced beyond their own subsistence needs. Since they produced their own subsistence, they were not dependent on the market for it. Under these conditions, the forces of production did not develop. O'Connor claimed that the family farm was an obstacle to the development of capitalism in antebellum America for two reasons. First, the family farm was an alternative to wage labor and thus blocked the formation of an American working class. This view is strongly consistent with the Turner thesis on the role of the frontier in American history, the idea that the frontier was a safety valve for labor problems.[69] If a laborer were unhappy in the East, he could go west and farm, or, by threatening to, he could obtain higher wages or better conditions. Second, the family farm was no market for industrial capital because it produced its own means of production and means of subsistence. It is only after the Civil War, when the family farm was destroyed, according to O'Connor, that capitalist development could proceed.

Against O'Connor, Robert Sherry argued that the family farm was a petty-bourgeois form of capitalism and as such was regulated by the law of value.[70] He claimed that the farm family marketed nearly the whole product it produced in the antebellum period. The law of value caused the family farm to develop the forces of production via competition and accumulation. Thus the farmers were dependent on the market for both the means of subsistence and for the means of production. The family farm was a central mechanism in the development of capitalism in antebellum America. Because the family farm was adopting agricultural technology that it purchased in the market, the costs of setting up a viable farm rose beyond the reach of working people. Thus the family farm was not a safety valve, à la Turner. In fact, following Sherry, competition in the market led to social differentiation among farmers into petty-bourgeois farmers on the one hand, and into propertyless wage earners on the other, providing labor for the industrial sector. The family farm system provided a massive home market for the means of production (the farm machinery they were buying), and for the means of subsistence (since, for Sherry, they were selling almost all of their production). Finally, the expansion of agricultural production provided a forward link to growth in the form of capitalist processing of agricultural produce.

Post sided with Sherry in this debate, except that he did not want to call the family farm capitalist. To do so, he argued, would be to conflate two groups, family farmers and industrial capitalists, which had severe class differences before the Civil War. Moreover, it was the alliance of these two different classes in the Republican Party which led to the outbreak of the Civil War. Yet, Post still asserts that the family farm was regulated by the law of value by the 1840s and 1850s.

Post used three empirical studies from non-Marxist scholars to choose Sherry's vision of the family farm over that of O'Connor's. First, he cites the work of Paul Gates, who complained about how farmers were exploited by land speculators.[71] Federal land policy turned land into a commodity through public auction of the public domain and this caused the farmer to be dependent on markets. Second, Post offers evidence on the development of the forces of production under family farming. He cites William Parker and Judith Klein's study for the National Bureau of Economic Research on the increase in the productivity of labor in grain production.[72] This is used as further evidence for the family farm being regulated by the market. Third, Post cites Clarence Danhof on the cost of farm making with the advent of the new farm machinery. The study claims to demonstrate that farm ownership was beyond the reach of the common laboring person.[73] Post uses this as evidence to show that the family farm was not an alternative to wage labor and thus was not an obstacle to economic development. Thus Post concludes from these three empirical studies that the family farm was dependent on the market and thus was regulated by the law of value.

Going beyond Sherry, Post considers the expansion of the family farm system as *the* central mechanism in capitalist development in the nineteenth century. Like Sherry, Post sees the backward linkage from family farming to growth in the industries supplying the family farmer with machinery and implements as a great spur to capitalist development.

Post errs both theoretically and empirically. First, to side with Sherry and to reject O'Connor on the nature of the family farm is to miss the transition of the family farm from one nature into another. The family farm was transformed from a medium-sized mode of production into simple commodity production. The family farm system was in transition in the decade before the Civil War, the 1850s. The family farm had been a subsistence unit in its early days (up to the early 1840s, later in some areas as one moves west), as O'Connor would have it. But the industrialization of the East from 1843 on, the construction of the Erie Canal in the 1830s, and the construction of the railroad system connecting New York City and Chicago in the 1850s gave the family farmers the opportunity to produce for the market and they did so in increasing amounts and proportions. They specialized in cash crops, such as wheat, and moved away from general or subsistence farming into commercial farming, as Sherry would have it. Despite this, they were not regulated by the law of value, as they did not purchase labor on the market. For an economic production unit to be regulated by the law of value, the bulk of its output must be marketed, and the bulk of its inputs must be purchased on the market. Otherwise, market forces cannot force the economic agent to be efficient and to accumulate.[74] If the economic agent is not dependent on the market, the market cannot dictate to it. The family farmer could always withdraw from the market if need be and still be able to support the farm family by producing food on the family farm. Historically, the road to market dependence moved slowly from marketing the surplus beyond subsistence to marketing the whole product. It was not just a matter of the market dependence to sell the output, but of the dependence on the market for inputs. Historically, the first input to be monetized was land when the European peasants had to pay money rent to gain possession of land. The next input to be monetized was labor, as first occurred in England. We have already seen this as capitalist agriculture that was regulated by the law of value, as early as seventeenth century in England.

In the United States, the sequence was different. In the first place, the family farm was still not marketing its entire product on the eve of the Civil War. From 1820 to 1860, the family farm system increased the proportion of its output that was sold on the market from 30 percent to 60 percent.[75] This shows that the family farm was not a neoclassical firm since not many neoclassical capitalist firms produce 40 percent of their output for the subsistence needs of their employees.

Family farmers were dependent on the market for some of their inputs. Gates and Post are correct to emphasize the importance of land being a commodity and to attribute this to federal land policy. Gates saw the land speculators harming the farmers. Post saw land policy as *forcing* farmers to produce for the market and becoming forced to produce by the law of value. My study suggests a different account. Farmers *desired* to own land and they had the opportunity to finance it by producing for the market. Federal land policy was beneficial for the farmer who desired written legal title to his land. The French peasant and the English copyholder never obtained this security. It was also beneficial for the economy, in that it gave the farmer the incentive to produce for the market and, in time, to buy capital equipment on the market which was beneficial for capitalist manufacturers who process that raw material and produce those producer goods. This development of a market for land was unique in the nineteenth-century world and is an important factor in explaining the commercialization and mechanization of American agriculture.[76]

Family farmers came to be dependent on the market much later for their capital input than for their land input. Prior to 1850, the family farm used tools made by the village blacksmith or by themselves. In the 1850s, family farmers were just beginning to adopt the mechanical reaper for harvesting wheat. This was the beginning of a large-scale movement toward purchasing capital equipment on the market. The acceleration of demand for the purchase of capital equipment in the market was greatest between 1850 and 1870, but increases in demand continued unabated throughout the nineteenth century up until World War I. This capital was primarily in the form of horse-drawn machinery, of which the mechanical reaper was the most important.[77]

But one key input to family farming production was *not* market dependent. The family farm used the labor of the farm family, not a permanent wage-labor force. For this reason, the family farm was not regulated by the law of value as Post would have it, nor was it a neoclassical profit-maximizing firm as David and Fleisig would have it.[78] Without buying labor on the market, the family farm was not *forced* to compete or to accumulate like a capitalist firm. Later in the century, more dependence on the market for farm machinery would pressure the farmer to produce efficiently, to compete, and to accumulate; but, as of 1860, the family farmer was not forced or dictated to by the market.

Nonetheless, the forces of production in agriculture were developing before the Civil War. Post claimed, based on the Parker and Klein study, that the law of value had caused this in the 1840s and 1850s. But this will not do. This study measures the productivity of labor in grain production in the 1840-1860 period in order to compare it to the productivity of labor in the 1900-1910 period. Thus it cannot be used to show that the family farm was innovating technically in the 1840s and 1850s. There was, of course, an agricultural revolution on the family farms: the period of 1850 to 1870 saw an acceleration of the purchase of farm capital equipment on the market, amounting to the first American agricultural revolution, the mechanization of agriculture.[79] However, what needs to be explained is why the family farmers did, in fact, innovate and improve agricultural technique without the compulsion of the law of value.

The agrarian class structure of the family farm system caused the forces of production to develop. It was not the law of value. Through political struggle, family farmers persuaded federal land policy to give them access to large quantities of land, more than enough to support their families, and more than could be operated by the labor of the farm family. When the price of wheat rose in the 1850s, family farmers purchased capital equipment to spread that family labor over the land they owned. Their motive was to earn cash to finance the ownership of that land. The strength and staying power of the family farm meant that industrial capitalists would produce and sell a set of horse-drawn machinery for each farm family.[80] There was no social differentiation of the family farm population. The family farm system, a single class system, has survived to this day and is still the major supplier of the U.S. food needs. This is not to say that O'Connor is right to say that the family farm system was an obstacle to the development of capitalism because it blocked the formation of an American working class. In the early period, up to 1843, industrial capitalism did not develop because there were so many opportunities within merchant capitalism.[81] Once industrialization got underway after 1843, the binding constraint on industrial capitalists was the political power of southern slaveowners who prevented them from using immigration to supply a wage-labor force.

Post is also wrong to accept Danhof's evidence on the costs of farm making. Danhof calculates how much it cost to make a farm in the 1850s. It seemed to be too much for a wage laborer to ever afford, given the wage rates. He concludes that farming was not a safety valve. But Danhof calculates the cost of constructing a commercially viable farm including the new farm machinery available as of the 1850s. But one does not need a commercially viable farm to be a subsistence farmer. Look at the French peasants and how they resisted working full time for wages by living off their subsistence plots. Many American family farmers were subsistence farmers in the 1850s. Family farming was an alternative to wage labor. That is why industrialist capitalists wanted to open up contract labor and massive immigration, and did so during the Civil War. The family farm was an alternative to wage labor but this was not the binding constraint on the transition to capitalism. The family farm propelled the transition to capitalism in spite of the fact that it was holding back the development of a market in labor.

The third form of production in antebellum America was capitalist manufacture and industry. This sector of the economy was expanding between 1843 (after the depression that followed the Panic of 1837) and 1857 (when the Panic of that year interrupted the 14-year boom). The sector was also being transformed from production in small mills to production in large factories. For example, the production of horse-drawn mechanical reapers in workshops by skilled craftsmen was transformed into their mass production in factories by wage laborers. Flour milling and meat processing were also being transformed into large scale and continuous processing production.[82] The transformation of the production of farm tools and machinery led to new production techniques in the production of iron, as the iron needed by farmers and blacksmiths was of high quality and expensive whereas the industrial producer of farm tools needed only a lower quality cheap iron.[83] The interaction of the capitalist manufacturing sector with the expanding and transforming family farm sector generated an agro-industrial complex which, both before and after the Civil War, constituted the leading sector of the American industrial revolution.[84] This is in contrast to the English model of industrialization through textiles and iron. The

United States imported its cotton and iron technologies whereas the technologies for the agro-industrial complex were of American invention.[85]

In sum, on the three forms of production in antebellum America, the growth and transformation of family farming and of capitalist manufacture and the interaction between the two shifted the balance of power from the slave mode of production to the capitalist mode of production and the allied family farm form of production.

The Role of the Civil War in the Transition to Capitalism

We turn now to the Beards-Hacker thesis on the role of the Civil War in the transition to capitalism in the United States. As mentioned above, the Beards argued that the Civil War was the American bourgeois revolution that brought the industrial capitalists to power in the federal government. Thus it is the American counterpart in the nineteenth century of the English Civil War in the seventeenth century and the French Revolution in the eighteenth century. Hacker argued that the true agents of change in the Republican Party were the conservatives with their plan for reconstruction of the North, not the radicals with their plans for reconstructing the South. As described above, the conservatives' economic policy package included removing the constraint on industrial capitalism's development and adding five spurs to that development. The constraint, of course, was slavery. The spurs were reform of money and banking, protective tariffs, liberalized immigration, a transcontinental railroad to the Pacific Ocean, and the Homestead Act.

As further evidence on the importance of the agrarian class structure for the capitalist transition, consider sharecropping which replaced slavery after the Civil War in the reconstruction of the South. Sharecropping as a form of production in the South was not an obstacle to the transition to capitalism in the North, but it was an obstacle to the transition in the South. The Emancipation Proclamation freed the slaves in the Confederacy and the Thirteenth Amendment to the Constitution prohibited slavery in the United States. Slavery was replaced not by capitalist plantations nor by black family farms. Rather sharecropping was the outcome of class struggle between the southern landowners—who wanted capitalist plantations—and the freedmen—who wanted family farms.[86] Sharecropping was not geographically expansionary and thus was no threat to the development of the west and thus to the transition to capitalism in the North. However, it was not a spur to development in the South. There was no pressure for the adoption of farm machinery, thus there was no market for the capitalist production of the means of production. The sharecroppers did have to buy their means of subsistence in the market because the landlords and the sharecroppers' creditors forced the sharecroppers to grow only cotton. But the poverty of the sharecroppers was so great that this was not much of a market for capitalist production of the means of subsistence. Sharecroppers were exploited by the landowners and by the country storekeepers through usury. And so we see that agrarian class structure—in this case, sharecropping—held back southern development, just as serf agriculture held back Eastern Europe after the fourteenth century and peasant property held back France after the seventeenth century.

Charles and Mary Beard called the American Civil War the Second American Revolution and the American counterpart to the French Revolution and the English Civil War. American historians have tried to revise this "history," denying the Civil War an economic interpretation. Because the Civil War is crucial to the transition to capitalism in the United States, we turn now to this debate. The debate began in 1961 with Thomas Cochran's attempt to revise the Beards and Hacker's account of American history by asking, "Did the Civil War retard industrialization?"[87] Using Robert Gallman's new statistical series, Cochran provided two pieces of evidence for his affirmative answer to the question. He proclaimed that American industry grew at a slower rate in the 1860s than during the 1850s (measured by value added by manufacturing). Moreover, he asserted that pig iron, textiles, and railroad production grew at a slower rate in the 1861-65 period than in the five years preceding and following that period.[88] There are problems with this specification of the question. First, using the 1860s is misleading because the first half were the war years and the second half were postwar years. Growth rates averaged for the whole decade hide more than they show. Moreover, using averages for the 1850s will not do either. The 1850s were, in fact, a boom decade. However, the boom died with the Panic of 1857 and the subsequent recession. Thus I reject the first piece of evidence. On the second piece, at least Cochran separates out the war years. But just comparing five years before and after Civil War trivializes the claim of the Beards and Hacker. The five years before should not be averaged because of the Panic of 1857 and recession. The five years afterwards, besides being postwar and thus unusual, was a short period of time. The Beards and Hacker were arguing about the effects of the Civil War on the rest of the nineteenth-century's development.

Arguing against Cochran's position, and using the same data compiled by Gallman, Salsbury demonstrates that iron, coal, and railroad lines grew considerably faster between 1865 and 1875 than between 1850 and 1860.[89] Jeffrey Williamson argued that the federal debt financing of the Civil War resulted in mobilizing capital after the war when the interest and principle repayments were made. He quantifies this contribution to capital formation at 1 percent of the GNP annually in the period between 1866 and 1872 and at 0.8 percent annually between 1872 and 1878.[90] Roger Ransom reports from statistical data compiled by Gallman that the rate of gross capital formation in the 1850s was 16 percent of GNP and in the 1870s was 19 percent.[91] Further, the percent of the labor force in manufacturing was 14 percent in 1860 and 19 percent in 1870.[92] In 1820 four in five people were in agriculture and in 1900 there were only two in five.[93] Compare that with England at the end of the seventeenth century, when only two in five were in agriculture. This is evidence that an agricultural revolution of similar proportion occurred in the two countries in two different centuries and with different agrarian class structures: family farms in the nineteenth-century United States and capitalist farms in seventeenth-century England. All this evidence implies that the Civil War was a watershed in the transition to capitalism in the United States.

In addition to this statistical evidence, Engelbourg discusses the impact of wartime inflation on the relationship between merchant capitalists and the fledgling industrial capitalists.[94] Inflation increased the cash flow to the industrialists and enabled them to liquidate their debts with merchants who had financed their development. Inflation also reduced the real value of that debt. The merchants were ultimately aligned with the slave power in the South and with pre-capitalism. As Hacker analyzed it, the American Revolution changed the nationality of merchant capitalism here from English to American. The Civil War marked the defeat of merchant capitalism by industrial capitalism. So in this sense, the Civil War helped industrial capitalists become free from the domination of merchant capitalists. Moreover, this made room for the new banking capital, reformed by Civil War legislation in 1863 and 1864.

Needless to say, this evidence has not affected the received wisdom of the economic history profession in the United States. Even though they provide the very evidence that I have used here in support of the Beards-Hacker thesis, most conventional economic historians deny its interpretation and blunt its power with qualifications. We can see this in the standard textbooks, such as Jonathan Hughes's *American Economic History*,[95] and in the latest scholarly works, such as Roger Ransom's *Conflict and Compromise: the Political Economy of Slavery, Emancipation and the Civil War*.

The family farm system in America was an agrarian class structure which enabled industrial capitalism to become the dominant mode of production in the United States. It did not hold back capitalism as serfdom did in Eastern Europe from the fourteenth century onward, nor as peasant agriculture held back France from the seventeenth century onward. Like capitalist agriculture in England from the seventeenth century onward, the American family farm system was progressive—it developed with industrial capitalism, but unlike English capitalist agriculture, in the American family farm system was egalitarian—there was no exploitation. The American Civil War put capitalists in power just as the French Revolution and the English Civil War did.

The remainder of the book is a case study of the family farmers adopting the horse-drawn mechanical reaper. It demonstrates that market forces alone cannot explain this revolutionary event and that only by looking at the agrarian class structure of the family farm system can we explain the agrarian roots of American capitalism.

The organization of the book is as follows. In Chapter 1, I introduce the empirical study that constitutes the rest of the book. In Chapter 2, I argue against the idea that family farmers were profit maximizers. In Chapter 3, I argue that they were not labor-constrained profit maximizers either. The family farm thesis is discussed in more detail in Chapter 4 and I present empirical evidence on the predominance of the medium-sized commercial family farm in the farm economy of the Old Northwest in 1860. An econometric analysis of the family farmer adopting the reaper is presented in Chapter 5. I draw conclusions from my research and infer implications for policy in Chapter 6.

NOTES

1. Maurice Dobb, *Studies in the Development of Capitalism* (London: Routledge & Kegan Paul, 1963, original edition 1946), hereafter *Studies*; and Paul Sweezy, "A Critique," in Rodney Hilton (ed.), *The Transition from Feudalism to Capitalism*, (London: New Left Review Editions, 1978, originally 1976), hereafter *Transition*.

2. T. H. Aston and C. H. E. Philpin (Eds.), *The Brenner Debate: Agrarian Class Structure and Economic Development in Pre-Industrial Europe* (New York: Cambridge University Press, 1985), hereafter *Debate*.

3. Charles A. Beard and Mary R. Beard, *The Rise of American Civilization* (New York: Macmillan, 1930, originally 1927); and Louis M. Hacker, *The Triumph of American Capitalism: The Development of Forces in American History to the End of the Nineteenth Century* (New York: Columbia University Press, 1947, originally 1940).

4. Guy Bois, "Against the Neo-Malthusian Orthodoxy," in Aston and Philpin (Eds.), *Debate*, p. 109, fn. 7.

5. John Locke, "Second Treatise of Civil Government," in *Two Treatises of Government* (London: Everyman's Library, 1924, originally 1690); and E. P. Thompson, *The Making of the English Working Class* (New York: Random House, 1963).

6. Eric Foner, *Free Soil, Free Labor, Free Men: The Ideology of the Republican Party Before the Civil War* (New York: Oxford University Press, 1970).

7. Matthew Josephson, *The Robber Barons: The Great American Capitalists, 1861-1901* (New York: Harcourt Brace Jovanovich, 1934).

8. See Chapter 6 on the implications for the Third World. In the 1980s and even in 1990, it is argued that inequality is good for growth and that it encourages work effort, saving, and investment. Thus policy to increase the inequality of incomes is fought for. The role of equality in the family farms system in the transition to capitalist development and growth in the nineteenth century suggests that the ideology of the 1980s is false.

9. Paul A. David, "Mechanization of Reaping in the Ante-Bellum Midwest," in

Henry Rosovsky (Ed.), *Industrialization in Two Systems: Essays in Honor of Alexander Gershenkron* (New York: John Wiley & Sons, 1966), pp. 2-39.

10. Karl Marx, *Capital*, 3 vols. (New York: International Publishers, 1976); and John Weeks, *Capital and Exploitation* (Princeton, NJ: Princeton University Press, 1981).

11. Heywood Fleisig, "Slavery, the Supply of Agricultural Labor, and the Industrialization of the South," *Journal of Economic History* 36 (September 1976):572-97.

12. Sweezy, "A Critique," in Hilton, *Transition*, pp. 33-56.

13. Dobb, "A Reply," in Hilton, *Transition*, p. 62.

14. Barrington Moore, Jr., *Social Origins of Dictatorship and Democracy: Lord and Peasant in the Making of the Modern World* (Boston: Beacon Press, 1966).

15. Hilton, "Introduction," in *Transition*, p. 30.

16. See Archives Municipales, et al., *Nice et la provence orientale à la fin du moyen-age* (Nice: Mairie de Nice, 1989).

17. Dobb uses this expression ("A Reply," in Hilton, *Transition*, p. 63). *Petty* is as opposed to a grand mode of production on the lord's demesne. Recall that half of the serf's week was spent on the lord's large-scale agricultural unit and half of the week on his own small-scale unit, which was further divided into strips.

18. While the European peasant and the American farmer both possessed enough land to support a family, there were differences. The European peasants' land was divided into strips whereas the American farmers had consolidated farms. The European peasants farmed communally and the American farmers individually. European peasants lived in villages; American farmers lived alone on their isolated farmsteads.

19. This is my own term developed to show the similarity and the difference of the European peasant and the American farmer. Both had enough land to support a family, but the American farmer had enough land to occupy the labor of the farm family whereas the European peasant used the extra labor time of family members to work for his lord. The European peasants were exploited. Thus petty and medium-sized are not just quantitative modifiers. Since American farmers were not exploited, they could farm more land for themselves.

20. Sweezy, "A Critique," in Hilton, *Transition*, p. 41, fn. 10.

21. Ibid., p. 42.

22. Ibid., pp. 42-43.

23. Ibid., pp. 44-45.

24. For historical documents of medieval towns agreeing not to allow runaway serfs to live within their walls, see M. Lapasset, "Menton sous les Vento," *Bulletin de la Société d'Art de d'Histoire du Mentonnais* no. 54 (Juin 1990).

25. Dobb, *Studies*, pp. 42, 46.

26. Georges Lefebvre, in *La Penseé in 1956, reprinted as "Some Observations,"* in *Hilton, Transition*, p. 123.

27. Later we will see that in the aftermath of the American Civil War, ex-slaves resisted capitalist agriculture because it included supervision. The struggle of black freedmen led to sharecropping, an unsupervised form of farming.

28. Dobb, "A Reply," in Hilton, *Transition*, p. 60.

29. See Hilton, in his 1953 "Comment," on the debate in *Science and Society*, reprinted in Hilton, *Transition*, p. 115.

30. Dobb, *Studies*, p. 32.

31. Weeks, *Capital and Exploitation*, pp. 27-49.

32. See Fernand Braudel, *The Mediterranean and The Mediterranean World in the Age of Philip II*, 2 vols., translated from the French by Sian Reynolds (New York: Harper and Row, 1972). Also see Jacques Bernard's "Trade and Finance in the Middle Ages, 900-1500," in *The Middle Ages*, The Fontana Economic History of Europe (Glasgow: Collins/Fontana, 1972).

33. *Società in 1955, reprinted as "A Survey of the Debate," in Hilton, Transition*, p. 133.

34. Dobb, "A Reply," in Hilton, *Transition*, p. 61.

35. Kohachiro Takahashi, "A Contribution to the Discussion," in Hilton, *Transition*, pp. 68-97.

36. Also see Moore, *Social Origins of Dictatorship and Democracy*.

37. Dobb, *Studies*, p. 20.

38. Hilton, "Capitalism--What's in a Name?," in *Transition*, p. 149.

39. The family farm remained a medium-sized mode of production in quantitative terms. When it began producing for the market, it was engaged in commodity production, but not of the capitalist sort, hence, I call it simple commodity production, of Marx's invention. It differs in that it has not evolved into the capitalist mode of production. It should also be noted that Marx used the term, simple commodity production, as a theoretical device and did not identify any historical example of it. Also note that the family farm is agrarian simple commodity production, whereas in Marx's exposition, it was artisan, urban simple commodity production.

40. For an explanation of the law of value, see Marx, *Capital*. For a coherent and concise explanation of the law of value, see Weeks, *Capital and Exploitation*.

41. Douglass C. North, *Growth and Welfare in the American Past* (Englewood Cliffs, NJ: Prentice-Hall, 1974).

42. D. C. North and R. P. Thomas, *The Rise of the Western World* (New York: Cambridge University Press, 1973); and North and Thomas, "The Rise and Fall of the Manorial System," in *Journal of Economic History* 31 (1971).

43. M. M. Postan, "The Chronology of Labor Services," *Transactions of the Royal Historical Society*, 4th ser., 20 (1937); and Postan, "The Rise of a Money Economy," *Economic History Review* 14 (1944).

44. *Possessed* means having the power and the right to use the land. This was not legal ownership with a written title.

45. A second market model was used by Marc Bloch to explain the rise of capitalist agriculture in the seventeenth century. The rise of market forces, he argued, led to the consolidation of landholdings and the rise of large-scale capitalist agriculture. Brenner criticizes this view by offering a counterexample. The rise of market forces in the sixteenth and seventeenth centuries did lead to consolidation and capitalist agriculture in England; but in France, market forces led to fragmentation of landholdings and to an agricultural and population crisis.

46. Robert Brenner, "Agrarian Roots of European Capitalism," in Aston and Philpin (Eds.), *Debate*, pp. 246-264. This article is Brenner's response to the reaction of the European economic historians to his original article.

47. Emmanuel Le Roy Ladurie, *The Peasants of Languedoc*, translated from the French by John Day (Chicago: University of Chicago Press, 1976).

48. As we will see, this is similar to Genovese's description of the antebellum South in the United States, see below.

49. Brenner, "Agrarian Roots," in Aston and Philpin (Eds.), *Debate*, p. 234.

50. Brenner, "Agrarian Class Structure and Economic Development in Pre-Industrial Europe," hereafter "Agrarian Class Structure," in Aston and Philpin (Eds.), *Debate*, p. 48.

51. Ibid., p. 61.

52. Perry Anderson, *Lineages of the Absolutist State* (London: New Left Review Press, 1974).

53. The large capitalist tenants were successful peasants who were wealthy enough to rent land and hire labor.

54. Quesnay's *fermiers* in the northern provinces of France were the French exception to the disaster described above.

55. Brenner, "Agrarian Class Structure," in Aston and Philpin (Eds.), *Debate*, p. 52.

56. Brenner, "Agrarian Roots," in Aston and Philpin (Eds.), *Debate*, pp. 213-327.

57. Charles Post, "The American Road to Capitalism," *New Left Review* 133 (May-June 1982):30-51.

58. Eugene D. Genovese, *The Political Economy of Slavery: Studies in the Economy and Society of the Slave South* (New York: Random House, 1965).

59. See Perry Anderson on this problem for the Roman Empire in *Passages from Antiquity to Feudalism* (London: New Left Review, 1974).

60. Robert William Fogel and Stanley L. Engerman, *Time on the Cross: The Economics of American Negro Slavery* (Boston: Little, Brown, 1974).

61. Gavin Wright, *The Political Economy of the Cotton South: Households, Markets, and Wealth in the Nineteenth Century* (New York: W. W. Norton, 1978).

62. Rodney Green, "Urban Industry, Black Resistance, and Racial Restriction in the Antebellum South: A General Model and a Case Study in Urban Virginia," (Ph.D. diss., American University, Washington, D.C., 1980).

63. Post, "American Road," pp. 31-38.

64. American mercantile capitalism dates from 1776 when the colonists broke from English mercantilism. It ends in 1843 when one may date the beginnings of American industrial capitalism as the economy pulled out of the depression and took off for an expansion that would last until the Panic of 1857. See Hacker, *Triumph of American Capitalism*.

65. Post, "American Road," p. 37.

66. See Green, "Urban Industry," on this.

67. See James M. McPherson's *Battle Cry of Freedom: The Civil War Era* (New York: Ballantine Books, 1988).

68. James O'Connor, "The Twisted Dream," *Monthly Review* 26,10 (March 1975).

69. Fredrick Jackson Turner, *The Frontier in American History* (New York: Henry Holt, 1920).

70. Robert Sherry, "Comments on O'Connor's Review of *The Twisted Dream*: Independent Commodity Production Versus Petty-Bourgeois Production," *Monthly Review*, 28,1 (May 1976). For an explanation of the law of value, also known as the labor theory of value, see Marx or see Weeks. Also, see below in the text for an explanation of what is required for the law of value to function.

71. Paul Gates, "The Role of the Land Speculator in Western Development," in G. D. Nash (Ed.), *Issues in American Economic History* (Boston: Heath, 1964).

72. W. N. Parker and J. L. Klein, "Productivity Growth in Grain Production in the United States, 1840-1860 and 1900-1910," in Dorothy S. Brady (Ed.), *Output,*

Employment and Productivity in the U.S. after 1800, vol. 30 of *Studies in Income and Wealth* (New York: National Bureau of Economic Research, 1966), pp. 523-46.

73. Clarence Danhof, "Farm-Making Costs and the 'Safety-Valve': 1850-1860," *Journal of Political Economy* 49 (June 1941).

74. Weeks, *Capital and Exploitation*.

75. Clarence Danhof, *Changes in Agriculture: The Northern United States, 1820-1870* (Cambridge, MA: Harvard University Press, 1969), p. 10.

76. Cynthia Taft Morris and Irma Adelman, *Comparative Patterns of Economic Development, 1850-1914* (Baltimore: Johns Hopkins University Press, 1988).

77. Parker and Klein, "Productivity Growth," in Brady (Ed.), *Output, Employment, and Productivity*.

78. Weeks, *Capital and Exploitation*, pp. 27-49, on how the law of value does not operate until labor power is purchased on the market.

79. Marvin Towne and Wayne Rasmussen, "Farm Gross Product and Gross Investment During the Nineteenth Century," in *Trends in the American Economy in the Nineteenth Century*, vol. 24 of *Studies in Income and Wealth*, National Bureau of Economic Research (Princeton, NJ: Princeton University Press, 1960), pp. 255-312.

80. William N. Parker, "Agriculture," in Lance E. Davis et al. (Ed.), *American Economic Growth: an Economist's History of the United States* (New York: Harper and Row, 1972), pp. 369-417.

81. See Hacker's *The Triumph of American Capitalism*.

82. See Alfred D. Chandler, *The Visible Hand: The Managerial Revolution in American Business* (Boston: Harvard University Press, 1977).

83. Post, "American Road," p. 49.

84. Ibid., p. 48.

85. Nathan Rosenberg, *Technology and American Economic Growth* (White Plains, NY: M. E. Sharpe, 1972).

86. Roger Ransom and Richard Sutch, *One Kind of Freedom: The Economic Consequences of Emancipation* (New York: Cambridge University Press, 1977); Eric Foner, *Reconstruction: The Unfinished Revolution, 1863-1877* (New York: Harper and Row, 1988); and Gavin Wright, *Old South, New South: Revolutions in the Southern Economy Since the Civil War* (New York: Basic Books, 1986).

87. Thomas Cochran, "Did the Civil War Retard Industrialization?" *Mississippi Valley Historical Review* 48 (September 1961) cited in Post, "American Road."

88. Post, "American Road," p. 50.

89. Cited in Ibid., p. 50.

90. Jeffrey Williamson, "Watersheds and Turning Points: Conjectures on the Long-Term Impact of Civil War Financing," *Journal of Economic History* 34, 3 (September 1974) and cited in Jonathan Hughes, *American Economic History*, 3rd ed. (Glenview, IL: Scott, Foresman, 1990), p. 254.

91. Roger Ransom, *Conflict and Compromise: The Political Economy of Slavery, Emancipation, and the American Civil War* (New York: Cambridge University Press, 1989), p. 264.

92. Ibid., p. 259.

93. Ibid.

94. Cited by Post, "American Road," p. 50.

95. Hughes, *American Economic History*.

1

INTRODUCTION TO
THE EMPIRICAL STUDY

The adoption of the horse-drawn mechanical reaper by family farmers in the American Midwest in the nineteenth century was a major economic revolution. It dramatically increased the productivity of agricultural labor, and it stimulated the spread of mass production in U.S. industry. It provided a case of successful economic development and a model of fruitful interaction between field and factory. I contend that family farm agricultural institutions played a crucial role in this event, and they offer lessons for current problems of economic development. My central thesis is that family farm agricultural institutions were a favorable initial condition for the adoption of farm machinery because they were based on a relatively equal distribution of abundant land which generated many farmers with a sufficient surplus and incentive to purchase capital goods. Without the farm machinery, the food needs of U.S. industrialization probably would not have been met. But without the family farm system, the mass production of that machinery probably would not have been taken on.

I shall defend the thesis that family farm agricultural institutions were favorable to adoption of farm machinery by showing their role in the adoption of the horse-drawn mechanical reaper, the most important agricultural machine in the nineteenth century. This study includes agricultural institutions, the family farm system, in a formal econometric analysis that relates them to agricultural performance and its interaction with U.S. industrialization.

THE PROBLEM WITH TREATING THE FAMILY FARM AS A PROFIT-MAXIMIZING FIRM

With the exception of plantation slavery in the antebellum South, the agricultural institutions in the nineteenth-century United States took the form of the family farm system.[1] David applied the neoclassical theory of the firm to the problem of explaining the adoption of the reaper in the antebellum Midwest, but without any specific reference to the institutional features of the family farm system.[2] There would be no need for an institutional explanation of the adoption of the reaper if David's explanation worked. The most serious challenge to David's profit-maximizing model came from Alan Olmstead, who criticized the model on empirical grounds.[3] These are discussed in Chapter 2. Olmstead argues that David underestimated the capital costs of the reaper attributable to interest costs and to depreciation. Thus, in Olmstead's view, the threshold of profitability for reaper adoption should be much higher than David had it. Olmstead then claims that, on the basis of the revised thresholds, few farmers in the American Midwest in the 1850s would have found it rational to adopt the reaper because most were producing substantially below the profit-maximizing scale.[4]

Olmstead's critique leaves matters in an anomalous state, since my own research shows that many farmers who were producing below the profit-maximizing scale did, in fact, adopt the reaper. Rather than conclude that they were not rational to do so, I suggest that family farmers were not profit maximizers, but risk-averse utility maximizers. As such, it was rational for these farmers to adopt the reaper in the 1850s even though they were producing below the threshold of profitability. I call this alternative view the family farm thesis. It holds that risk-averse utility-maximizing farmers rationally adopted the reaper in the 1850s when producing an output below the threshold at which profit maximization would have dictated its adoption.

To defend the family farm thesis, I shall test David's model using Olmstead's revised thresholds on new data and with new methods. Where David tested his model on wheat-producing counties in Illinois, I shall use data from the whole Old Northwest, where the first wave of popular reaper adoption took place. Instead of using averages, I shall use observations on individual farms. In this way, I determine how many farmers and what proportion were producing below the estimated profit-maximizing level. If a substantial number and proportion of reaper adopters were producing under the estimated profit-maximizing scale, this anomaly suggests the need for an economics of the family farm that would explain this behavior. I carry out this quantitative task in Chapter 2.

Along with the family farm thesis, I shall consider another possible explanation for the anomaly. This is suggested by the work of Fleisig, who assumes that the farmer is a profit maximizer facing a labor constraint.[5] As the farm increases its scale of production, the labor constraint becomes binding. Thus the farmer must substitute capital for labor to expand, and this means mechanization. However, the binding labor constraint prevents the farm from producing at the profit-maximizing scale. Accordingly, family farmers could have been labor-constrained profit maximizers who adopted the reaper when the labor constraint became binding, while the labor constraint prevented them from attaining the profit-maximizing scale. This might explain the anomaly.

I take exception with Fleisig's explanation because it ignores what I consider to be the crucial characteristic of the family farm, its choice to rely on family labor and to avoid the risks of employing a year-round wage-labor force. It is the lack of demand for wage labor and the corresponding choice to rely on family labor that caused the family farm to adopt the reaper when its opportunities and cash needs led it to desire to produce more output than family labor force could produce with hand tools. In addition, due to the family farm system, there was not much labor supplied to the market as most families owned farms. Moreover, if the family farm had been a profit-maximizing firm facing a labor constraint, it would have paid a higher wage to attract labor from other regions and industries and even other countries through immigration. We now turn to a more detailed statement of the family farm thesis.

THE FAMILY FARM THESIS

The family farm thesis is comprised of elements of an economics of the family farm coupled with elements of a theory of the institutional structure of the family farm system. Together they constitute a political economy of the family farm. It is an alternative to the neoclassical economic theory of the profit-maximizing farm found in the work of David and Fleisig. I shall also measure the economic, institutional, and resource characteristics of the family farm system in the Old Northwest at mid-nineteenth century. Together, this theorizing and evidence can be used to explain the adoption of the reaper by family farms.

The family farm thesis is about one of the important causes of the adoption of agricultural improvements in the nineteenth-century United States. It holds that the economics and the institutional structure of the family farm system were important initial conditions accounting for the responsiveness of nineteenth-century U.S. agricultural institutions to the spread of markets--a responsiveness evident in their adoption of productivity raising improvements. The family farm thesis is offered in conjunction with two other major causes of reaper adoption, which will be discussed below: (1) economic changes and opportunities due to the industrialization of the American northeast, and (2) relative abundance of agricultural resources in the United States.

Definition of the Family Farm

The family farm is defined as an agricultural production unit (producing food and fiber) based on land resources in which both labor and management are supplied by the family household, the residence of which is on the farm. The first necessary condition for a family farm is: (1) there must be enough land on the farm to support the family.[6] The second necessary condition for a family farm is: (2) there is not more land on the farm than the labor force of the family can work, with the exception of harvest time, when hired labor may be used. If condition (1) is not fulfilled, then it is not a farm, but a holding. The implication is that a family using this holding must supplement its income, for example, by hiring out the labor of some members of the family. If condition (2) is not fulfilled, then it is a business farm. The implication is that this farm must hire labor to operate this much land.

There are two consequences of these various land-labor relationships. One consequence of a family farm so defined is that the family controls production, that is, is the manager of the farm. The same economic agents labor and manage. This is not the case on the business farm. Here the manager hires labor. The other consequence of a family farm so defined is that the family resides on the farm. It is a household residence in addition to being a production unit. The manager and the hired workers on the business farm need not, and probably do not, reside on the farm. Thus, a third necessary condition for a family farm is: (3) the predominant kind of labor on the farm is that of the family, with hired labor used only at the harvest. If this condition is not fulfilled, and the predominant kind of labor on the farm is hired labor, that is, labor purchased in the market, then it is a business farm. The fourth, and final necessary condition for a family farm is: (4) the family which operates the farm and supplies the labor for farm production resides on the farm. If this condition is unfulfilled it is not a family farm. The set of sufficient conditions for the definition of a family farm includes all four of the necessary conditions.

Assuming that this is a closed system, the demand for labor on the large business farms must be met by the supply of labor from farm households with land-holdings insufficient to support the family. I distinguish family farms into small and medium-sized family farms. Small family farms are those with just enough land to support the farm family. Medium-sized family farms are those with more than necessary to support the family, but no more than can be worked by the labor force of the farm family. Small family farms do not supply much labor to the market. Medium-sized family farms do not demand much labor. The labor constraint experienced by the large farm (and to a lesser extent by the medium-sized family farm at harvest) is due to the fact that there were only a few farm households offering labor in the market. No other important sources of labor were available in this period. This is what is meant by the labor constraint being caused by the institutional structure of the family farm system, rather than by market forces alone.

Under certain conditions individual farms could be transformed from one type to another. The small family farm could grow into a medium-sized family farm or it could be reduced to a holding. The holding could increase into a small family farm or even into a medium-sized family farm. How a medium-sized family farm becomes a large business farm is more complicated. Through a process of increasing commercialization, quantitative changes might result in qualitative change. Historically, commercialization begins with output. If a family farm sells its surplus, it is still a family farm. Even if it specializes and sells its whole output, it is still a family farm. Historically, the first input to be commercialized was land. As the case of family farms in the United States shows, even the purchase of land does not change its family farm status. Furthermore, the commercialization of the input capital, that is, the purchase of the capital in the market (the adoption of farm machinery) does not change the status of the farm; it is still a family farm. What does change is the amount of land that can occupy the labor force of the farm family. A family farm is quite large when it uses machinery, but it is still a family farm. For example, I estimate that in 1860 in the Old Northwest, a family farm could operate 160 acres. Today, it is said that a farm family can operate a farm of 2,000 or 3,000 acres of wheat.

The major qualitative change occurs with the commercialization of labor. When all inputs, including labor, are purchased on the market, and all output is sold on the market, it is no longer a family farm. It becomes a business farm. This process can be traced historically as follows. First, labor was hired at the harvest, which was a traditional transaction. Second, in the northern United States, the permanent hired hand appeared on the family farm. As long as most of the labor on the farm was family labor, it was still a family farm. As the hired labor force increased on a family farm, the working farmer tended to stop doing manual labor and specialized in the management function. Exceptions might be rich peasants in nineteenth-century Russia or France where working and managing peasants worked alongside their hired workers. Third, when most of the labor on the farm was hired labor, it became a full business farm in which all the labor was purchased in the market.[7]

Economics of the Family Farm

I assume that the farm family is a utility maximizer, rather than a profit maximizer. I assume that the farm family derives utility not only from consumption but also from the benefits of farm ownership and family control of the farm.[8] Part of the reason that the farm family wants to own the farm is to maximize current and future consumption. Owning the farm reduces risk and thus increases the discounted present value of the future income stream from the farm. However, there is an independent source of utility in farm ownership. This is demonstrated by the fact that the farm family is willing to give up consumption in order to obtain or maintain farm ownership. For example, in the downswing of the agricultural cycle, the farm family continues operating the farm even though their implicit wage is lower than what they could obtain from alternative employment.

I also assume that farm families are risk averse. They are willing to have a lower level of consumption, current and future, in order to avoid the risks of fluctuations in the level of consumption. It is the level of consumption in bad times that is their concern. Owning and operating a farm means that in periods of unemployment, sickness, or old age, the level of consumption of the family can be maintained at a minimum acceptable to the family. They produce their own food and have shelter on the farm. This level is higher than the level of consumption they would attain in bad times if they did not own and operate their own farm. They might be unemployed. But this level is lower than the level of consumption they could have obtained in good times if they hired a permanent, year-round labor force to help them on the farm. This minimum level of consumption is lower than that which they could have obtained in alternative employment.

The economic problem of the family farm is to use given resources and allocate them to achieve their goals. In the case at hand, there was a relative abundance of agricultural resources, which had been relatively equally distributed. The family farm is characterized by this relative abundance of land resources. I stress this abundance where Fleisig stresses the market labor constraint. I believe this abundance affected the behavior of the family farms more than the market-determined labor constraint that Fleisig posits. A second characteristic of the family farm is that it faces a type of risk in agriculture that is not present in industry and commerce. This is due to the organic nature of agriculture and its dependence on the weather. A third characteristic of the family farm is that it faces fluctuations in the demand for labor over the seasons. Family labor may be enough to operate a farm in slack times, but at wheat harvest there is a peak demand for labor.

The family farm allocates its abundant resources to achieve its goals. It decides what level of output to produce. The family farm selects its level of output initially by a labor constraint. In contrast to Fleisig who takes the labor constraint to be determined by the market, I take this labor constraint to be self-imposed: To avoid risk, the farm family limited the use of labor to that of the farm family. Although this labor constraint was binding in terms of the number of workers, there was a range of output based on two other major factors. First, the medium-sized family farm allocated more labor time per family member to work instead of leisure than did the small family farm, because it was under pressure to earn more cash to finance its larger farm. Second, the medium-sized family farm had access to a higher quality of labor than the large business farm based on a permanent, year-round labor force. Hired labor did not have the incentive to do quality work. Family labor did. While the maximum level of output was determined by the labor constraint (because the family farm was risk averse and chose a labor level at which, in downturns, labor could be underpaid and paid no cash), cash needs to finance the mortgage provided a strong incentive to approach the maximum level of output that family labor can produce. This incentive operated to help avert the risk of having no cash to pay the mortgage in the downturn. I hypothesize the following observable behavior:

Hypothesis 1: Risk-averse utility-maximizing family farms rationally adopted the reaper in the 1850s at a scale of production below the threshold at which profit maximization would have dictated the adoption of the reaper. When the farm family wanted to produce more than they currently were based on family labor, it had to decide whether to hire labor or to adopt machinery. At harvest time, the labor constraint becomes a problem. There was not much labor in the market, as Fleisig states. In addition, the family farmer had to compete with large business farms that had already collected a labor force and wanted more for the harvest. Thus it was a risk that he would not command the limited labor that was in the market. The decision to plant wheat was made months before the harvest, so there was the risk that by harvest time the labor would not be there. I contend it was the riskiness of obtaining labor, more than the limited amount that the family farmer had to compete for, that turned his decision to machinery. There are other reasons for this. Money and credit were available to finance machinery purchase but not to finance a wage bill. Furthermore, workers cannot wait until after the harvest to be paid, unlike machinery producers who can and do wait. The family farmer was cash constrained. He rarely had cash except when he has sold his harvest. The farm family could have achieved a higher level of income if they expanded their farm and collected a labor force, but they preferred to avoid the risks of agricultural fluctuations by not relying on hired labor. I hypothesize the following observable behavior:

Hypothesis 2: Risk-averse utility-maximizing family farms rationally adopted the reaper in the 1850s when they wanted to produce more wheat than they could with family labor.

The Institutional Structure of the Family Farm System

Intimately related to the economics of the family farm is the institutional structure of the family farm, to which we now turn. The two major features of the institutional structure of the family farm system were: (1) the system of land holding and tenure, the fact that ownership was available to families through the purchase of land for a farm; and (2) the system of land distribution, the fact that land was relatively equally distributed. These agricultural institutions were, in part, caused by the political institutions in the nineteenth-century United States. Farmers were represented in the legislative part of the federal government in the United States, a rare phenomenon in the nineteenth-century world. In addition, there was the relatively egalitarian federal land policy which was liberalized throughout the nineteenth century. This mainly took the form of decreasing the minimum amount of unimproved land that could be bought from the federal government. This meant access to the abundant land resources for cultivator families.[9]

Hypothesis 3: The institutional structure of the family farm system was a favorable initial condition for the adoption of farm machinery because it made ownership possible for many farmers through the purchase of land. To purchase land for a farm, the family needed cash. Thus they increased their production for the market. In the case of the medium-sized family farm, the level of production required to finance owning this size farm brought the family up to its capacity to operate the farm with hand tools and without recourse to hired labor. Whereas the economics of the family farm led to the desire to own a farm, the institutional structure of the family farm led to the real possibility of owning a farm.

Hypothesis 4: The institutional structure of the family farm system was a favorable initial condition for the adoption of farm machinery because it was based on a relatively equal distribution of abundant land which generated many farmers with a sufficient surplus and incentive to purchase capital goods. The sheer number of farms with an investible surplus made for a broad market for capital goods. Continuing egalitarian federal land policy in the 1850s resulted in a rapidly growing market. And the expectation for the future was a continually growing market for capital goods. Without this mass market for farm machinery, the mass production of farm machinery probably would not have been taken on. Without mass production of farm machinery, it would not have been so abundant and so reasonably priced and thus not adopted. In addition, the institutional structure of the family farm system was so strong and predominant in the farm economy, that the producers of farm machinery adapted the machinery to the family farm scale, hence encouraging its adoption.

Note that unlike the two economic hypotheses which are directly observable, these two institutional hypotheses are not. However, there are behaviors that we can observe directly which will suggest that these hypotheses should be retained in our explanation or that we should reject them. That is, they are testable.

In the small, I am arguing that the family farm system was an important cause of the adoption of the reaper and other farm machinery. In the large, I am arguing that the family farm system was an important cause of the widespread nature and the great extent of industrialization in the United States in the nineteenth century. Following Adelman and Morris, I believe that the path of industrial development is the outcome of the interaction of two sets of influences: initial conditions and dynamic economic developments.[10] The family farm system, as a kind of agricultural institution, is one of the several initial conditions, which also include natural resource constraints, favorableness of political institutions to the spread of market activities, and the level of subsistence of the rural population. In the case of the United States, there were also the favorable initial conditions of relatively abundant agricultural resources and a high level of subsistence of the rural population. There was a high level of subsistence of the rural population because, in part, the relatively abundant agricultural resources were widely distributed to families. As to the dynamic economic forces, Adelman and Morris include: the spread of domestic markets, the dynamics of export expansion, and the pace and direction of the movement of productive factors. If there had been no spread of the market for food, the family farm system would not have had the economic opportunity for commercialization and mechanization. There was "export" of food from the Old Northwest to the Northeast. There was a tremendous flow of capital and labor from Europe and the American Northeast to the Old Northwest. There were many reasons why the United States industrialized so early, rapidly, and widely, but the family farm system was clearly one of those reasons.[11]

A BRIEF QUANTITATIVE ECONOMIC HISTORY OF THE OLD NORTHWEST IN THE 1850S

The Ordinance of 1787 set up the first colony of the United States, the Northwest Territory, which was the territory northwest of the Ohio River. When the border of the United States extended to the Pacific Ocean, this territory became the Old Northwest.[12] In this eastern half of the Upper Mississippi Valley, a large agricultural surplus grew and was exported.[13] The Old Northwest, the present census region of the East North Central, had the most rapid economic growth per capita of any U.S. region for which we have data. Consequently this portion of the U.S. can be viewed as being perhaps the most significant single region from the standpoint of understanding the nature of economic growth in the nineteenth century. It is the heart of the national experience in the beginning of the movement toward sustained growth in per capita national income.[14]

The Old Northwest is the eastern half of what we call the American Midwest today.[15]

The Old Northwest region is bordered on the east by the states of the American Northeast, on the west by the Mississippi River and the American West, on the north by the Great Lakes and Canada beyond, and on the south by the American South. By the 1850s the territory had become the states of Ohio, Indiana, Illinois, Michigan and Wisconsin. It was "climatically temperate and generally endowed with the indented coast lines and river networks which alone at the time [before the railroad] made possible the long distance transport of cereals."[16] The area of the territory was 248,283 square miles, which is larger than France at 210,038 square miles, and much larger than the United Kingdom, at 94,399 square miles.[17]

In order to return mentally to the region and to the mid-nineteenth century, I offer these two facts. In the 1850s in Indiana "one half of the rural population still dwelt in log cabins."[18] "In any given month for a full half-century there was a demand for 40,000 axes in North America."[19] In the case of the Old Northwest, nearly all the land was virgin woodlands that had to be cleared of trees by ax and fenced before farming could begin.

As to the decade of the 1850s, the focal point of this study, the following two tables document the economic boom that was taking place. Table 1.1 shows regional growth. First we can see the farm-making process in the statistic that there was a 45 percent increase in total acres in farms. This represents the distribution and sale of land by the federal government. The 80 percent increase in improved acres represents the clearing and fencing of land that was put into production. Capital formation was rapid: the value of farms in the region rose 158 percent due to rising land values and to the farm-making process. This was basically a corn and livestock economy; the value of livestock rose 138 percent and the production of corn rose 58 percent. However, with the price of wheat rising in the 1850s many farmers turned to wheat production and this increased 102 percent over the 1850s. The value of farm implements and machinery rose 90 percent, reflecting the beginnings of the mechanization of agriculture.

The number of farms increased by 59.4 percent over the 1850s and this accounts for much of the growth of the regional aggregates given above. However, the individual farm also grew. Table 1.2 shows the growth of the individual farm via statistics on the mean farm. The mean size of farm in total acres actually declined because of the availability in the later period

Table 1.1
Growth of the Regional Economy of the Old Northwest

	1850	1860	Growth Rate (percent)
Total acres	50 m	73 m	45
Improved acres	23 m	41 m	80
Value of farms	$672 m	$1,736 m	158
Value of implements	$30 m	$57 m	90
Value of livestock	$99 m	$236 m	138
Wheat (bushels)	39 m	80 m	102
Corn (bushels)	177 m	280 m	58

Source: U.S. Census, *The Seventh Census of the United States, 1850, Agriculture* (Washington, D.C.: Robert Armstrong, 1853), pp. 729, 791, 863, 904, 930 for TA, IA, VOF and VOI and pp. 731, 792, 864, 905, 931 for VOLS, wheat and corn. (Hereafter cited as *Printed Census, 1850*); U.S. Census, *Agriculture of the United States in 1860: Compiled from the Original Returns of the Eighth Census* (Washington, D.C.: Government Printing Office, 1864), pp. 34, 42, 76, 116, 166 for TA, IA, VOF and VOI, and pp. 35, 43, 77, 117, 164 for VOLS, wheat and corn. (Hereafter cited as *Printed Census, 1860*.)

Table 1.2
Growth of the Average Farm in the Old Northwest

	1850	1860	Growth Rate (percent)
Number of farms	368,177	586,717	59
Total acres	136	124	- 27
Improved acres	62	70	13
Value of farm	$1,825	$2,957	62
Value of implements	$83	$97	17
Value of livestock	$282	$402	43
Wheat (acres)	8.8	11.1	27
Corn (acres)	15.8	14.6	- 8

Source: Printed Census, 1850, for number of farms: pp. 220, 226, 232, 256, 286, 292, 328, 334; *Printed Census, 1860*, for number of farms: pp. 197, 198, 204, 211, 219; and Table 1.1 sources. Yields: 12.2 bushels of wheat per acre and 32.7 bushels of corn per acre, W. N. Parker and J. L. Klein, "Productivity Growth in Grain Production in the U.S., 1840-60 and 1900-10" in Dorothy S. Brady (Ed.), *Output, Employment and Productivity in the U.S. After 1800*, vol. 53 of *Studies in Income and Wealth* (New York: National Bureau of Economic Research, 1966), p. 532.

of smaller holdings of land for purchase. However, the actual size of a functioning farm (in improved acres) rose by 13 percent. This represents the farm-making process of transforming virgin land (total acres) into improved acres ready to be planted. The value of the average farm rose by 62 percent, the value of the livestock by 43 percent, and the value of farm implements and machinery rose by 17 percent. The production of wheat on the mean farm rose by 27 percent and the production of corn actually declined by 8 percent. It should be noted that the scale of production of wheat on the individual farm rose, from 8.8 acres to 11.1 acres, or 26.1 percent. This was caused by the increase in the price of wheat from 1850 to 1860 from 80 cents to $1.02, or 27.5 percent.[20] This is near unity elasticity.

David argued that one of the causes of the adoption of the reaper was the increase in production of small grains up to the profit-maximizing level of 36 acres. Olmstead, correcting for empirical errors, revised this to 78 acres of small grains. As I shall argue in Chapter 2, the threshold of profitability should be measured in the cash crop only, and thus the threshold should be 78 acres of wheat. The scale of wheat production rose over the 1850s and in some way did cause the adoption of the reaper. The issue is what was the nature and magnitude of the threshold, beyond which a farmer must desire to produce, that would put pressure on him to adopt the reaper.

Labor statistics are harder to come by. We know from Gates's analysis of the printed census that there were 956,244 men in the farm labor force in the Old Northwest in 1860. Of these, 588,717 were farm operators, leaving 367,527 farm workers without farms that were either unpaid sons of the farm operators or farm workers for hire.[21] It has been estimated that in Indiana there were as many farm workers as industrial workers, but that each group constituted only one-eighth of the number of independent farmers. Furthermore, the economic status of the farmer was said to be the same as an industrial worker except for the ownership of land.[22] In the 1850s there was a rise in day wage for cradlers of 47 percent. The cradler who cut wheat by hand made $1.27 a day in Illinois in 1849-1853 and by 1854-1857 he was making $1.87 a day.[23] The index of farm wage rates (1910-14 = 100) rose from 49 to 62 between 1850 and 1860.[24]

This is the second cause given by David for the adoption of the reaper. He argues that an increasing demand for labor in other sectors of the economy caused the wage for farm workers to rise relative to the price of capital goods. Thus farmers adopted the reaper to substitute inexpensive capital goods for expensive labor. However, David did not see this as a matter of the choice of the least-cost technique alone but rather this coupled with the increase in the scale of production to profit-maximizing levels. The wage did rise, but was it an important cause of reaper adoption?

From Tables 1.1 and 1.2, we can see that the farm economy of the Old Northwest was growing rapidly in the 1850s. It was also being transformed qualitatively via commercialization and mechanization. First, we look at commercialization. The Old Northwest rose to be the major producer of wheat in the United States in 1840 when it overtook the region of the North Atlantic (New England plus New York, New Jersey, and Pennsylvania) as producer of the largest share of U.S. wheat production. In the 1850s the Old Northwest was producing between 46 and 49 percent of the U.S. wheat crop.[25] The farm economy of the northern part of the United States had increased its marketed farm product from 30 percent of its total product in 1820 to 60 percent in 1860.[26] In the Old Northwest, there was an increase in specialization in wheat at expense of corn of ten percentage points. In value terms, in the Old Northwest in 1850, the average farm was 29 percent specialized in wheat, whereas by 1860, the average farm was 39 percent specialized.[27]

Second, we look at mechanization. The machines of the first agricultural revolution included machines to plant corn and wheat, machines to cultivate corn, machines to harvest wheat (the reaper), and machines to thresh the wheat. The most important machine was the horse-drawn reaper because the wheat harvest was a weather-related bottleneck for the farmer. In the Old Northwest in the 1850s, the pace of the adoption of the horse-drawn mechanical reaper accelerated. In 1849 less than 1 percent of farmers in the Old Northwest had adopted reapers and were cutting 2 percent of the wheat crop there. In 1859, 5 percent of the farmers had adopted the reaper and were harvesting one quarter of the wheat crop.[28] The Old Northwest was the major site of the first popular wave of reaper adoptions. The adoption of the reaper caused a rise in the productivity of labor including a decrease in man-hours required per bushel of wheat. One can infer the rise in productivity in the Old Northwest in the 1850s due to the adoption of the reaper from the statistic on the rise of productivity in wheat production in the American West (including the Old Northwest) between 1840 and 1910, the period in which the mechanical reaper was adopted across the continent. The hours of labor required to harvest a bushel of wheat fell from 15 hours in 1840 to 2.3 hours in 1910.[29] The adoption of the reaper was part and parcel of the first agricultural revolution in the United States. From 1850 to 1870, "the real farm gross output rose from $1.4 billion to $2.5 billion . . . [and] real farm gross product per worker in agriculture rose from $294 in 1850 to $362 in 1870."[30]

The farm economy of the Old Northwest in the 1850s was growing and being transformed by commercialization and mechanization. A third crucial aspect of this economy was its interaction with the American Northeast that was industrializing. If we define industrialization of the factory sector (where factory is an enterprise using inanimate power), then we can say that the Northeast was industrializing in this decade of the 1850s.[31] Machinery was the seventh most important sector of the U.S. economy in value-added terms in 1860, indicating the extent of factory production of machinery.

Textile production was mechanized and cotton goods were the number one sector of the economy and woolen goods were the eighth. A wide range of consumer goods were being produced mainly in factories: boots and shoes were the third sector in value-added terms and men's clothing was the fifth most important sector. Iron was the sixth most important sector.[32] In the 1850s the American Northeast and Old Northwest were connected by railroads and feeder railroads built within the Old Northwest.[33]

Two other interactions between the agricultural and industrial sectors should be mentioned. The most important was the demand and supply of food. Without this demand for food, the farm economy would never have adopted farm machinery. They did not need it to feed themselves. To see how important food was in the economy, note that the fourth leading branch of manufacture in the United States in 1860 in value-added terms, was flour and meal. Liquor was tenth.[34] The other interaction was the demand and supply of money and credit. Without this, farmers could not have financed farm ownership or the purchase of machinery. Also eastern (and British) investment was important in financing the construction of the railroads.

The 1850s saw an increase in the production of reapers. In 1849, only 1,684 reapers were produced in the United States. In the year 1859, 16,574 reapers were produced. This represents a growth rate of 9 percent per annum sustained over a period of ten years.[35] This represents a backward linkage from agriculture to the suppliers of machinery and subsequent economic growth of the whole U.S. economy.[36] The index of farm machinery prices (1910-14 = 100) fell from 187 to 161 from 1850 to 1860.[37] However, the price of the reaper rose 11 percent from $124 to $138.[38] It should also be noted that the scale of production of reapers increased with the initiation of factory production by McCormick in Chicago from 1848.[39]

In sum, the farm economy of the Old Northwest in the 1850s was rapidly growing, commercializing and mechanizing with important interactions with the industrializing American Northeast.

NOTES

1. On slavery, see Gavin Wright, *The Political Economy of the Cotton South: Households, Markets, and Wealth in the Nineteenth Century* (New York: W. W. Norton, 1978). On family farms, see William Parker, "Agriculture," in Lance Davis, et al. (Eds.), *American Economic Growth: An Economist's History of the U.S.* (New York: Harper and Row, 1972).

2. Paul David, "Mechanization of Reaping in the Ante-Bellum Midwest," in Henry Rosovsky (Ed.), *Industrialization in Two Systems: Essays in Honor of Alexander Gershenkron*, (New York: John Wiley and Sons, 1966).

3. Alan Olmstead, "The Mechanization of Reaping and Mowing in American Agriculture, 1833-1870," *Journal of Economic History* 35 (June 1975).

4. My study focuses on the eastern half of the Midwest because that is where the first wave of popular reaper adoption took place. The Old Northwest is the region of the United States that today is called East North Central by the U.S. Bureau of the Census. It includes the states of Ohio, Indiana, Illinois, Wisconsin, and Michigan. The American Midwest includes the states of the Old Northwest plus the states west of the Mississippi River, such as Iowa, Kansas, and Minnesota.

5. Heywood Fleisig, "Slavery, the Supply of Agricultural Labor, and the Industrialization of the South," *Journal of Economic History* 36 (September 1976).

6. To be precise, this condition would be stated as just enough land to just support the family. This is the minimum amount of land to qualify as a family farm. A family farm is identified at just that point where there is just enough land to just support a family. The maximum amount of land before disqualifying a farm from being a family farm is just as much land as the farm family can handle.

7. My work on the family farm was greatly benefitted by the generosity of Wayne Rasmussen, recently retired historian at the U.S. Department of Agriculture. See his "Mechanization of Agriculture," *Scientific American* 247 (September 1982): 82. To gain a wide perspective on the mechanization of agriculture, see this entire issue of *Scientific American* which is devoted to the topic of mechanization of work.

8. The benefits of farm ownership include liberty, independence, security, status, and control of the labor process.

9. My work on the measurement of institutional variables was greatly benefitted by the generosity of Cynthia Taft Morris. See Irma Adelman and Cynthia Taft Morris, "Patterns of Industrialization in the Nineteenth and Early Twentieth Centuries: A Cross-Sectional Quantitative Study," *Research in Economic History* 5 (1980).

10. Cynthia Taft Morris and Irma Adelman, *Comparative Patterns of Economic Development, 1850-1014* (Baltimore: Johns Hopkins University Press, 1988).

11. My thesis is the same principle only in reverse as that of Fred Bateman and Thomas Weiss, in *A Deplorable Scarcity: The Failure of Industrialization in the Slave Economy* (Chapel Hill: University of North Carolina Press, 1981). My thesis could be stated as a laudable equally distributed abundance was a cause of the success of industrialization in the family farm economy.

12. R. Carlyle Buley, *The Old Northwest: Pioneer Period, 1815-1840*, 2 vols. (Indianapolis: Indiana Historical Society, 1950), p. vii.

13. A. L. Kohlmeier, *The Old Northwest as the Keystone of the Arch of the American Federal Union* (Bloomington, IN: The Principia Press, 1938), p. iv.

14. David C. Klingamon and Richard Vedder, *Essays in Nineteenth Century Economic History: The Old Northwest* (Athens, OH: Ohio University Press, 1975), pp. ix-x.

15. William N. Parker, "From Northwest to Midwest: Social Bases of a Regional History," in David C. Klingamon and Richard Vedder (Eds.), *Essays in Nineteenth Century Economic History: The Old Northwest* (Athens, OH: Ohio University Press, 1975), p. 3.

16. E. L. Jones and S. J. Woolf (Eds.), *Agrarian Change and Economic Development: The Historical Problems* (London: Methuen and Co., 1969), p. 5.

17. *World Atlas*, Hammond, 1981.

18. Harvey L. Carter, "Rural Indiana in Transition: 1850-1860," *Agricultural History* 2 (April 1946):107.

19. Jones and Woolf, *Agrarian Change*, p. 18.

20. Marvin W. Towne and Wayne E. Rasmussen, "Farm Gross Product and Gross Investment During the Nineteenth Century" in *Trends in the American Economy in the Nineteenth Century*, National Bureau of Economic Research, vol. 24 of *Studies in Income and Wealth* (Princeton: Princeton University Press, 1960), p. 297.

21. Paul W. Gates, *The Farmer's Age: Agriculture 1815-1860*, vol. 3 of *The Economic History of the United States* (New York: Harper and Row, 1960), p. 273.

22. Carter, "Rural Indiana," p. 108.

23. David, "Mechanization of Reaping," in Rosovsky, *Industrialization*, pp. 35-36.

24. Towne and Rasmussen, "Farm Gross Product," p. 269.

25. Parker, "Agriculture," in Davis, *American Economic Growth*, p. 381.

26. Clarence Danhof, *Changes in Agriculture: The Northern U.S., 1820-1870* (Cambridge, MA: Harvard University Press, 1969), p. 10; and U.S. Census, *Historical Statistics of the United States, Colonial Times to 1957* (Washington, D.C.: Government Printing Office, 1960), pp. A202-203.

27. The price of corn rose from 40 cents to 46 cents and the price of wheat from 80 cents to $1.02 over the 1850s, according to Towne and Rasmussen, "Farm Gross Production," p. 297. Specialization was measured by taking the quotient of the value of wheat and the combined value of wheat and corn for the average farm. This index can be interpreted in two ways. On one hand, it shows the temporary switch from corn to wheat and on the other hand, it shows the long run trend of increasing production for the market, as wheat was sold on the market and corn was produced for on-farm use, to feed livestock and the family.

28. See my Chapter 2 and Appendix A for the procedure used to make these estimates.

29. W. N. Parker and J. L. Klein, "Productivity Growth in Grain Production in the U.S., 1840-60 and 1900-10," in Dorothy S. Brady (Ed.), *Output, Employment and Productivity in the U.S. after 1800*, vol. 53 of *Studies in Income and Wealth* (New York: National Bureau of Economic Research, 1966), p. 532. Another comparison is that in 1822-1825: "About 50 to 60 man-hours of labor were required to produce 1 acre of wheat with a walking plow, a bundle of brush for harrow, hand broadcast of seed, harvesting by sickle, and threshing by flail." Whereas in 1890: "To produce 1 acre of wheat with a gang plow, a seeder, a harrow, a binder [an advance on the reaper], a thresher, wagons and horses, 8 to 10 man-hours of labor were required." U.S. Department of Agriculture, *Chronological Landmarks in American Agriculture*, compiled by Marvanna S. Smith, Agricultural Information Bulletin No. 425 (Washington, D.C.: U.S. Department of Agriculture, 1979), pp. 10, 32.

30. Towne and Rasmussen, "Farm Gross Product," p. 260.

31. See for example, Adelman and Morris, "Patterns of Industrialization," pp. 44-42.

32. Douglass C. North, *Growth and Welfare, in the American Past: A New Economic History*, 2nd ed. (Englewood Cliffs, NJ: Prentice-Hall, 1974), p. 80 on sectors of U.S. economy in 1860.

33. Albert Fishlow, *American Railroads and the Transformation of the Antebellum Economy* (Cambridge, MA: Harvard University, 1965) and Robert Fogel, *Railroads and American Economic Growth: Essays in Economic History* (Baltimore: The Johns Hopkins University Press, 1964).

34. North, *Growth and Welfare*, p. 80.

35. These statistics are based on numbers given in Leo Rogin, *The Introduction of Farm Machinery in its Relation to the Productivity of Labor in the Agriculture of the U.S. during the Nineteenth Century* (Berkeley: University of California Press, 1931). See my Appendix A for estimating procedures.

36. Albert Hirschman, *The Strategy of Economic Development* (New Haven: Yale University Press, 1958).

37. Towne and Rasmussen, "Farm Gross Product," p. 269.

38. David, "Mechanization of Reaping," in Rosovsky, *Industrialization*, pp. 34-35.

39. William T. Hutchinson, *Cyrus McCormick*, 2 vols., (New York: D. Appleton Century Co., 1930).

2

ATTAINMENT OF PROFIT-MAXIMIZING SCALE AS A CAUSE OF REAPER ADOPTION

Four articles have appeared in the *Journal of Economic History* in response to David's 1966 article on the mechanization of reaping in the American Midwest. In 1975, Olmstead found some empirical errors in David's analysis and offered an alternative explanation of the timing of the adoption of the reaper. In 1976, Pomfret tested David's model on Canadian data and found it lacking.[1] In 1977, Jones attempted to defend David's model by retesting it on new data and with new techniques.[2] Olmstead replied to Jones's challenge in 1979 by finding empirical errors in Jones's analysis.[3]

In the first section of this chapter, David's profit-maximizing model as modified by Olmstead's revised thresholds is tested. If I can show that family farmers adopted the reaper before they had reached the profit-maximizing scale of wheat output, then there is reason to believe that they were not profit maximizers. This would support Hypothesis 1: Risk-averse utility-maximizing family farms rationally adopted the reaper in the 1850s at a scale of production below the threshold at which profit maximization would have dictated the adoption of the reaper.

In addition to the empirical errors that Olmstead found in David's analysis, he also questioned David's assumption that there was no sharing of reapers. If farmers did share a reaper, then the reason why they were observed to adopt the reaper at levels of output less than that which would have dictated reaper adoption for profit maximizers is that together with their neighbors they did produce at the profit-maximizing scale. Thus, in this chapter's second section, I investigate this possibility. If I can show that the amount of reaper sharing that was occurring in the Old Northwest in 1860 is not quantitatively important, then we are still left the need to explain the behavior of family farmers in terms that do not assume that they were profit maximizers.

Olmstead's alternative explanation for the timing of reaper adoption is that the reapers were not reliable until the 1850s. I wish to push causality back a step and ask why they were reliable in the 1850s. My answer is that they were being mass-produced then. And there was mass production because there was a mass market for them. There was a mass market because the land had been distributed to so many tillers of the soil. In the third section of this chapter, I present evidence for Hypothesis 4: The institutional structure of the family farm system was a favorable initial condition for the adoption of farm machinery because it was based on a relatively equal distribution of abundant land which generated many farmers with a sufficient surplus and incentive to purchase capital goods.

TESTING THE PROFIT-SCALE MODEL
WITH REVISED THRESHOLDS

David's argument begins with the claim that there was a threshold size beyond which profit maximizing would dictate reaper adoption. His formula for this is:

$$ST = \frac{d + 0.5\,(r)}{LS} \cdot \frac{C}{w} \quad \text{where}$$

- ST is the threshold size in acres of small grain (wheat, oats, rye);
- d is the depreciation rate of the reaper and the reciprocal of its useful life;
- r is the interest rate, in annual terms;
- LS is labor-saving of the reaper in man-days of labor over 11 acres; the difference in labor time over 11 acres when reaper used instead of the cradle used by hand;
- C is purchase price of the reaper; and
- w is the farm wage per day for cradlers.[4]

The comparative static test of the model consists of a comparison of the threshold size with the actual size of farms before the 1850s and in the mid-1850s. The claim is that when the relative price of labor rose, the threshold fell and farmers adopted the reaper in order to maximize profits. A second cause was the increase in the actual scale of production on individual farms which moved them up toward the threshold size.

David tested his model using printed census data on farm averages in Illinois, but only those counties where most of the state's wheat crop was produced. His findings were that the threshold size fell from 47 acres to 35 acres over the decade of the 1850s and the actual scale of production on the average farm rose from 25 to 30 acres. On this basis, David claims that his model is confirmed.

Olmstead proposed a revision in David's threshold calculation because he argues that the depreciation rate and interest rate that David used are incorrect.[5] Olmstead claims that the useful life of the reaper in the 1850s was five years, not ten years as David has it. As the depreciation rate is the reciprocal of the length of the useful life of the machine, the depreciation rate is 0.2, not 0.1.

If Olmstead is correct, the threshold size in the earlier period rises from David's calculation of 47 to 82 acres, and in the latter period the threshold rises from 35 to 62 acres.[6] But the gap between the threshold and the actual scale in the 1850s is 32 acres, and thus it would not be rational for farmers to adopt the reaper. They were not producing at the profit-maximizing scale of production.

Here is Olmstead's evidence and argument. David had cited as his sources Hutchinson (vol. 1, *Seed Time*, pp. 73, 311, and 365) and Rogin (*Introduction of Farm Machinery*, p. 95). Olmstead, citing elsewhere in Hutchinson (vol. 1, *Seed Time*, p. 471), argues that if the reaper was not treated with good care, Hutchinson revises downward the useful life to a range of from five to ten years. As to the Rogin reference, Olmstead claims that the ten-year useful life refers to the decades of the 1870s and 1880s, the conditions of which differed greatly from the 1830s, 1840s, and 1850s. I confirm that Rogin's statement of the ten-year useful life of the reaper refers to the period at the end of the Civil War until the 1880s.

Olmstead argues that the appropriate depreciation rate is 0.2 because the useful life of the reaper in the period of David's study was five years. He bases this claim on Danhof (*Changes in Agriculture*, p. 235) who cites contemporary farm journals. Olmstead also cites *Transactions* of the Illinois State Agricultural Society for 1856-1857 (p. 120) that the useful life was five years. I confirm both of these references. The other evidence that Olmstead provides refers to post-Civil War period or to mowers and thus is not relevant to the problem at hand. However, on balance, I think that there is reason to believe that the average life was five years and not ten.

Next on the issue of the correct interest rate to use, Olmstead claims that the effective interest rate was 18 percent, not 6 as David uses. If this is correct, and along with the change in the depreciation rate, then the thresholds have to be revised upward again. If we accept Olmstead's argument for the interest rate, then we obtain in the earlier period a threshold of 104 acres (compared to David's 47) and in the later period a threshold of 78 acres, compared to David's 35.[7] The gap between the threshold size and the actual size, while it narrows, is still substantial in the mid-1850s and thus it was not rational for the farmers to adopt the reaper.

Here is Olmstead's evidence and argument. As to the appropriate interest rate to use, David accepted what McCormick advertised and what was reported in farm journals at the time which was that McCormick gave the farmers credit for 6 percent, citing Hutchinson (vol. 1, *Seed Time*, pp. 337, 369, n. 31). Olmstead probes deeper than what was said and asks if that was the real effective interest rate. He looks into the sources used by Hutchinson (Hutchinson, vol. 1, *Seed Time*, pp. 362-63, 337 fn.31, 369, and vol. 2, *Harvest*, pp. 71-75).

In Hutchinson, (vol. 1, *Seed Time*, opposite p. 330) there is a McCormick advertisement which states that the price of the reaper was "$115 if cash is paid on delivery . . . or $120 when $30 is paid on delivery . . . and the balance on the first December next, with six percent interest after first July next." It was rare that the farmer had cash in the period before the harvest, which in the Old Northwest was the end of June and beginning of July. After harvesting, threshing, and selling his wheat (end of November), the farmer would have cash. Olmstead correctly removes the five dollars from the credit price and uses it to calculate the effective interest rate. The farmer was borrowing $85 ($115-$30) and he paid $5 interest for it. That alone represents 6 percent of what he borrowed, but he borrowed it not for a year but for six months only; thus the annual rate of interest would be 12 percent. In addition to this "service-charge" for using credit, the farmer paid 6 percent interest. On December first the farmer had to pay the balance of $90 ($85 principle and five dollars effective interest) and the 6 percent interest owed. Six percent explicit interest plus 12 implicit interest makes the effective interest rate 18 percent. Using this reasoning Olmstead obtains a rate of 19 percent but does not give his assumptions nor his calculations.

There is one reason not to accept Olmstead on the interest rate and this is based upon one's conception of neoclassical price theory. If price theory is to explain conscious decisions on the part of economic agents, then what matters is what they expected the interest rate to be. They appear to have thought the interest rate was 6 percent (Rasmussen takes this position). If we reject Olmstead's argument on the interest rate, the depreciation rate argument alone is still strong enough to push the threshold up way beyond the actual scale of production and still is a potential reason to reject the ability of the threshold model to explain. On the other hand, if price theory describes how successful economic agents actually behave and are rewarded for following price signals in the market, then the effective interest rate is the one to use. The question is not whether the farmers consciously made profit calculations but did they behave as if they did. Because the issue is whether or not the farmers were rational profit maximizers, I believe that we must expect them to calculate the real effective interest rate.

Accepting both arguments, together the new depreciation rate and the new interest rate cause the capital costs of a reaper to rise and thus the threshold of profitability to rise. Olmstead concludes that "the threshold model provides a basis for concluding that few if any midwestern farmers would have rationally adopted the reaper in the 1850s." The fall in the threshold caused by the change in the relative factor prices "facilitated the adoption of the reaper, but one could no longer explain diffusion by comparing the threshold with the actual acreage in small grains on each farm." The change in relative factor prices "created tremendous incentive for mechanization, but other problems restricted individual adoption of the reaper."[8] I argue that farmers were rational to adopt the reaper at this time and at this scale of production, because they were risk averse utility maximizers, not profit maximizers.

I revise David's threshold formula by arguing that the threshold and the actual scale of production should be calculated in terms of wheat alone, not in terms of small grains. There are three reasons for this. First, wheat was the predominant small grain. David concedes that hardly any rye was produced before the Civil War. The only other small grain was oats and not much of it was grown. See Table 2.1. Second, it is possible that the reaper could not be used to harvest oats because the heads of oats droop. Thus it may not be accurate to include oat output in the threshold.[9] Third, and most important, is the fact that wheat was the cash crop and the basis of the farmer's cash income for the year.[10] His decision to adopt the reaper

Table 2.1
Wheat as a Proportion of Small Grains Produced

percentile	Small Grains	Wheat	Oats	Rye	Wheat/Small Grains
Mean	11.8	9.8	2	0	0.83
Median	6.4	6.4	0	0	1.00
75	15.6	13	2.6	0	0.83
90	32.0	25.0	7.0	0.0	0.78
95	44.0	33.0	10.0	1.0	0.75
99	75.0	57.0	16.0	2.0	0.76
100	398.0	298.0	89.0	11.0	0.75

Source: Fred Bateman and James D. Foust, *Agricultural and Demographic Records for Rural Households in the North 1860* (Ann Arbor, MI: Inter-University Consortium for Political and Social Research, 1976).

Note: Table given in acres: Yields, 12.2 bushels of wheat per acre and 30.5 bushels of oats and rye per acre, Parker and Klein, p. 532.

would be based on wheat calculations alone. Oats were grown for his horses and were not sold in the market.

Next, I want to change the basis of comparison from Illinois, counties which produced most of the state's wheat, to the entire Old Northwest.[11] There are several reasons for this. First, the Old Northwest was the producer of the top share of wheat in the United States.[12] Second, the literature, including David himself, refers to the fact that the adoption of the reaper took place predominantly in the Old Northwest.[13] A state, in this case, Illinois, is not an economic unit, it is a political unit. The Old Northwest, on the other hand, can be considered an economic unity and thus an appropriate unit of economic analysis. Furthermore, rather than use statistics from the printed census and thus be forced to use averages, by using the manuscript census sample, we can use statistics on individual farms.[14] As Parker writes, "the only comprehensive source of nineteenth-century microeconomic data . . . [is] the manuscript returns of the federal censuses . . . [which] exists only for 1840 through 1880.[15]

We turn now to three tests of David's threshold model, with the above revisions: (1) threshold based on the useful life of the reaper being five years, not ten; (2) threshold based on the interest rate being 18 percent, not 6; and (3) threshold in terms of wheat, not small grains.

The first test is a comparison of the number of reapers in the reaper stock in the Old Northwest in 1859 and the number of farmers that were producing more than 78 acres of wheat.[16] To be consistent with David's model these two estimates should be similar in magnitude. If the number of reapers in the reaper stock is substantially greater than the number of farmers producing over 78 acres of wheat, then this is inconsistent with David's model.

First we must calculate the stock of reapers. Rogin claimed that there were 73,200 reapers on western farms in 1859.[17] David says that Rogin misinterpreted this figure, that it actually refers to the quantity of reapers produced in the United States between 1845 and 1858. David discounts the figure to estimate the stock net of replacement. Since the useful life was ten years, in David's opinion, all production before 1848 should be disregarded. David discounts the stock further to obtain the stock net of depreciation, which at a useful life of ten years is a discount or depreciation rate of 0.1. This gives David the stock of 50,000 reapers in the United States in 1858. However, we have accepted Olmstead's revision on the useful life as being only five years, so we have to disregard production prior to 1853 and we must discount at 0.2 for stock net of depreciation. In addition, David points out that Rogin incorrectly assumed that all the U.S. reapers were used in the West. I correct for this by assuming that the reapers were distributed across the United States in the same proportion as the wheat harvest.

I calculate the reaper stock available for the wheat harvest of 1859 in the Old Northwest in Appendix A. I use Rogin's monograph for the facts we have on reaper production and present them in the appendix. Using a series of explicit assumptions, I construct a time series of reaper production from the Rogin facts, which are presented in the appendix. Using the time series for the years 1854 to 1859, I calculate the stock net of replacement and net of depreciation. I obtain a figure of 46,706 for the United States. In 1859 the Old Northwest produced 46 percent of the wheat in the United States and assuming that reapers were similarly distributed, that makes 21,485 reapers available for the wheat harvest in 1859 in the Old Northwest.[18]

Next we need to determine what number of farms were producing 78 acres of wheat or more. Table 2.2 shows the top of the distribution of wheat output on the 5,756 farms in the manuscript census sample, Old Northwest, 1860.[19] The census gives wheat output in bushels, so we must convert it to acres, using 12.2 as a yield, based on Parker and Klein. The first farm in the table produced 960 bushels or 79 acres and was the first farm beyond the threshold. Below this was a farm that produced 900 bushels of wheat or 74 acres and was below the threshold. The table shows that there were only 30 farms that produced over 78 acres of wheat. Out of 5,756 farms, that is 0.5 percent of farms that produced beyond the threshold. To compare this to the reaper stock we have to infer from the sample to the universe of farms. There were 586,717 farms in the Old Northwest in 1859. Taking 0.5 percent of this figure gives us 2,934 farms in the Old Northwest that were producing more than 78 acres of wheat.[20]

We now make the comparison test. There were 21,485 reapers available for the harvest in the Old Northwest in 1859 but there were only 2,934 farms producing more than 78 acres of wheat. The reaper stock is substantially greater than the number of farmers producing over 78 acres of wheat. This is inconsistent with David's model.

In conclusion, I believe that the threshold should be 78 acres of wheat and only 2,934 farms in the Old Northwest were producing above this threshold, which is only 14 percent of the number of reapers in the stock. I believe on this basis that only a few farmers adopted the reaper because of attaining the scale of profit-maximization.

In the second test, we compare the proportion of farms that adopted the reaper with the proportion of farms that were producing beyond the threshold of 78 acres of wheat.[21] By comparing the two estimates, we can test David's model. If the two estimates are equal, this is consistent with his model. If the proportion of farms that adopted the reaper is substantially greater than the proportion of farms producing more than the profit-maximizing threshold of 78 acres of wheat, this suggests that many reaper adopters were not profit maximizers.

There are no estimates of the proportion of farmers who adopted the reaper in the literature. The census enumerators did not ask the farmers if they had reapers. Thus we have to infer this. I developed a threefold criterion for inferring that a farmer had adopted a reaper based upon how

Table 2.2
The Top of the Wheat Distribution of All Farms

Value		Count	Percents	
Bushels	Acres		Cell	Cumulative
960	79	1	0.0	99.5
1000	82	10	0.2	99.7
1020	84	1	0.0	99.7
1030	84	1	0.0	99.7
1050	86	1	0.0	99.7
1070	88	1	0.0	99.7
1100	90	1	0.0	99.8
1110	91	1	0.0	99.8
1123	92	1	0.0	99.8
1150	94	1	0.0	99.8
1200	98	1	0.0	99.8
1285	105	1	0.0	99.8
1300	107	1	0.0	99.9
1400	115	1	0.0	99.9
1500	123	1	0.0	99.9
1600	131	1	0.0	99.9
1700	139	1	0.0	99.9
2000	164	2	0.0	100.0
3000	246	1	0.0	100.0
3616	296	1	0.0	100.0

Source: Fred Bateman and James D. Foust, *Agricultural and Demographic Records for Rural Households in the North 1860* (Ann Arbor, MI: Inter-University Consortium for Political and Social Research, 1976).

Note: Yield: 12.2 bushels of wheat per acre, Parker and Klein, p. 532. N = 30 farms.

much wheat he produced, the value of his farm implements and machinery, and the number of horses.[22] In Appendix A I give a detailed account of how I determined this criterion. First, the farmer had to have reported at least 20 acres of wheat because this is how much a single farmer could harvest himself with hand tools and the help of his family. It is not likely that a farmer producing less than 20 acres of wheat would even consider adopting a reaper. Using the manuscript census sample for the Old Northwest, this criterion eliminated 86.1 percent of the farms because they produced under 244 bushels or 20 acres of wheat. Conversely, the criterion included 13.9 percent of the farms. In addition, the farmers must have reported a value of farm implements and machinery of at least $200. The reaper was the first farm implement or machine which represented a substantial amount of value. Thus once one estimates the value of standard farm equipment, the value of the reaper should stand out. This criterion alone eliminated 88 percent of farms, as only 12 percent of farms had $200 or more in farm implements and machinery. The third requirement was that the farmer must have reported two or more horses. Without two horses, the reaper of the 1850s could not have been used. Combining all three aspects of the criteria for inferring the adoption of the reaper, we obtain 268 farms, or 4.7 percent of the farms in the sample.

Next, we need the proportion of farms that were producing 78 acres of wheat or more. From Table 2.2, we know that 30 out of 5,756 farms were producing beyond the profit threshold, which is 0.5 percent of all farms.

Comparison test two has the result that while 5 percent of the farms are inferred to have adopted the reaper, only 0.5 percent of them were producing 78 acres of wheat or more. This is inconsistent with David's profit-threshold model.

The third test is to determine what proportion of the actual farmers that did adopt the reaper were producing 78 acres of wheat or more. This is a very important test because all other tests by other authors have been based on assuming that the farms that adopted the reaper were the same farms that were claimed to be producing beyond the profit threshold. No one ever was able to show that it was those large farms that were the reaper adopters. Since I have inferred the farms that adopted the reaper, we can look at the distribution of their wheat production and see whether or not they were producing above the threshold, as David would have us believe, or whether only a small proportion at the top of the distribution was producing wheat at the threshold, as I suspect. Table 2.3 shows this distribution. Seventy-eight acres of wheat, assuming a yield of 12.2 bushels per acre, is 951.6 bushels of wheat as the threshold. The farmer who produced 1,000 bushels of wheat or 82 acres, was beyond the threshold as were all farmers above him in the distribution. Below the profit threshold was a farmer who adopted the reaper and produced 900 bushels of wheat which was below the threshold. He was at the 94.8 percentile of wheat producers. That means that only 5.2 percent of the farms that adopted the reaper were producing over the threshold. This is inconsistent with David's threshold model.

Further information on the wheat production of the farmers inferred to have adopted the reaper gives a picture of wheat production substantially below the threshold. The mean of wheat production of farmers who adopted the reaper was 40 acres, the median was 33, and the mode was 25

Table 2.3
The Top of the Wheat Distribution of Farms Inferred to Have Adopted the Reaper

Value		Count	Percents	
Bushels	Acres		Cell	Cumulative
1000	82	4	1.5	96.3
1020	84	1	0.4	96.6
1030	84	1	0.4	97.0
1070	88	1	0.4	97.4
1100	90	1	0.4	97.8
1285	105	1	0.4	98.1
1300	107	1	0.4	98.5
1400	115	1	0.4	98.9
1700	139	1	0.4	99.3
2000	164	1	0.4	99.6
3000	246	1	0.4	100.0

Source: Fred Bateman and James D. Foust, *Agricultural and Demographic Records for Rural Households in the North 1860* (Ann Arbor, MI: Inter-University Consortium for Political and Social Research, 1976).

Note: Yield used is 12.2 bushels of wheat per acre, from Parker and Klein, p. 532. N = 14 farms.

Table 2.4
Results of Test 3

Threshold	Percent of Farmers Inferred to Have Adopted the Reaper Who Were Producing Beyond Threshold
78 wheat	5.2

Wheat Production of Farmers Inferred to Have Adopted the Reaper (acres)	
Mean	40
Median	33
Mode	25

Source: Fred Bateman and James D. Foust, *Agricultural and Demographic Records for Rural Households in the North 1860* (Ann Arbor, MI: Inter-University Consortium for Political and Social Research, 1976).

acres of wheat. None of these "average" farms were producing beyond the threshold of 78 acres of wheat. The results of test 3 are given in Table 2.4. I conclude that the predominant proportion of farms inferred to have adopted the reaper did so at a scale of production substantially below the threshold which profit maximization would have dictated the adoption of the reaper. This is strong evidence for my first hypothesis.

We can now use the findings of these tests to quantify the anomaly discussed in Chapter 1. Table 2.5 gives the statistics obtained from the

Table 2.5
Inferences from Sample to Universe

Set of Farms	Sample	Universe
All farms	5,756	586,717
Inferred to have adopted the reaper	268	27,576
That produced beyond 78 acres of wheat	30	2,934
Inferred to have adopted the reaper and that produced beyond 78 acres of wheat	14	1,434
Inferred to have adopted the reaper but that did not produce beyond 78 acres of wheat	254	26,142
Inferred not to have adopted the reaper, but did produce beyond 78 acres of wheat	16	1,555

Source: Fred Bateman and James D. Foust, *Agricultural and Demographic Records for Rural Households in the North 1860* (Ann Arbor, MI: Inter-University Consortium for Political and Social Research, 1976). *Printed Census 1860*, Old Northwest.

manuscript census sample of the Old Northwest, 1860. We inferred that 268 farms adopted the reaper and this is 4.7 percent of all 5,756 farms in the sample. Taking 4.7 percent of farms in the universe, 586,717 from the *Printed Census 1860*, we obtain the estimate that 27,576 farms in the Old Northwest had adopted the reaper in 1859.

From Table 2.2 we found that 30 farms produced more than 78 acres of wheat and this is 0.5 percent of all farms. We can infer from this that 0.5 percent of the 586,717 farms in the Old Northwest were producing beyond the threshold, or 2,934 farms. Notice that the set of farms that produced beyond the threshold of 78 acres of wheat is much smaller than the set of farms that adopted the reaper. It is 9.4 times smaller; that is, the quantity of farms that were producing beyond the threshold was less than one-ninth the quantity of farms that adopted the reaper. To be consistent with David's model, these two quantities should have been the same.

From Table 2.3, we found that 14 farms had both adopted the reaper and had increased wheat production beyond the profit threshold of 78 acres. Fourteen compared to 268 is 5.2 percent of all farms that adopted the reaper and also produced beyond the threshold. The intersection of the two sets represents the farms whose behavior can be explained by David's threshold model (as revised by Olmstead and modified by this study). Inferring to the whole Old Northwest, the behavior of 1,434 farmers can be explained by the threshold model.

In Table 2.5, the number of farms that adopted the reaper but that did not produce beyond 78 acres of wheat is obtained by subtracting 14 from 268. These 254 farms represent 94.8 percent of all farms that adopted the reaper. That makes 26,142 farms in the Old Northwest. The family farm thesis is an explanation of why these farmers adopted the reaper even though they were not producing beyond the profit threshold.

Finally, the other side of the anomaly. In the sample there were 16 farms that were producing beyond the profit threshold but did not adopt the reaper. We obtain this from subtracting 14 from 30. They represent 53 percent of farms that produced beyond the threshold. In the Old Northwest universe of farms, 1,555 farms produced more than 78 acres of wheat and yet did not adopt the reaper. This side of the anomaly is explained neither by David's model nor by the family farm thesis. However, these farms represent only 0.3 percent of all farms.

Only 5.2 percent of all the farmers who adopted the reaper appear to be profit maximizers and 94.8 percent appear not to be profit maximizers. As I will argue in Chapter 4, these latter farmers were risk averse utility maximizers.

One final argument on the threshold model. It was designed to explain why the reaper was adopted in the 1850s rather than earlier, since the machine was available before this. That is, we are interested in a change over time. The three tests presented above are based on a cross-section analysis in 1859 based on the manuscript census sample. Manuscript censuses exist for 1840, 1850, 1860, 1870, and 1880. The National Science Foundation financed the taking of a sample from the 1860 census manuscripts. Until samples are taken from the other years, the only way to do a comparison over time is to go to the individual states and take one's own sample. Jones has done this for the state of Illinois for 1849 and 1859.[23] Furthermore, he has used this data base to test David's threshold model.

The test of the model is whether or not the growth of the number of farms above the threshold is consistent with the growth of reaper stock between 1849 and 1859. If the two growth rates are similar, then the threshold model is supported. If the growth rate of the number of farms over the threshold is less than the growth rate of the net reaper stock, then we need further causal mechanisms in addition to the profit-threshold model to explain this additional adoption.

Unfortunately, Jones has made a number of empirical errors. In order to evaluate his model, we must retest it with the empirical errors corrected. Jones accepted the challenge of Olmstead's higher thresholds and responded with an approach that attempts to find farms which are that large, utilizing the whole distribution of farms, instead of the mean farm. Jones takes his own samples from the manuscript census schedules for Illinois in 1850 and 1860. The first sample for 1850 has 1,021 farms which is 1.3 percent of the farms (76,208) and the second sample for 1860 has 1,081 farms which is 0.75 percent of (143,310) farms in Illinois at that time. Jones does not explain how he took the sample nor provide any tests of its representativeness.

The first error in Jones's analysis is the selection of the interest rate of 10 percent, hence he uses the wrong thresholds, 89.4 acres and 67.6 acres. Olmstead had hypothetically used an interest rate of 10 percent to demonstrate the sensitivity of the thresholds to minor changes in the values of some of the constants, but later in his research he argues that the empirical evidence supports an actual interest rate of 19 percent or even higher. I corrected this to 18 percent which generates thresholds of 104 acres and 78 acres.

The second error, found by Olmstead,[24] was that much of Jones's time series on reaper production is incorrect. Confirming this, I made my own estimates of reaper production over time and net stocks in 1849 and 1859 in Appendix A. In order to reconstruct Jones's argument with these errors corrected, we first want to estimate the percentage of farms that were greater than the threshold in each of the two periods. We use the percentage frequency distribution in small grains provided by Jones.[25] Using the correct profit threshold of 104 acres in the earlier period, we obtain 0.8 percent of farms in the sample were 100 acres or more in small grain production. Using the correct threshold of 78 acres in the later period, we obtain 4.33 of the farms in the sample greater than the range 75-79.9 and above.

Next we assume that the sample is representative and thus we use the proportion of the sample to represent the proportion of the universe of Illinois of farms over the threshold. The number of farms in Illinois in 1850 was 76,208, and in 1860 it was 143,310. Thus, 0.8 percent of the 76,208 total farms is 610 farms over the threshold in 1850. Taking 4.33 percent of 143,310 total farms is 6,205 farms over the threshold in 1860. That is an increase of 917 percent over the decade.

The test of the model is that the growth rate of the estimated number of farms over the threshold should be consistent with the growth rate of the reaper stock. Because of errors in Jones's estimates, I recalculated the net reaper stock in 1849 and 1859 (see Appendix A). In 1849 the net reaper stock was 2,178 and in 1859 it was 46,706, a growth rate of 2,044 percent.

Comparing the two growth rates we find that the rate of growth of number of farms over the threshold is only half of the rate of growth of the net reaper stock (917 percent compared to 2,044 percent). I conclude that the threshold model can at most explain half of the increase in reaper adoption, using Jones's approach. Results are presented in Table 2.6.

One objection to the foregoing analysis could be that the farmers who were not producing at the profit-maximizing level of output achieved a

Table 2.6
Results of Test 4

	Farms Beyond Threshold*	Growth Rate (percent)
1849	610	
1859	6,205	
		917

	Net Reaper Stock**	
1849	2,178	
1859	46,706	
		2,044

Source: See text.

Note: *In Illinois; **in the United States; if we assume distribution of reapers to be similar to distribution of grain production, and if we are interested in the growth rate, then it is permissible to make the comparison this way. Jones does the same.

similar arrangement by cooperating with their neighbors and that together they produced at the profit-maximizing scale and then they shared a reaper. Olmstead has made this argument and in the next section I shall try to estimate the extent of sharing.

SHARING TO ATTAIN PROFIT SCALE

If several farmers cooperated, they could put their land together, attain the threshold of profitability, and buy a reaper and share it. It would be rational for them, given that together their wheat fields were more than 78 acres, the estimated threshold scale of profitability. This is a way to explain the anomaly. It does mean that the threshold model would not work to explain the timing of the adoption of the reaper, because farmers could have shared before 1850 as well as in the 1850s. This sharing explanation was offered by Olmstead and defended with evidence from the historical literature. In this section I examine this evidence and then make an argument against the quantitative importance of sharing.

David assumed that the reaper was an indivisible fixed capital cost and thus the farmer had to attain the threshold scale alone. However, if the threshold could have been attained by two or more farmers sharing, then the attainment of the threshold by one farmer in the later period cannot be a reason why he adopted the reaper, and likewise the non-attainment of the threshold in the earlier period cannot be a reason for him not adopting.

Olmstead challenged David's assumption that there was "no sharing" of the reaper. If there had been sharing, then fixed costs would have varied across farmers and there would have been no uniform threshold size. This is a serious challenge to David's threshold model as a predictor of adoption and deserves careful consideration. Olmstead claims that sharing was widespread and therefore the threshold model should be rejected.

The first set of evidence that Olmstead presents is from McCormick Reaper sales records of legal joint purchases. On this basis Olmstead claims that this phenomenon was widespread, one in four cases. Olmstead does not explain how he randomized his sample or if he tested it for representative-ness.[26] Furthermore, it is possible that some of the purchases made by two people were cases in which one of the individuals was the financial backer although it was not so recorded or made explicit. Hutchinson states that McCormick's agents were told to be "aware of a homesteader who had not yet acquired a title to his holding, and of a renter unless he could secure the endorsement of a substantial landowner on his reaper note."[27] Olmstead does state that if the second individual was identified as a financial backer securing the note of the other, that he tabulated it as a single, not a joint purchase. However, it is possible that this information was not recorded systematically and that some of the two-name purchases could have been cases of one user and one backer, and that there was little sharing via joint purchase.

Next Olmstead presents evidence on informal sharing and contracting which he claims was more widespread than the official legal joint purchase. The problem with this evidence is that except for one case in Illinois, all the evidence comes from outside the Old Northwest region (Ohio, Indiana, Illinois, Michigan, and Wisconsin).[28] It is generally agreed that this is the region where the first wave of popular acceptance of the mechanical reaper took place in the 1850s. The evidence is for Iowa, Minnesota, and Massachusetts. Olmstead generalizes on sharing when he states that it was more important in developing areas (Iowa, Minnesota) where labor was more scarce and it was more often found in New England (Massachusetts), where the farms were too small to warrant individual ownership.[29] The upshot is that we are left with one reference to a case in Illinois on sharing. Ironically, it is on Illinois alone that David tests his model.

Another problem with Olmstead's evidence is that some of it is on mowing, not reaping. There was no time constraint or bottleneck in mowing and no one argues that mowing could not be done cooperatively. It is the sharing in reaping alone which is in dispute. Nearly all farm operations could be done cooperatively, by sharing equipment and exchanging labor, except for harvesting wheat. Mechanizing the wheat harvest is unique because of the time constraint which inhibits sharing. Mowing, threshing, even harvesting oats could be done at the farmer's leisure. Wheat must be harvested immediately upon ripening or it can be lost. Ripened grain can fall to the ground and thus never be retrieved. Wind, rain, and hail can (and often did) destroy the wheat crop but are not so damaging of other heartier grains and field crops. This is one reason why family farmers did not share reapers.

Gates argues that unique to wheat and its harvest is the fact that this represented the farmer's cash income for the year and was thus more critical to the farm household than other farm operations done for on-farm use.[30] Rasmussen argues that this is the most important reason why sharing was not an important or widespread phenomenon.[31]

I do not think Olmstead's evidence warrants us to assume that in the Old Northwest, where in the 1850s the reaper was being adopted, sharing was important. But there is an even more important reason why the sharing argument should be discounted. Olmstead does show that sharing existed but he does not demonstrate that the proportion could be judged to be decisive. My major argument against the importance of sharing is as follows. The proportion of the wheat harvest that was cut mechanically when calculated from the number of reapers available, what they could have cut, regardless of who owned them, calculated as if the Old Northwest were one giant farm, is about the same proportion as one obtains if one infers reaper

Table 2.7
Estimates of the Extent of Mechanization

Estimates	Number of Acres	Proportion of Acres
Reaper Stock: Sharing Irrelevant	1,675,830	25.6
Census: Assume "no sharing"	1,433,115	25.2
Sharing	242,715	0.4

Source: See Appendix A.

adoption for individual farms and assumes that they do not share. The fact is that both of the two procedures result in estimates of essentially the same proportion of wheat mechanically cut, implying that sharing was not quantitatively important. See Table 2.7 and description of the procedures.

My sharing argument is as follows. First, I describe the procedure based upon the reaper stock for which the issue of sharing is irrelevant. Second, I describe the procedure based on inferring individual reaper adoption for which it is assumed that there was no sharing.

The reaper stock estimate procedure was developed by Leo Rogin,[32] modified by David, and again modified for this study (see Appendix A). First, one has to estimate the U.S. reaper stock for the year 1859. I did this in Appendix A. This must be adjusted for the Old Northwest. I assigned the region the same proportion of reapers as their proportion of the wheat production. This biases the results against my case because more reapers were adopted in the Old Northwest due to the flat land, and other reasons, than in other regions. Third, assume that reapers were not used to full capacity, but rather used to 78 percent of capacity. There is much evidence to suggest that reapers were not used to full capacity (approximately 100 acres). I quote Gates and Parker on this in Appendix A. Below I test the robustness of the results by relaxing this assumption. I used 78 acres because this is the estimated threshold of profit-maximizing scale. Fourth, the number of reapers in the reaper stock is multiplied by 78 acres of wheat to obtain the amount of wheat which could have been cut mechanically. This then is compared with the amount of wheat which was produced, regardless of how it was harvested, which gives the proportion of the wheat which could have been cut by the reaper stock. My estimate is that 25.6 percent of the wheat harvest in the Old Northwest in 1859 was mechanically cut. In this procedure it does not matter if the reapers were shared or not.

The estimate is made as if the reaper stock were used on one large farm, the Old Northwest.

The census estimate procedure is based on inferring individual farmers adopting the reaper and implicitly I assume that there was no sharing. I used the manuscript census sample of the Old Northwest, 1860. First, I assumed that a farmer had adopted the reaper if all three of the following criteria were met: the farmer reported to the census enumerator at least 20 acres of wheat, at least two horses, and at least $150 of farm implements and machinery (see Appendix A for a defense of this set of criteria). Second, I took the sum of the wheat produced (transformed from bushels into acres) by the farmers inferred to have adopted the reaper. Here I am assuming that there was no sharing, that is, that only the farmers that are inferred to have adopted the reaper were the ones using those reapers. Because the sample is approximately 0.01 of the population, I multiplied this acreage by 100.[33] Third, I compared the amount of wheat produced by the farmers inferred to have adopted the reaper with the amount of all the wheat produced by the farmers in the sample to obtain a proportion of wheat cut mechanically. Using this procedure I obtained 25.2 percent.

Using the procedure based on the reaper stock, for which sharing is irrelevant, I found that 25.6 percent of the wheat in the Old Northwest was cut mechanically and using the procedure based on individual reaper adopters, for which it was assumed that there was no sharing, I found that 25.2 percent of the wheat was cut mechanically. If these estimates are correct, then this does not leave much room for sharing.

In the census estimate, I assumed that the inferred reaper adopter did not share. If the reaper stock estimate is correct, then 242,715 acres of wheat were cut mechanically by sharers. That represents 0.4 percent of all mechanically cut wheat. This suggests that sharing was not quantitatively important. Thus the anomaly remains that most reaper adopters were producing below the estimated profit-maximizing scale.

A SUPPLY-SIDE EXPLANATION OF THE TIMING OF THE ADOPTION OF THE REAPER

Olmstead offered an alternative explanation for the timing of the adoption of the reaper, as he rejected David's analysis. Olmstead claimed that before adoption the reaper was not a reliable machine and that is why farmers did not adopt it. However, as soon as it did become a reliable machine farmers did adopt it. The cause of the timing is that in the 1850s the horse-drawn mechanical reaper had become a reliable machine.

One problem with Olmstead's analysis is that the reliability of a machine is a necessary condition for its adoption, but not a sufficient one. The historical record is full of examples of machines that were reliable but not adopted. There must also be economic incentives to use a reliable machine.

The appearance of a reliable machine on the scene in the 1850s may be a proximate cause, but really not an independent explanatory variable. What caused the appearance of a reliable machine? Jones argues that it was the acceleration in reaper sales which caused the reaper to become reliable.[34] I would add that it was the acceleration in production behind the sales that finally ironed out the kinks in the harvesting machine. This can be seen in the time series of reaper sales and production presented in this section.

The increased production led to three characteristics of the reaper: reliability, durability, and reasonable price, all at approximately the same time. Once the reaper was being mass-produced, two results followed. On one hand, the mass producers of the reaper could capture economies of scale in reaper production. This in turn resulted in a reasonably priced reaper. This increased the demand for the reaper and caused its adoption. On the other hand, the mass producers of the reaper adopted new technology for the production of the reaper, that is, used inanimate power and machinery to produce machinery. This is a second cause of the availability of a reasonably priced reaper. Third, mass production of the reaper led to technical change in the design of the reaper. The new design provided a reliable and durable reaper that caused its adoption, as Olmstead pointed out.

The cause of the timing of the adoption of the reaper is an issue of invention and innovation. The mechanical reaper was invented in the 1830s. It allowed the farmer to cut 100 acres of wheat whereas by hand with hand tools he could only harvest 20 acres. The technical argument is that an invention is not innovated until it is reliable and durable. Reliability and durability were achieved in the process of increased production of mechanical reapers after 1848 in McCormick's factory and four or more years to learn by doing and work out the kinks. The cause of this supply arriving in the 1850s was the movement of industrial production from the American Northeast into the trans-Allegheny region, the Old Northwest.[35] In particular, McCormick set up his factory in Chicago in 1848. By the next year, he increased his production by 88 percent. In 1854 Manny entered the market and sold nearly as many reapers as McCormick. In 1855 McCormick increased his production by 117 percent. Also in 1855, Manny increased production by 127 percent; Atkins entered the market with his self-rake reaper; and 5,000 other reapers were produced. In terms of total production 1855 was the year of the greatest spurt in production. Production was even higher in the rest of the decade.

This increased production was achieved by the transfer of production from workshops and mechanics to factories with inanimate power and machinery. This represents technological change in reaper production (process), as opposed to in reaper design (product). Mass production required the simplification of the machine. It also sped up the process of learning by doing for reaper producers.

Mass production meant simplification and increased efficiency in producing a useful machine. Alan Bogue refers to the mechanization of agriculture as "the application of the achievements of the industrial revolution to agriculture."[36] Nathan Rosenberg describes technical change in the long run as a progressive loosening of supply-side constraints.[37] All of the technical changes described by Olmstead could be seen as caused by changes in the production of the mechanical reaper and thus just this loosening of supply-side constraints. It is generally accepted that the producers of those days could sell all the reapers they could produce and that demand was usually greater than supply. If we assume that the mechanical reaper was in the farm production function, then the farmer would not be constrained by the imperfection of the reaper. The suppliers of the reaper were profit maximizers and would have ironed out the kinks as they learned by doing. From the time of the first industrial revolution there have always been kinks. Industrialists start factories and participate in a learning process. Kinks should not be considered a constraint. Technical change occurs from where one is on the production function.

Why did production accelerate? In the 1850s the industrial revolution moved across the Alleghenies to the Midwest and McCormick set up a factory to mass produce reapers in 1848. Finally, why was the mass production of farm machinery and the reaper in particular taken on in the Midwest? I believe it was because of the family farm system there that provided a mass market. This is discussed in Chapter 4.

We turn now to the evidence and documentation. First, the acceleration in reaper sales can be seen in the time series given in Table 2.8.

Was it true that the mechanical reaper was reliable by the mid-1850s and not before? Evidence suggests that the horse-drawn mechanical reaper was a reliable machine as of 1852-57. Danhof states that "in 1852 the harvester had been developed to a sufficiently high degree to ensure consistent production of satisfactory machines."[38] Rogin dates it later, claiming that the machines of 1855, 1856, and 1857 were the first to give general satisfaction.[39] Danhof concurs when he states that the major reaper trial of the decade was in Syracuse in 1857 and it was generally agreed that after this contest, in which 40 different kinds of reapers were demonstrated, that the reaper was seen as technologically and economically desirable. Danhof considered the era of 1848 to 1852 as the experimental era of reaper production.[40]

Was the mechanical reaper a durable machine by the mid-1850s and not before? Evidence suggests that the horse-drawn mechanical reaper was more durable after 1848: Before 1848 the useful life of the reaper was only two years.[41] After 1848 the useful life was five years.[42] Before 1848 the depreciation rate was 0.5 and after 1846 it was 0.2. The effect of this

Table 2.8
Time Series of American Reaper Production

Year	Hussey	McCormick	New Yorker	Manny	Atkins	Non-McCormick	Total
1833	1						1
1834	7						7
1835	7						7
1836	7						7
1837	7						7
1838	7						7
1839	9						9
1840	36	2					38
1841	36						36
1842	36	6					42
1843	36	39					75
1844	36	50					86
1845	36	200					236
1846	36	275					311
1847	36	500					536
1848	36	800					836
1849	34	1,500	150				1,684
1850	97	1,128	150				1,375
1851	275	1,150	500				1,925
1852	275	1,150					1,425
1853	275	1,150					1,425
1854	275	1,150			1,100		2,525
1855		2,500		2,500	1,200	5,000	11,200
1856		3,932				12,642	16,574
1857		3,932				12,642	16,574
1858		3,932				12,642	16,574
1859		3,932				12,642	16,574
Total	1,600	2,732	800	3,600	1,200	55,568	90,096

Source: Based on Rogin, 1931. See Appendix A for how facts from Rogin were used
to construct this time series.

change, ceteris paribus, was a dramatic fall of the threshold from an
extremely high level of 211 acres in the pre-factory era down to 104 acres
in the factory era. The former threshold of 211 was greater than the
capacity of the machine (100 acres), hence farmers did not adopt. The
increase in the useful life of the machine after factory production caused
the threshold of profitability to fall from the impossible demand of using it

on more acres than the machine could harvest in a year to the possible threshold of 104 acres, about the capacity of the machine.[43]

Is it true that by the mid-1850s the price of the mechanical reaper was reasonable? The long-run trend of the price of farm machinery in the second half of the nineteenth century was downward.[44] The reason for this was that factory production involves capturing economies of scale, the use of new technology, both the use of inanimate power and the use of machinery to make machinery, that is, machine tools. This replaced the workshop method utilizing the expensive skilled labor of mechanics.

In conclusion, on the supply side of the matter, the timing of the adoption of the reaper can be explained by the taking on of mass production of the mechanical reaper that in turn caused the development of a reliable, durable, and reasonably priced reaper. This conclusion supports Hypothesis 4 on the family farm system providing a mass market for farm machinery.

Obviously there was an interaction between the decision to adopt the reaper (demand) and expanded mass production (supply). On the demand side, there was an acceleration in the mid-1850s due to the rise of the price of wheat in turn due to the completion of the Midwestern railroad links to the East and development of the feeder railroads within the Old Northwest. In Chapter 4, a further development of the explanation of the timing, on the demand side, will be presented.

CONCLUSION

The evidence presented in section one suggests that David was incorrect to assume that the family farmers who adopted the reaper were profit maximizers. These family farmers seem to have adopted the reaper before it was profitable. Thus we have reason to accept Hypothesis 1: Risk-averse utility-maximizing family farms rationally adopted the reaper in the 1850s at a scale of production below the threshold at which profit maximization would have dictated the adoption of the reaper.

The evidence presented in section two suggests that Olmstead was incorrect to argue that sharing was widespread enough to explain the farmers adopting the reaper below the profit-maximizing threshold.

In section three, we saw that the adoption of the reaper coincided with the mass production of the reaper in factories. This gives us reason to retain Hypothesis 4: The institutional structure of the family farm system was a favorable initial condition for the adoption of farm machinery because it was based on a relatively equal distribution of abundant land which generated many farmers with sufficient surplus and incentive to buy capital goods.

In Chapter 3, I turn to Fleisig's analysis of farm mechanization because it offers a possible explanation for the anomaly of farms producing below the estimated level of profit maximization and adopting the reaper.

NOTES

1. Richard Pomfret, "The Mechanization of Reaping in Nineteenth-Century Ontario: A Case Study of the Pace and Causes of the Diffusion of Embodied Technical Change," *Journal of Economic History* 36 (June 1976):399-415.

2. Lewis R. Jones, "'The Mechanization of Reaping and Mowing in American Agriculture, 1833-1870': Comment," *Journal of Economic History* 37 (June 1977):451-55.

3. Alan Olmstead, "The Diffusion of the Reaper: One More Time!" *Journal of Economic History* 39 (June 1979):475-76.

4. Paul A. David, "Mechanization of Reaping in the Ante-Bellum Midwest," in Henry Rosovsky (Ed.), *Industrialization in Two Systems* (New York: John Wiley and Sons, 1965), p. 30.

5. Alan Olmstead, "The Mechanization of Reaping and Mowing in American Agriculture, 1833-1870" *Journal of Economic History* 35 (June 1975):330-34.

6.

$$ST0 = \frac{d + 0.5\,(r)}{LS} \cdot \frac{C}{w} = \frac{0.2 + 0.5(.06)}{0.273} \cdot \frac{124}{1.27} = 82 \text{ acres}$$

$$ST1 = \frac{d + 0.5\,(r)}{LS} \cdot \frac{C}{w} = \frac{0.2 + 0.5(.06)}{0.273} \cdot \frac{138}{1.87} = 62 \text{ acres}$$

7.

$$ST0 = \frac{d + 0.5\,(r)}{LS} \cdot \frac{C}{w} = \frac{0.2 + 0.5(.18)}{0.273} \cdot \frac{124}{1.27} = 104 \text{ acres}$$

$$ST1 = \frac{d + 0.5\,(r)}{LS} \cdot \frac{C}{w} = \frac{0.2 + 0.5(.18)}{0.273} \cdot \frac{138}{1.87} = 78 \text{ acres}$$

8. Olmstead, "Mechanization," pp. 352, 328, and 342, respectively.

9. Interview with Wayne Rasmussen, June 1984. Qualified in letter of May 1985.

10. Paul Gates, *The Farmer's Age: Agriculture 1815-1860*, vol. 3 of *The Economic History of the United States* (New York: Harper and Row, 1960), p. 156.

11. Jones performed a test of David's model using micro farm data from the state of Illinois alone.

12. William Parker, "Agriculture," in Lance Davis et al. (Eds.), *American Economic Growth* (New York: Harper and Row, 1972), p. 381.

13. David, "Mechanization of Reaping," p. 5; Clarence Danhof, *Changes in Agriculture* (Cambridge, MA: Harvard University Press, 1969), pp. 243-249.

14. Jones used the census manuscripts and thus had observations on individual farms. By taking his own sample of the manuscript census, Jones could compare 1850 and 1860. The sample I use is from 1860 only, the only year that the National Science Foundation financed the taking of a sample.

15. Parker, "Agriculture," p. 369.

16. Rationale for this test: Pomfret compared the reaper stock in 1850, 1860, and 1870 in Ontario with the number of farms over the threshold in those three years, "The Mechanization of Reaping in Nineteenth-Century Ontario," p. 399. Jones also compared the reaper stock and the farms over the threshold in 1849 and 1859 Illinois.

17. Leo Rogin, *The Introduction of Farm Machinery in its Relation to the Productivity of Labor in the Agriculture of the U.S. during the Nineteenth Century* (Berkeley: University of California Press, 1931), p. 76.

18. Jones calculated the reaper stock and used both David's ten-year useful life and Olmstead's five-year useful life. However, he made errors in his time series of reaper production, which was pointed out by Olmstead in his second article, "The Diffusion of the Reaper: One More Time!" *Journal of Economic History* 39 (June 1979):475-76. It was for this reason that I constructed my own time series on reaper production.

19. In Chapter 5 I present evidence on the representativeness of the sample I use to establish this argument.

20. Pomfret used the printed census which gives only the size distribution when he tested David's model on data from Ontario, Canada. This gives a rough approximation. Jones used the manuscript census and thus had access to observations on individual farms, as I have. However, he took his own small sample and just from Illinois. I use the manuscript census sample which is a large sample and it was taken with an explicit methodology, for which see again Chapter 5. I use the Old Northwest subset of this sample and thus have five states instead of Jones's one state of Illinois.

21. This use of the proportion of farms beyond the threshold is an important move in the literature. It represents moving beyond comparing the scale of production of the mean farm and moving to looking at the whole distribution of farms. Pomfret was the first to do this. He revised David's model by calculating the proportion of farms in the distribution that were beyond the threshold. The threshold cuts the distribution above the mean.

22. Atack and Bateman have used a twofold criterion of wheat output and value of farm implements and machinery, written communication, June 1983. I added the number of horses upon the advice of Dr. Rasmussen, interview, April 1983.

23. Jones, "Mechanization of Reaping," pp. 451-455.

24. Olmstead, "Diffusion of the Reaper," pp. 475-76.

25. Jones, "Mechanization of Reaping," p. 453.

26. Olmstead, "Mechanization," p. 337.

27. William T. Hutchinson, *Cyrus Hall McCormick*, vol. 2, *Harvest* (New York: D. Appleton Century Co., 1930), p. 72.

28. Olmstead, "Mechanization," p. 340, fn. 33.

29. Ibid., pp. 242-43.

30. Gates, *The Farmer's Age*, pp. 156, 166.

31. Wayne Rasmussen, "The Mechanization of Agriculture," *Scientific American* 247 (September 1982):76-89 and personal communication.

32. Rogin, *Introduction of Farm Machinery*, pp. 78-79.

33. In Chapter 4 I present evidence on the representativeness of the sample I use to establish this argument.

34. Jones, "Mechanization of Reaping," p. 455. I extend the argument from sales to production.

35. David, "Mechanization of Reaping," in Rosovsky, *Industrialization*, p. 8.

36. Allan G. Bogue, *From Prairie to Corn Belt: Farming on the Illinois and Iowa Prairies in the Nineteenth-Century* (Chicago: University of Chicago Press, 1963), p. 148.

37. Nathan Rosenberg, *Technology and American Economic Growth* (White Plains, NY: M. E. Sharpe, 1972), p. 55.

38. Danhof, *Changes in Agriculture*, p. 234.

39. Rogin, *Introduction of Farm Machinery*, p. 91.

40. Danhof, *Changes in Agriculture*, pp. 234-35.

41. Ibid., p. 236. This is based on the assumption that the reaper was used for at least 20 acres, but not to full capacity.

42. Ibid., p. 335.

43.

$$ST0 = \frac{d + 0.5\,(r)}{LS} \cdot \frac{C}{w} = \frac{0.5 + 0.5(.18)}{0.273} \cdot \frac{124}{1.27} = 211 \text{ acres}$$

$$ST1 = \frac{d + 0.5\,(r)}{LS} \cdot \frac{C}{w} = \frac{0.2 + 0.5(.18)}{0.273} \cdot \frac{124}{1.27} = 104 \text{ acres}$$

44. Marvin Towne and Wayne Rasmussen, "Farm Gross Product and Gross Investment During the Nineteenth Century," in *Trends in the American Economy in the Nineteenth Century*, vol. 24 of *Studies in Income and Wealth* (Princeton: Princeton University Press, 1960), p. 269. The index of farm machinery prices was 100 for the years 1910-1914, and the index for 1850 was 187 and for 1860 it was 161.

3

LABOR CONSTRAINTS DUE TO MARKET FORCES AS THE CAUSE OF MECHANIZATION

In the first section we look at Fleisig's model of labor-constrained profit maximizers who mechanize their farm operations when they want to expand their output beyond that allowed by the available labor supply. I will test this model on the micro data of the Old Northwest in 1859. If we cannot find correlations between the labor available in a township and the capital per farm, then we have reason to doubt Fleisig's model of the family farm.

In the second section, I present a model of the farm household that allocates labor to its production activities for the market and for on-farm use. My alternative explanation of mechanization stresses the abundance of land more than the scarcity of labor. The family farm as a household is defined as a farm with enough land to support the family. The family farm as a firm is defined as a farm with enough land to occupy the labor force of the farm family. In most of world history, the two definitions were the same quantity. Families spent all their time on the land to support themselves. But in the northern United States in the nineteenth century, there was a relative abundance of agricultural resources that were distributed to families. The soil was so rich that the labor force of a farm family could produce more than was needed to support the family. I will test this model on the same data as I test Fleisig's model. If we can find correlations between the proportion of medium-sized family farms in a township and the capital per farm, then we have reason to believe my model of the family farm.

In the third section, I estimate the quantitative importance of the market labor constraint. I accept the idea that there were labor-constrained profit maximizers in the Old Northwest in the 1850s, but how many and what proportion of total farms? If there were not many, then we can say that Fleisig's explanation cannot account for northern mechanization.

If the tests come out as I expect them to, then we can argue that the preference not to hire labor on the part of the family farm is a more important reason for mechanization than the labor constraint in the market. This would suggest that we should retain Hypothesis 2 from the economics of the family farm: Risk-averse utility-maximizing family farms rationally adopted the reaper in the 1850s when they wanted to produce more wheat than they could with family labor.

If the tests on "equal distribution of abundance" come out stronger than the tests on "labor scarcity," then we will want to retain Hypothesis 4 from the institutional structure of the family farm system analysis: The institutional structure of the family farm system was a favorable initial condition for the adoption of farm machinery because it was based on a relatively equal distribution of abundant land which generated many farmers with a sufficient surplus and incentive to purchase capital goods.

LABOR ALLOCATED BY THE MARKET

Fleisig explains mechanization in the antebellum North by the market labor constraint faced by individual farms. He assumes that the farm is a profit maximizer facing a fixed supply of labor, due to scarcity in the labor market. He implicitly assumes that labor in the farm economy is allocated by the market. In order to expand, the farm must substitute capital for labor. Think of the production function of the farm. Assume that the farm is producing within the labor constraint and with hand tools, but desires to increase production beyond that quantity that can be operated with the constrained supply of labor in the market. It must produce using horse-drawn machinery because there is no labor to hire. On the other hand, the unconstrained farm can increase production without mechanizing because there is labor to hire.

Because Fleisig has no direct measures of the market labor constraint, nor of mechanization, he tests his theory via the intermediate predictions. He predicts that farms assumed to be labor constrained will have less farm employees (including slaves) per farm operator, less output, less land, and less capital than farms assumed to be unconstrained. Fleisig tests his propositions by comparing averages for the North, representing the labor-constrained farms, and for the South, representing the unconstrained farms. Table 3.1 presents Fleisig's evidence, which is consistent with his predictions. The South had more labor available, 1.92 employees or slaves

Table 3.1
Fleisig's Evidence on the Labor Constraint

Variable	North	South
FE/FO	0.35	1.92
Output	$532.10	$879.50
Land	69.00	97.00
Capital	$111.00	$136.00

Source: Fleisig, "Slavery," p. 596-97 using *U.S. Census, the Eighth Census of the U.S., 1860, Population* (Washington, D.C.: Government Printing Office, 1864), hereafter *Printed Census, 1860, Population*; and Towne and Rasmussen on output.

Note: FE/FO is farm employees per farm operator; Output is average value of farm output; Land is average number of acres of improved land; Capital is average value of farm implements and machinery.

per farm operator, where as the North had less labor available, 0.35 employees per farm operator. The labor-constrained farm in the North had less output, $532.1 to the South's $879.5. The labor-constrained farm had less land, 69 improved acres, to the 97 improved acres on the slave farm. The northern farm had $111 in farm implements and machinery to the $136 on southern farms. I retested Fleisig's propositions on townships in the Old Northwest in 1860. I constructed a measure of labor availability similar to Fleisig's measure of labor per farm for each township: farm employees per farm operator. I have observations on the average amount of wheat output (proxy for value of total output as Fleisig used), land and capital per farm, and reaper adoption rates. The propositions become:

- The lower the farm employee per farm operator ratio is in a township, the lower the number of acres of improved land per farm there is in the township.
- The lower the farm employee per farm operator ratio is in a township, the lower the number of bushels of wheat per farm there is in the township.
- The lower the farm employee per farm operator ratio is in a township, the lower the value of capital equipment per farm there is in the township.
- The lower the farm employee per farm operator ratio is in a township, the higher the proportion of farms that adopted the reaper there is in a township.

The propositions are tested by running correlations between each set of variables predicted to vary together or inversely. Correlations were run two at a time between labor available and one each of wheat output, land per farm, capital per farm, and reaper adoption rates.

First we must address the problem of estimating the farm employees per farm operator. We look at three estimates, one from Fleisig, one using data from Gates, and my own estimates. Fleisig only used the population census and its reported occupations. He used the occupation farmer for the farm operator, which he inappropriately calls farm proprietor. He used the occupation farm laborer for farm employee. He obtains the farm employee per farm operator ratio of 0.32 for the Old Northwest in 1860. The problem is that he ignores the fact that some people who reported the occupation farmer did not have farms. He ignores the "farmers-without-farms" problem. This results in a bias toward a greater labor constraint than there really was. He has implicitly put farmers without farms in his farm operator denominator when they should be in his farm employee numerator. See Table 3.2.

From Gates we obtain the number of farms in the system from the agricultural census. This enables us to correct for farmers-without-farms. In Table 3.2 we see that there were 724,361 people reporting the occupation farmer. Fleisig uses this number for farm operators. There were only 588,717 farms. That makes for 135,644 farmers-without-farms that should be added to farm employees and subtracted from farm operators. Fleisig overestimated the farm operators by 23 percent and underestimated the farm employees by 37 percent. Making this correction, we obtain a farm employee per farm operator ratio of 0.62.

The availability of the manuscript census sample on computer tape makes it possible to make a third estimate of the farm employee per farm

Table 3.2
Estimates of Farm Employees per Farm Operator

Procedure	Farmers	Farm Operators (Farms)	Farmers Without Farms	Farm Laborers	Farm Employees	FE/FO
Fleisig	724,361			231,883	231,883	0.32
Gates	724,361	588,717	135,644	231,883	367,288	0.62
New	8,377	5,756	2,621		2,621	0.46

Source: Fleisig, "Slavery," pp. 596-97; Gates, *The Farmer's Age*, p. 273; Fred Bateman and James D. Foust, *Agricultural and Demographic Records for Rural Households in the North, 1860* (Ann Arbor, MI: Inter-University Consortium for Political and Social Research, 1976).

operator. The Old Northwest subset of this sample includes 9,494 rural households of which 3,738 are non-farm rural households who may report their occupation as farmers, meaning farm employee, or at least farmer-without-farm. A farm operator lives on the farm. There were 5,756 farm households each of which we assume had a farm operator. A mature son or a hired hand may live in the farm household and he would report a farm occupation. In the sample, 8,377 people reported a farmer occupation. If we subtract 5,756 farm operators (farms) from this, we obtain 2,621 farmers-without-farms. See Table 3.2. That makes for a farm employee per farm operator ratio of 0.46. A possible explanation for the fact that this is lower than the Gates's ratio is that Gates uses the whole universe of farms and the manuscript census sample is biased toward farms not near urban areas. This explanation assumes that the labor constraint was tighter away from urban areas. In Chapter 5 I discuss in full the bias of the sample. But my bias toward more of a labor constraint is not as great as Fleisig's bias.

Using the new procedure for estimating the farm employee per farm operator in the Old Northwest, I estimated the ratio for each of the 46 townships. There is considerable variation in the labor available, but in 22 of 46 townships, under 0.50 employees were available on average per farm operator, and in 35 townships there was one or less farm employee per farm operator on average.

The sample gives the wheat output, land in improved acres, and capital value of farm implements and machinery for each of the 5,756 farms in the Old Northwest in 1860. When the farms are grouped by townships, the aggregate wheat output for each township can be calculated. Divided by the number of farms in each township, aggregate wheat output is transformed into the average wheat output per farm (see Appendix C). The average wheat output per farm in the mean township was 8.7 acres, in the median township 7.0 acres, and in the mode township, 0 acres. The range was from a maximum of 29.8 acres of wheat to a minimum of zero.

Land in improved acres is given for each of the 5,756 farms. This data can be grouped and averaged for townships. The average land per farm in the average township was 65 acres, in the median township 57 acres, and the mode township 49 acres. The maximum was 187 acres and the minimum was 1 acre (see Appendix C).

Capital per farm (value of the farm implements and machinery) is given for each of 5,756 farms. One can calculate averages for each township (see Appendix C). The average capital per farm in a township ranges from $233.9 to $16.2.

Having constructed these variables and observations, I ran correlations to test the propositions. The results are given in Table 3.3. None of the correlation coefficients are statistically significant and the R-squares show that variation in the average output and land and capital inputs are not explained very much by variation in the farm employee per farm operator

Table 3.3
New Evidence on the Role of the Labor Constraint

Variable X	Variable Y	Correlation Coefficient	R-square
FE/FO	Wheat Output	- 0.15	0.02
FE/FO	Land	0.02	0.00
FE/FO	Capital	0.14	0.02
FE/FO	Reapers	0.01	0.00

Source: Fred Bateman and James D. Foust, *Agricultural and Demographic Records for Rural Households in the North, 1860* (Ann Arbor, MI: Inter-University Consortium for Political and Social Research, 1976). See Appendix C.

Note: N = 46 townships. FE/FO is farm employees per farm operator in a township; Wheat Output is average bushels on a farm in a township. Land is average number of improved acres per farm in a township; Reapers is the proportion of farms in a township that adopted the reaper, see Appendix A and Chapter 5.

ratio. Townships with less farm employees available per farm operator on average are not necessarily producing less wheat, using less land, nor using less capital on average. Fleisig's propositions are not consistent with this evidence. I also tested this proposition by running a correlation on 46 townships between the farm employee per farm operator ratio and the proportion of farmers inferred to have adopted the reaper (see Appendix C). The correlation coefficient was 0.01 and R^2 was 0.00. This evidence suggests that the adoption of the reaper was not caused by the market labor constraint. I did not expect this.

I offer a different line of reasoning on why Fleisig's intermediate predictions did not work. I agree that the family farm was labor constrained. However, within that limit, they had room to maneuver. True their labor force was constrained to the members of their family. However, they could increase the number of hours worked, the intensity of labor, and the efficiency of labor. They could move their farm to the production frontier. They maximized output to the physical limit of the capacity of the farm family. This was not true for small family farms or for large business farms, so I contend. Thus, the medium-sized family farm, as the predominant kind of farm in the system, was able to produce large outputs, using large amounts of land, and then, meeting the labor constraint of the farm family, adopted the reaper.[1]

LABOR ALLOCATED BY THE FARM HOUSEHOLD

An alternative to Fleisig's market labor-constraint model on northern mechanization is the farm household model that is based on the assumption that labor was allocated predominantly by the farm household, not by the market as in Fleisig's model. The farm household allocates family labor among three options: work, leisure, and non-farm work.[2] The farm household is assumed to be a utility maximizer; this is the principle that guides the decisions to allocate the family labor to the three options. Allocation of family labor to leisure leads directly to utility. Allocation of family labor to non-farm activity, such as making clothing, leads directly to utility. Most important is the allocation of family labor by the farm household to work on the farm. This labor leads to farm output. The revenue from sold output is used either to (1) buy consumer goods on the market which gives utility or (2) invest in farm ownership which leads to utility.[3] Farm ownership enters the utility function of the farm household because the goal of the farm household is to attain the security of farm ownership as a hedge against risk and uncertainty of farming and of life in general.[4]

The cause of mechanization in the North in this farm household model is the self-imposed labor constraint of limiting the labor on the farm to that of the farm family and the desire of the medium-sized farm household to produce more food for the market than the capacity of the labor force of the farm family allowed. Another way to express this is that family farmers to a large degree were "unwilling to bid for wage labor."[5]

The family farm is assumed to be a risk averse utility maximizer. The risk aversion caused them to limit the labor on the farm to that of the farm family. This allowed them to avoid the fluctuations of consumption, by sacrificing a higher level of consumption. Given this labor constraint, there was pressure to maximize output with that family labor. They produced to the physical limit of the capacity of the family and operated the farm on the production frontier. They worked long hours, they worked intensely, and they worked efficiently. This is different from small family farms and large business farms, as I shall explain below.

To illustrate this, I selected out of the Bateman-Foust manuscript sample of farms a farm with 160 total acres. I call it medium sized as defined by being made up of 41 to 160 total acres, enough land to occupy the labor force of the family farm.[6] Here is how the labor force of the farm family can operate this farm. I found that 96 of the 160 total acres (TA) are improved (IA), leaving 64 acres unimproved. The farm allocates family labor to clearing and fencing this unimproved land for investment purposes, for capital formation in land. This is the farm-making stage of a medium-sized family farm in the Old Northwest in 1860 and is at the 81.3 percentile of the manuscript census sample. On the 96 acres of improved land (IA), the farmer grows 16 acres of wheat (W) and 22 acres of corn (C). The 16 acres of wheat is assumed to be for the market, and can be harvested by hand by the family. The 22 acres of corn has two implications: on one hand, this is probably more corn than a family needs for its food supply; therefore it is being grown for feed to sell meat or dairy on the market. In addition, some of the corn is for the family food supply as corn bread and feed for family meat and dairy. On the other hand, this is probably more than the family can plant and cultivate unless the family had a mature son.[7] Otherwise this farm would have to adopt corn planter and corn cultivator horse-drawn machinery. The remaining 58 acres of improved land are in general farming which includes pasture, meadow, garden, orchard, farm residence, farm structures, and so on.

To illustrate a farm at the fully-developed stage, I selected out of the Bateman-Foust manuscript sample, a farm with 160 improved acres. Although this was a real farm (computer-generated from real farm data) at the 95.3 percentile of the manuscript census sample Old Northwest, 1860, it was part of a larger farm in total acres, and it can be used to see the future potential and the structure of land use of a 160-improved acre farm. *Fully-developed* means that all the land on the farm is improved; farm making is complete, there are no unimproved acres. I found that 46 acres are in corn and 28 acres are in wheat. Both of them are being produced in large part for the market and both are beyond the capacity of the labor force of the family farm. This medium-sized family farm mechanized because it wanted to produce more than 20 acres of wheat and/or more than 20 acres of corn. The two are not competitive because corn planting and cultivating is in the spring and wheat harvest is in the summer. Why the farm wants to produce beyond the capacity of the labor force of the farm family using hand tools is investigated in Chapter 4. General farming takes up 86 acres [160 IA - (28W + 46C) = 86].

I present here the same tests that Fleisig uses to support his market labor-constraint model carried out on my farm household model. The farm household propositions are:

- The higher the proportion of farms in the 41- to 160-improved-acre range is in a township, the higher the value of capital equipment per farm there is in a township.
- The higher the proportion of farms in the 41- to 160-improved-acre range is in a township, the higher the proportion of farms adopting the reaper there is in a township.
- The higher the proportion of farms in the 41- to 160-improved-acre range is in a township, the higher the number of bushels wheat per farm there is in a township.

The family farm variable was constructed as follows: The 5,756 farms were sorted into their townships and arranged by size in improved acres per farm. Then the number of farms in the range of 41 to 160 improved acres was counted for each township. This was divided by the number of farms in the township to obtain a proportion of farms of this size. In 12 of the 46 townships the proportion of medium-sized farms was between 61 and 80 percent. An additional 16 townships had 41 to 60 percent of farms in the medium-size range.

The results of running the correlations are given in Table 3.4. The proportion of medium-sized farms in a township is correlated with the capital per farm in a township. The correlation coefficient is 0.68. The R^2 is 0.46 which means that 46 percent of the variation in the amount of capital per farm in a township is explained by the proportion of medium-sized farms in that township. Even the proportion of farms adopting the reaper can be "explained" by the proportion of medium-sized family farms, at least 16 percent of the variation in adoption is so explained. The correlation coefficient is only 0.41 and thus not statistically significant, but compared with the coefficient that Fleisig obtained for the labor available, 0.01, it is substantially more. Furthermore, the market labor constraint was Fleisig's complete and only explanation. I do not claim that all mediumsized farms adopted the reaper, only that most farmers who did adopt the reaper were medium-sized, not small (as Fleisig claims) and not large (as David claims). I claim that given the predominance of this size farm, the

Table 3.4
Results of Testing Propositions on Medium-Sized Farm Households

Variable X	Variable Y	Correlation Coefficient	R-square
Medium Farm	Capital	0.68	0.46
Medium Farm	Reaper	0.41	0.16
Medium Farm	Wheat	0.41	0.17

Source: Fred Bateman and James D. Foust, *Agricultural and Demographic Records for Rural Households in the North, 1860* (Ann Arbor, MI: Inter-University Consortium for Political and Social Research, 1976).

Note: N = 46 townships. Medium Farm is the proportion of farms in a township that are in the range of 41 to 160 improved acres per farm. Capital is the average value of farm implements and machinery per farm in a township. Reaper is the proportion of farms in a township that adopted the reaper; Wheat is the average number of bushels of wheat per farm in a township.

mass production of farm machinery was taken on. Then, further explanation of which medium-sized farms mechanized or adopted the reaper is accounted for by other variables, such as size of debts for mortgage, land, livestock, and implements. Thus I do not expect the mere predominance of the medium-sized family farm in a township to explain all the mechanization. In this case, to obtain such a large part of the variance explained is significant.

The same case can be made for wheat production. An R^2 of 0.17 means that 17 percent of the variation in the average wheat production in a township can be explained by the proportion of medium-sized farms in that township. The correlation coefficient of 0.41 is not statistically significant but it is larger than the coefficient for labor available, - 0.15. I do not claim that all medium-sized farms produced a large amount of wheat, but I do claim that medium-sized farms account for most of the wheat production. I defend this in Chapter 4.

In conclusion, the evidence is consistent with the proposition that mechanization was located in the North because of the predominance of medium-sized family farms there and that the labor in the farm economy was allocated by the farm household. Although they were labor constrained, the medium-sized family farm allocated its labor to market production. They worked long, hard, and efficiently. They produced on the production frontier. They maximized output with family labor. When they got to the physical limit of the family's capacity, they purchased capital on the market, that is, they adopted the reaper. In Chapter 4, we look at the pressures on the medium-sized family farm to adopt the reaper. But first, we turn to specifying and quantifying the labor constraints in the farm economy of the Old Northwest in 1860.

PREDOMINANT LABOR ALLOCATOR

The labor that went into the gross farm product was predominantly labor allocated by the farm household and the smaller proportion was allocated by the market. If this proposition is true, then the farm household model is the explanation of the predominant mechanizers, and the market labor constraint model explains the mechanization of only a small percent of farms.

Gross farm output is constituted by the following factors: productivity, hours per worker, employment, labor force, and population.[8] First, let us look at the population. In the Old Northwest, population was growing at a rate of 53.1 percent from 1850 to 1860.[9] The natural rate of population increase is greater on the farm and in rural areas than in the urban areas. Most of the population lived in rural areas, and on farms. As to labor force participation of the rural non-farm population, it helped at the harvest. As to labor force participation of the rural farm population, it includes nearly all men, mature sons, women, and children. As to employment, there was a labor market for farm employees. The people who are in the farm labor force are "employed" or allocated by the farm household; there is really no unemployment here.

How many farm workers were allocated by the farm household and how many by the market? In the manuscript census sample of the Old Northwest, 1860, 8,377 men over the age of 16 reported their occupation as farmer. If we assume that each farm has a farm operator, we can subtract the number of farms from the number of farmers to obtain the number of farm workers allocated by the farm household, as the farm operator is the main worker. This makes for 5,756 farm operators, allocating their own labor from within the farm household. That leaves 2,621 farmers without farms, potentially available for hire. Inferring from the sample to the universe, there were 269,890 potential available workers for hire, to 586,717 farm operators laboring on their own farms. Based on these statistics, we can say that 31 percent of the farm workers were employees and 69 percent were farm operators who laborered. See Table 3.5.

The claim that the predominant proportion of labor in the farm economy of the Old Northwest in 1860 was allocated by the farm household is stronger when made in terms of labor time, instead of in numbers of

Table 3.5
Quantifying the Predominant Allocator of Labor

Predominance Judged by:	Percentage		Numbers in Sample	Numbers in Universe
Number of	FO	69	5,756	586,717
workers	FE	31	2,621	269,890
	TOTAL	100	8,377	856,607
Number of	FO	81	5,756	586,717
man-years	FE	19	1,311	134,945
	TOTAL	100	7,067	721,662

Source: Fred Bateman and James D. Foust, *Agricultural and Demographic Records for Rural Households in the North, 1860* (Ann Arbor, MI: Inter-University Consortium for Political and Social Research, 1976) and *Printed Census, 1860, Population*.

Note: N = 9,494 rural households of which 5,756 were farm households; Universe of 586,717 farms; FO is farm operator; FE is farm employee.

workers. The farm operator worked 12 months a year. The farm employee was usually hired for six months.[10] The proportion of labor-time in man-years that was allocated by the market was 19 percent and that allocated by the farm household was 81 percent. See Table 3.5.

If we accept the idea that the predominant proportion of the labor in the farm economy was allocated by the farm household, the question remains why did they allocate so much. It is uncontroversial to state that farm families work long and hard. Recall that the farm household is allocating labor between work and leisure. They allocated family labor to work because they wanted to own their farm to increase the security and decrease the risk in their lives. They preferred work to leisure.

On the productivity component of the manpower in the farm economy, I would argue that family labor was more productive than market labor, judged in output per time unit of labor. This is because of the incentive to work hard, like the incentive to work long, that they would by so doing earn money to finance ownership of the family farm.

On farm output we know that in the north, 60 percent of the farm output went into the market.[11] This is family labor allocated to farm work for the market which leaves 40 percent for farm work for on-farm use. From the welfare point of view, average productivity of the farm economy can be broken down into the real hourly wage (opportunity cost for the farm household-allocated labor) and the inverse of labor share in the farm product.[12] Family labor worked for a lower wage than market labor. The share of labor in the earnings from farm production was total because the family laborer was also the farm operator and farm owner. This is part of the incentive system of the family farm. The farm household earns wages from labor, rent from land ownership, and profit on capital.[13]

The upshot of this analysis is that 81 percent of the labor time in man-years in the farm economy was allocated by the farm household. This labor worked harder and longer and for a lower wage. This labor was more productive. Furthermore, this 81 percent does not include the labor of mature sons over the age of 16, counted in the labor force of employees, but not known to be allocated by the farm household or by the market. In addition, the labor of women and children was allocated by the farm household.

Even more important is how much of the labor in marketed food output was family labor. I estimate that 68 percent of the labor time in the marketed output of food in the North as of 1860 was produced by family labor. I obtained this estimate in the following way. Assume the average farm household as having 100 units of labor-time. On average, 81 units were family labor and 19 units were hired labor. Now, assume the average farm household produces 100 units of output. On average, 40 units were for the support of the family and 60 units were for the market. Thus, of the 60 units of farm output produced for the market, 41 units were produced by family labor (81-40), and 19 by hired labor. Sixty-eight percent (41/60) of the labor in the marketed output was family labor and 32 percent (19/60) was hired labor.

We now turn to the major task of this section, to specify and quantify the labor constraints in the farm economy. We do this by examining the qualitative evidence that Fleisig used to support his assumption of the labor constraint.

Fleisig states, "The pivotal assumption is that the typical northern farmer could not hire all the labor he desired at the prevailing wage."[14] So far we have considered only the supply of labor. To quantify the market labor constraint we need to look at the demand for labor. Three sources of demand for hired labor will be investigated: to run a farm larger than 160 total acres; to harvest more than 20 acres of wheat; and to plant and cultivate more than 20 acres of corn.

First, let us look at the demand for hired labor to run a farm larger than 160 total acres. Parker suggests that a family could operate a 160-acre farm. Gates tells us that in 1850 people who protested against land speculators proposed in Ohio to limit the quantity of land to be owned by one man to 160 acres and that the surplus beyond that was to be sold. Heady says the typical farm was 160 acres and we know that the typical farm was run by a family.[15] I would qualify this by adding that a farm of 160 improved acres could be operated by a farm family if they did not grow over 20 acres of corn and if they did not grow over 20 acres of wheat.[16] In the second section of this chapter, I showed how a farm family could operate a 160-total-acre farm in the farm-making stage if they were engaged in general farming.

How many farms were larger than 160 acres of total acres, such that they would demand labor in the market to operate them? Using my sample, I found that only 1,077 farms were that large, or 18.7 percent. Inferring from the sample to the universe, there would be 109,717 farms over the size of 160 total acres and thus demanding hired labor. See Table 3.6. If the supply of labor for hire, 269,890 potential farm employees, were allocated to the farms that needed labor to run their more than 160 total acres, then each farm would obtain 2.5 employees.

Who were these large farms and what was their nature in terms of obtaining a labor force? First, there were the bonanza farms and Fleisig cites Gates on the 1850s: "Greatest of the bonanza farm makers on the prairies was Michael Sullivant. . . . In 1852 he began buying land in eastern Illinois until he held 80,000 acres. With the aid of 100 hired hands, 125 yoke of oxen, and 50 horses he had by 1857 3,000 acres in corn and a smaller number in wheat."[17]

Judging from my sample, only 2 percent of farms were 500 improved acres or more. While the individual demand for labor on the bonanza was large, the aggregate demand of all of them was not great with respect to the

Table 3.6
Quantifying the Constraint of Hired Labor

Source of Demand for Hired Labor	Farms		Supply of Hired Labor	Allocation per Farm
	Percent	Number		
OVER 500 TA	2.0	11,734	269,890	23.0
OVER 160 IA	4.7	27,576	269,890	9.8
OVER 160 TA	18.7	109,717	269,890	2.5
OVER 20 WHEAT	14.0	82,420	269,890	3.3
OVER 20 CORN	25.0	146,679	269,890	1.8

Source: Fred Bateman and James D. Foust, *Agricultural and Demographic Records for Rural Households in the North, 1860* (Ann Arbor, MI: Inter-University Consortium for Political and Social Research, 1976) and *Printed Census, 1860.*

Note: N = 5,756 farms. Universe of 586,717 farms. IA is improved acres of land on a farm; TA is total acres; WHEAT is number of acres of wheat on a farm; CORN is number of acres of corn on a farm.

supply of labor available. If we infer from the sample to the universe, then 11,734 bonanza farms "competed" for the 269,890 farmers without farms, also inferred from the sample to the universe. If they obtained all the labor for hire, then each would receive 23 farm workers. I do not know how many farm workers are needed per acre, thus I cannot say that on average 23 was enough. Another problem for the bonanza farm was that the incentives of the labor available were less than the incentives of family labor, hence bonanza farm labor costs were higher. This takes us back to David's high and rising wage, and not Fleisig's labor constraint as the cause of mechanization.

The business farm, defined as between 161 and 499 improved acres, is below the bonanza farm in acres of land, but above the family farm. In the Old Northwest, judged by the sample, there were 2.7 percent of this size farms. They needed less labor than a bonanza farm but would be competing for the same labor force. Inferring from the sample to the universe, that makes for 15,841 farms who would obtain 17 farm employees per farm. Fleisig cites Gates on 1815 New York: "The fear of losing tenants, purchasers of land, or even farm laborers was a factor that induced landowners to deal leniently with them, sell at lower prices, and pay higher wages."[18]

Fleisig also used as evidence of the labor constraint, the complaints of English gentlemen who came to Illinois in the 1817-18 period. Fleisig cites

Bidwell and Falconer:

The English farmers, Birkbeck, Flower, and others, who came to Illinois . . . with plenty of capital, expecting to carry on large-scale farming, found their plans upset by the lack of a class of farm laborers. . . . Finally, the English were forced to the conclusion that Illinois was a good location only for the small farmer who was willing to work his land without hired labor.[19]

If English gentlemen could not find labor in an area of U.S. farms, this indicates a labor scarcity, but there is one important difference. The English gentlemen did not labor themselves, they needed a complete labor force. The family farmer did 81 percent of the labor time on his farm and thus demanded much less labor from the market (if he had no sons, less if he had sons). The problem of the English gentlemen was more that they were unwilling to labor themselves, than the marginal problem of hired labor. The English gentlemen were like southern plantation owners who operated their plantations but did not labor on them like the family farmers did in the North and in the South. Fleisig includes the northern farm operator when he calculates the labor force for his capital-labor ratios and does not include the southern plantation operator when calculating the labor force in the South for this capital-labor ratio.[20]

The second way to quantify the market labor constraint is in terms of output. We look first at wheat. Fleisig cites Gates: "As farmers increased their acreage in wheat they became more dependent upon migratory labor or exchange labor, since it was not feasible for them to keep hired hands in sufficient quantity for more than the harvest and threshing season."[21]

Let us quantify the demand for market labor for the wheat harvest. From the sample, I calculate the number of farms that are producing more than 20 acres of wheat and find that 14 percent of the farms are. Inferring from the sample to the universe, that makes 82,420 farms in need of market labor to harvest their wheat. If the supply of potential market labor, 269,890 employees, were allocated to these farms, each would obtain 3.3 workers. See Table 3.6. We have not even included a large source of harvest labor in the rural towns.

Fleisig cites Gates: "In the better times of the fifties it was increasingly difficult to keep laborers at the old rates. . . . A . . . Michigan farmer complained in 1852 that he now had to pay $26 a month to keep hands who, only a few years earlier had cost him only $11 a month."[22] The reference to hiring by the month shows it is not for the wheat harvest, which was only two weeks long. Why else would a farmer want to hire labor? The quantity of time required for planting corn by hand and cultivating it by hand with a hoe was great, although it was not time constrained to two weeks as in the case of wheat harvesting.[23] Corn had a time constraint on planting and cultivating but was not so short nor so risky as in wheat harvesting. The need for labor to plant and cultivate corn was not competitive with the labor needed to harvest wheat as they did not occur in the same time of year. Corn planting and cultivating is in the spring and wheat harvest is in the mid-summer. How great was the demand for labor for the corn planting and cultivating? See Table 3.6.

In the sample, 25 percent of farms were producing more than 20 acres of corn. Inferring from the sample to the universe, that makes 146,679 farms that need hired labor to plant and cultivate their corn. If the supply of market labor, 269,890 employees, was distributed to these farms, each one would obtain 1.8 employees.

It is interesting to note that there was a greater shortage of labor for corn production than for wheat production, judged by the number of farms in need. In addition to the adoption of the horse-drawn reaper (to replace the harvest of wheat by hand with a cradle-scythe) this was the era of the horse-drawn corn planter (replacing the hand planting) and the horse-drawn corn cultivator (replacing the hand cultivation of corn with a hoe). Furthermore, there was a horse-drawn seed drill to plant wheat instead of hand sowing. The threshing machine in the barn was replacing hand threshing with the flail. The farmer had to wait until the twentieth century to get a machine to shell the corn.

If we assume that the evidence warrants the claim that in the aggregate that supply was equal to demand, the problem remains of the distribution of that labor. How was the labor available for hire distributed? We do not know. We do know that most farms had the farm operator, the head of the farm household, as the only laborer. If he was lucky, he had a mature son. However, the rich farmer could pay this mature son of his neighbor, and many sons were thus not at their father's disposal. Gates says that by 1860 the hired hand was a typical feature of the farm system.[24]

The distribution of labor on the farm had three typical forms: one per farm, two per farm, or many per farm. In the case of one worker per farm it was the farm operator who was the head of the farm household. In the case of two workers on the farm it was the farm operator, a mature son from his household, or a hired hand. The hired hand might be the son of a poor neighbor who allocated his son's labor to making a money wage. This hired hand would not stay for long. He would soon be off to the city, off to the west, and/or off to his own farm. The hired hand could also be a farm operator/owner whose farm was not yet developed enough to support the family. As soon as farm making had progressed enough for this man to support his family he would no longer offer his labor on the market. In the case of many workers on a farm, this is the business farm run by a profit maximizer, who when faced with a labor constraint, would mechanize.

In conclusion, yes, there was a market labor constraint, but it operated mostly for the few large farms at the top of the size distribution. The problem probably did not exist at the aggregate level, hence the accurate specification of the problem is barriers to mobility, that prevented that aggregate supply from being distributed to all parts of the aggregate demand. Large landowners preferred tenants to laborers, not because the latter were constrained, but because tenants were families and had stronger incentives to work. Most farms were family farms and only 19 percent of their labor was hired (less due to sons) on average. Sometimes a large family farm had a hired hand. I would argue that the labor of the hired hand was not to be replaced by machinery. The hired hand helped the farm operator with one set of machinery. This is one reason why mechanization is better represented by capital per farm than by the capital-labor ratio, which Fleisig prefers.

The business farms adopted farm machinery in the North because as individual profit-maximizing firms they were market labor-constrained. In order to expand for profit, they had to adopt machinery. But these farms did not account for a large proportion of all farms. As we will see in Chapter 4 they did not account for a predominant proportion of food production, land use, or capital equipment purchasers.

CONCLUSION

The analysis of this chapter suggests that we are dealing with a farm system that does not use much hired labor. We found that a farm operator on average had access to 0.46 of an employee. The labor in this farm economy was allocated by the farm household, not the market. We found that 81 percent of the labor time in the farm economy was allocated by the farm household and at most only 19 percent of the labor time was allocated by the market. The complaints about the labor scarcity seems to have come from a small proportion of the farmers, those with bonanza farms or at least farms so large that they could not be operated by the labor of the farm family. There were not very many of these farms.

Fleisig's labor-constrained model was not supported by the correlation tests. My medium-sized family farm household model was supported by the correlation tests. Most significantly, I found that townships with higher proportions of medium-sized family farms were also townships with higher capital per farm.

This evidence suggests that the preference of medium-sized family farms to not hire labor was a more important reason for reaper adoption than the scarcity of labor in the market. This supports Hypothesis 2: Risk-averse utility-maximizing family farms rationally adopted the reaper in the 1850s when they wanted to produce more wheat than they could with family labor.

In addition, the empirical evidence supporting the medium-sized family farm household model suggests that we should retain Hypothesis 4: The institutional structure of the family farm system was a favorable initial condition for the adoption of farm machinery because it was based on a relatively equal distribution of abundant land which generated many farmers with a sufficient surplus and incentive to purchase capital goods.

In Chapter 4 we look in more detail into the family farm system in the Old Northwest and its adoption of the reaper.

NOTES

1. Jeremy Atack and Fred Bateman, *To Their Own Soil: Agriculture in the Antebellum North* (Ames: Iowa State University Press, 1987), pp. 187-88. They state that "the family farm tended to employ more labor and operate at a greater scale for the same costs than a farm that relied upon hired labor," and that "the family farm had a greater propensity to mechanize and farm extensively than a purely commercial operation relying upon hired labor."

2. Conventional neoclassical economic literature uses the concept of leisure to represent all non-market activity. In the farm economy of the American North in the nineteenth century, we must distinguish between leisure and actual non-market work, because farm household did non-farm work such as producing housing, clothing, and footwear.

3. Some output was for food self-sufficiency and was not marketed, but this leads to utility via consumption. As to the output that was sold and exchanged, the top sectors of the economy in 1860 suggest that they bought cotton and woolen goods, men's clothing, boots and shoes, and lumber for housing. See Douglass C. North, *Growth and Welfare in the American Past*, 2nd ed., (Englewood Cliffs, NJ: Prentice-Hall, 1974), p. 80.

4. Conventional neoclassical literature sees utility as a function of consumption alone. However, the new literature on female participation in the labor force uses the idea that the woman in the household wants utility from consumption and from such non-consumption goals as childrearing. Neoclassical literature is being developed also to include risk and its effect on goals and behavior.

5. James A. Henretta, "Families and Farms: Mentalité in Pre-industrial America," *William and Mary Quarterly* 35, 3rd series (1978):3-32.

6. "Small" is defined by enough land to support the family. A large farm is not a family farm at all but defined as more land than a family labor force can operate.

7. See Allan G. Bogue on the estimate that a farmer could plant and cultivate 20 acres of corn by hand alone, *From Prairie to Corn Belt* (Chicago: University of Chicago Press, 1963), p. 165.

8. David Weir provides this framework in his "Stabilization Regained: A Reappraisal of the U.S. Macroeconomic Record, 1890-1980," presented to the Washington Area Economic History Seminar, Washington, D.C., October 11, 1985, pp. 41-42.

9. See Chapter 1 of this text on Regional Statistics.

10. Paul W. Gates, *The Farmer's Age: Agriculture, 1815-1860*, vol. 3 of *The Economic History of the United States* (New York: Harper and Row, 1960), p. 272; Fred Bateman and Jeremy Atack, "The Profitability of Northern Agriculture in 1860," *Research in Economic History* 4 (1979): 105-8.

11. *Historical Statistics of the U.S.*, A202-203.

12. Weir, "Stabilization Regained," p. 42.

13. Four of five farm operators owned their farms in the manuscript census sample.

14. Heywood Fleisig, "Slavery, the Supply of Agricultural Labor, and the Industrialization of the South," *Journal of Economic History* 36 (September 1976):573.

15. William Parker, "Agriculture," in Lance Davis et al. (Eds.) *American Economic Growth* (New York: Harper and Row, 1972), p. 393-394; Gates, *The Farmer's Age*, p. 86; Earl O. Heady, "Economic Policy and Variables: Potentials and Problems for the Future" in David Brewster et al. (Eds.), *Farms in Transition: Interdisciplinary Perspectives on Farm Structure* (Ames: Iowa State University, 1983), p. 24.

16. Bogue, *From Prairie to Corn Belt*, p. 165 on the ability of a farm family producing 20 acres of corn and my estimates on the ability of a farm family to produce 20 acres of wheat, in Chapter 2 of this text.

17. Gates, *The Farmer's Age*, pp. 192-93.

18. Ibid., p. 40.

19. Percy W. Bidwell and John I. Falconer, *History of Agriculture in the Northern United States, 1620-1860* (Washington, D.C.: Carnegie Institute, 1925), p. 164.

20. Fleisig, "Slavery," pp. 596-97.

21. Gates, *The Farmer's Age*, p. 165.

22. Ibid., p. 277.

23. W.N. Parker and J.L. Klein, "Productivity Growth in Grain Production in the U.S., 1840-60 and 1900-10," in Dorothy Brady (Ed.), *Output, Employment, and Productivity in the U.S. after 1800*, vol. 30 of *Studies in Income and Wealth* (New York: National Bureau of Economic Research, 1966), p. 532, Table 1.

24. Gates, *The Farmer's Age*, p. 272.

4

FAMILY FARM
SYSTEM AS A CAUSE
OF REAPER ADOPTION

In his 1965 article in *Agricultural History*, Wayne Rasmussen argued that the Civil War acted as a catalyst of agricultural revolution.[1] In his 1960 study for the National Bureau of Economic Research, Rasmussen identified the two decades of the 1850s and the 1860s as the time of the first agricultural revolution in the United States.[2] In my study I estimate that, by 1860, only 5 percent of farmers in the Old Northwest had adopted the reaper and accounted for only 25 percent of the wheat harvest. This represents the initial wave of popular acceptance of the horse-drawn mechanical reaper, a key machine in this agricultural revolution of mechanization, documented by Rasmussen in his article for the *Scientific American* in 1981.[3] The 1860s, the second decade of agricultural revolution, then, represent the diffusion of machinery from its initial popular acceptance. It was this diffusion which was sped up by the catalyst of the Civil War, according to Rasmussen.

The word *catalyst*—from the Greek for dissolve, loosen or release—refers to a substance that modifies, usually by increasing, the rate of reaction without being consumed in the process. To state that the Civil War was a catalyst, then, means that the reaction may already have begun and the arrival of the catalyst sped up that reaction. Continuing with the chemical analogy, the reactants and the catalyst exist in a physical environment which can prevent, encourage, or be neutral to, the reaction taking place. The environment could be frozen, airless, warm, and so on. My point is that family farm agricultural institutions were a favorable environment for the "chemical" reaction. This institutional framework engendered responsive economic agents. The Civil War, as catalyst, sped up the reactions that began in the 1850s and the initial wave of popular acceptance became a process of widespread diffusion. This diffusion is described by Rasmussen in his 1965 article. I believe that the family farm system, as a favorable environment, was an important cause of the initial acceptance of the reaper in the 1850s, as well as an important cause of the diffusion of the reaper during the Civil War.

In this chapter I seek to analyze the structure of family farm agricultural institutions and to measure its links with economic events in the Old Northwest in the 1850s. Both David and Fleisig explain why profit-maximizing farms adopted farm machinery. The family farm thesis explains why risk-averse utility-maximizing family farmers adopted farm machinery. Thus we need to know what proportion of farmers were profit maximizers and what proportion were family farmers. We need to know this about all farms and about reaper adopting farms in particular. I agree with David and Fleisig that there were some profit-maximizing farms that did behave in the way described by conventional neoclassical economic theory. I even think that family farmers behaved like profit maximizers on some decisions, but with important differences. These differences need to be modeled into a new kind of model of the family farm in which farmers are seen to be rational and which includes key features of the institutional structure of the family farm system. Without these rational family farmers, the environment would not have been conducive to agricultural improvements. There were not enough profit-maximizing farms in the United States to account for the agricultural revolution.

The evidence developed in this chapter will be used to test Hypothesis 4: The institutional structure of the family farm system was a favorable initial condition for the adoption of the farm machinery because it was based on the relatively equal distribution of abundant land which generated many farmers with sufficient surplus and incentive to purchase capital goods.

FAMILY FARM SYSTEM AS AN EXPLANATORY VARIABLE

The predominance of the medium-sized family farm in the farm economy of the Old Northwest in 1860 was, in part, the cause of the adoption of the reaper and mechanization. First, we must determine that the medium-sized family farm was the predominant farm size judged by numbers and proportion of farm land used. Second we investigate the source of the system, in the federal land policy for the public domain in the nineteenth century.

Predominant Land Users

The family farm system can be defined, in part, by the quantity of land on the farm. We look at the size distribution of farms in the Old Northwest in 1860 to see what size category had the most farms. The categories of the size distribution are designed to answer the questions: how many farms were of the size that could occupy the labor force of a farm family? which we will call medium-sized family farms; how many farms were of the size that could support a family or less? which we will call small family farms; and how many farms were of the size that was beyond the capacity of the labor force of a farm family? which we will call large business farms. Assuming the fertility of the soil and the technology of the period, I estimate a medium-sized family farm to be in the range of 41 to 160 improved acres, a small family farm to be 40 improved acres or less, and that a business farm to be larger than 160 improved acres. In my Chapter 3, I explain how a family could handle 160 acres.

Inferring from the manuscript census sample, 49.5 percent of the farms in the Old Northwest in 1860 were medium-sized family farms. See Table 4.1. The mean farm in the distribution had 64 acres, the median farm had 50

Table 4.1
Predominant Land Users

Range of Land in IA	No. of Farms	No. of IA of Land	Percent of Farms	Percent of Land Used
less than 41 IA	2,636	66,106	45.8	17.9
41-160 IA	2,849	228,092	49.5	61.7
more than 160 IA	271	75,473	4.7	20.4
TOTAL	5,756	369,671	100.0	100.0

Source: Fred Bateman and James D. Foust, *Agricultural and Demographic Records for Rural Households in the North, 1860* (Ann Arbor, MI: Inter-University Consortium for Political and Social Research, 1976).

Note: N = 5,756 farms. IA is improved acres.

acres, both had more than enough to support a family, but not too much that they could not be operated by a family. The mode farm, however, was a small family farm of 40 acres.

The second largest category of farm size was the small family farm. In Table 4.1 we see that whereas there were 228,092 medium-sized farms, there were 66,106 small family farms, or 45.8 percent of all farms in the sample of 5,756 farms. It should be noted that this was a temporary phenomenon in that as the farm-making stage progressed many of these small family farms would develop into medium-sized family farms. Farm making is the clearing and fencing of unimproved acres of land, transforming them into improved acres of land. In 1860, only 4.7 percent of farms were larger than 160 improved acres, accounting for only 271 of the 5,756 farms in the sample. Thus judged in terms of number of farms, the medium-sized family farm was predominant.

More important than the predominance of the medium-sized family farmer in terms of numbers of farms is his predominance in the proportion of land operated. Table 4.1 shows that of the 369,671 improved acres in production in 1860 in the sample, 228,092 were being operated by the medium-sized family farmers. This is 61.7 percent of all the land in operation, judged by the sample. As to the small family farmers, or 45.8 percent of the farmers, they operated only 66,106 improved acres, or only 17.9 percent of the land in cultivation. The large business farmers, 4.7 of the farmers, operated 75,473 improved acres, or 20.4 percent of the land in operation. The predominant land users were the medium-sized family farmers.

Egalitarian Federal Land Policy

In conventional neoclassical economic analysis, distribution is taken as given without explanation. Here, however, we investigate the sources of the findings on the nature of land distribution. I claim that economic behavior was affected by distribution. Fleisig had predicted that farms in areas with constrained market labor would have less land per farm than farms in areas without such a labor constraint. We found in Chapter 3 that this prediction was not confirmed in the case of townships with a variation in labor constraint in the Old Northwest. The family farm thesis holds that it was abundant land, not constrained market labor, that was associated with the adoption of farm machinery. The claim is that the land per farm (TA and IA) was not determined by market forces alone. We look now at how federal land policy determined, in part, the total acres of land per farm.

The medium-sized family farm system was created, in part, by egalitarian federal land policy. The total acres of land per farm and the number of farms in the farm economy in the public land states were greatly influenced by federal policy which distributed the relatively abundant agricultural resources in the United States. The family farm system was a result of the relatively abundant agricultural resources in the United States and the character of the liberal government policy in distributing those resources, among other influences.

Between 1785 and 1860 73 million acres (unimproved, virgin, raw land) was distributed in the Old Northwest by the U.S. federal government.[4] Land policy changed over this period of 75 years and I have grouped the changes into three eras. When the Northwest Territory was opened for official settlement in 1785, the land was surveyed, land offices were established to sell the land at auction, and the minimum purchase was 640 acres (one square mile, one of 36 sections of a township). The first era was from 1785-1803 and can be called the business farm land policy, in the sense that the resulting farms were larger than could be operated by a family. If this policy had held through to 1860, ceteris paribus, the 73 million acres distributed in 640 acre holdings would have generated 114,062 farms. See Table 4.2. Land policy was liberalized within this first era, in 1800, via lowering the required minimum purchase to 320 acres, still a

Table 4.2
Land Policy and Counterfactual Outcomes

Dates that Policy Held	Minimum Purchase(1) (total acres)	Percentage of Counties Formed(2) (no. of farms)	Counterfactual Outcome(3)
1785-1799	640		114,062
1800-1803	320	2*	228,124
1804-1819	160	20	456,250
1820-1832	80	30	912,500
1833-1869	40	48	1,825,000
Actual Outcome	124(4)		586,717(5)

Sources: (1) North, *Growth and Welfare*, p. 119; (2) Leon E. Seltzer (Ed.), *The Columbia Lippincott Gazetter of the World* (New York: Columbia University Press, 1952) for when counties formed and Fred Bateman and James D. Foust *Agricultural and Demographic Records for Rural Households in the North, 1860* (Ann Arbor, MI: Inter-University Consortium for Political and Social Research, 1976) for sample counties; (3) see text for explanation; (4) and (5) *Printed Census, 1860*.

Note: * Two percent refers to percentage of counties formed in the first two periods.

business size farm, given the technology of the day. If this policy had held sway for the entire period, then 228,124 farms of the 320 acres size would have been the outcome, a farm economy of a small number of large farms. This would be a farm system based upon a high degree of land concentration. However, in this era from 1785 to 1803 only 2 percent of the counties in the Old Northwest were formed, a proxy for the number of farms set up under a given land policy. Thus the farm economy that was to emerge in 1860 was not predominantly one made up of a few large estates or business farms.

The second era began with the Jefferson administration. In 1804, the minimum purchase was reduced to 160 acres, which could be operated by a family. The goal of Jefferson's land policy was to establish a nation of family farm owners. We can call this the era of Jeffersonian family farm land policy. If this policy had held for the whole 75 year period, then there would have been 456,250 farms of the 160-acre size. The law was made even more egalitarian in 1820 by reducing the minimum purchase to 80 acres. This generates a counterfactual estimate of 912,500 farms if this 80-acres minimum policy had held for the whole 75-year period. The result would have been (and was) an economy of many, medium-sized farms. It would be a system of moderate land equality. Twenty percent of the counties were formed under the 160-acre minimum and 30 percent under the 80-acre minimum. In this Jeffersonian era, 50 percent of the counties were formed. The outcome of this policy would have been (and was, in fact) the medium-sized family farm system, where family farm means a farm of a size such that the labor force of the farm family could operate this amount of land.

The third era began in the Jackson administration when the minimum land purchase was lowered to 40 acres. A 40-acre farm was a small family farm in the sense that it was enough land to support a family, given the conditions in the Old Northwest in 1850s. We can call this the era of the Jacksonian family farm land policy. If this policy had held from the beginning in 1785, then 1,825,000 farms of the 40-acre size would have been the result, that is, an economy of many, small farms. This is relatively extreme equality of land distribution. Forty-eight percent of the counties in the Old Northwest were formed under the Jackson policy.

The actual result of the 75 years of land distribution of 73 million acres of public domain in the Old Northwest was 586,717 farms which, on average, were 124 acres (see Table 4.2).[5] The outcome was a farm economy made up of many, medium-sized farms and a system based on a relatively equal distribution of abundant land. The actual result shows the predominance of the Jeffersonian land policy of relatively egalitarian distribution of land.

In addition to this progressively liberalized land policy on selling land, the federal government gave land away in family farm size grants. In the 1850s, the U.S. government granted as much land as it sold in the public domain states (North and South, including the Old Northwest). Fifty million acres were granted to individuals and 50 million were sold to individuals. Of these 100 million acres, 57 percent was alienated (given or sold) to individuals in holdings of from 40 to 160 total acres, the family farm size range.[6]

Not only was the mean size farm a medium-sized family farm, the majority of farms were of this size. See Table 4.3. Sixty-one percent of farms were in the range of 40 to 160 total acres, in the range in which there was more land than needed to support the family, but not too much land that they could not operate it. The median farm was 89 acres and the mode farm was 80 acres. The typical farm was more than enough to support a family, at least potentially, in that total acres could be turned into improved acres.

Table 4.3 shows that the medium-sized family farm constituted 3,523 of the 5,756 farms in the manuscript census sample. There were 1,156 farms of the small family farm size or less, and this was 20.1 percent of all farms. The business farms were 18.7 percent of all farms, and numbered 1,077. The table reveals the one statistic that I found in which the medium-sized family farm was not predominant: the 18.7 percent of farms that were larger than 160 total acres held 58.8 percent of the land. The medium-sized family farms, while constituting 61.2 percent of all farms, held only 37.4 percent

Table 4.3
Predominant Land Holders

Range of Land in TA	No. of Farms	No. of TA of Land	Percent of Farms	Percent of Land Held
less than 41 TA	1,156	33,012	20.1	4.6
41-160 TA	3,523	265,947	61.2	37.4
more than 160 TA	1,077	418,158	18.7	58.8
TOTAL	5,756	711,117	100.0	100.0

Source: Fred Bateman and James D. Foust, *Agricultural and Demographic Records for Rural Households in the North, 1860* (Ann Arbor, MI: Inter-University Consortium for Political and Social Research, 1976).

Note: N = 5756 farms; TA is total acres.

of all the land. The 20.1 percent of farms that were small family farms or less held only 4.6 percent of the land. I believe that the reason for this is that the business farm held much land for speculation purposes and that in time this large land-holding would be sold off, and sold off as medium-sized family farms. The fact remains that there was some degree of concentration in land-holding, although in terms of land in cultivation, there was less, such that land use was dominated by the medium-sized family farms.

The initial conditions of the abundance of land in the United States and egalitarian federal land policy were influences on the determination of the quantity of total acres of land per farm. The inheritance of the past, from 1785 onwards, determined behavior in the 1850s of this family farm system, defined by the predominant farms being of the medium-sized family farm size. Most important was the medium-sized family farm, 41 to 160 acres, because it represented a surplus beyond the land needed to support the family, but not too much to be run by the labor force of the farm family.

In the sample of 5,756 farms in the Old Northwest in 1860, I obtained a correlation coefficient of 0.57 between the total acres per farm and the improved acres per farm. That is a R^2 of 0.33. That is to say, 33 percent of the variation in the quantity of land per farm in improved acres is explained by the quantity of land per farm in total acres. In the next section we investigate the possible explanations for the other 67 percent of the variation in land per farm in improved acres. I expect that this depended upon pressures to commercialize due to goals and debts of farmers.

The evidence of this section suggests that the medium-sized family farm, defined as a farm using 41 to 160 improved acres, accounted for 49.5 percent of all farms and more importantly operated 61.7 percent of all land in cultivation. This is consistent with the claim that the predominant land users in the farm economy of the Old Northwest in 1860 were the medium-sized family farms. This system was generated, in part, by egalitarian federal land policy, although land holding was found to be more concentrated than land use. Yet 33 percent of the variation of land in cultivation on a farm was explained by the quantity of land held.

WHEAT PRODUCTION AS AN INTERVENING VARIABLE

The intervening variable between the cause, or the explanatory variable, the medium-sized family farm system, and the effect, or dependent variable, the mechanization and adoption of the reaper, is the commercialization of the medium-sized family farm system. When the medium-sized family farm commercialized to a certain threshold level, the pressure to mechanize began. The medium-sized family farm commercialized because it was a utility maximizer of a novel sort. In the first part of this section I present a model of the utility-maximizing medium-sized family farm, which in the process of commercializing, ran up against pressures to mechanize. Some illustrative evidence is given for this from computer-generated farms from the manuscript census sample. In the second part of this section I provide evidence for the claim that the medium-sized commercial family farm was the predominant wheat producer among farms that mechanized. This utility-maximizing pressure was a more important cause of reaper adoption than the labor constraint or the rising wage pressure on the profit-maximizing large business farm because the utility-maximizing farmer was the predominant land user and predominant wheat producer.

Utility Maximization as Pressure to Mechanize

Let us assume that the family farmer was a risk-averse utility-maximizing economic agent, a rational pursuer of his goals in a market economy. The attainment of consumption and the benefit of owning and operating his own farm were his two goals. Because of his goal of farm ownership, the farmer went into debt and to pay off the debt he had to produce for the market, that is, commercialize. The three sources of pressure to mechanize were:

- debt for owning medium-sized family farm
- debt for the livestock and farm implements and machinery for the farm
- desire to increase consumption beyond food self-sufficiency.

When the farmers' debt or desire for cash was a certain magnitude representing the need to produce a given amount for the market, the capacity of the labor force of the farm family was reached, and the pressure to mechanize began. The alternative of hiring a permanent labor force was rejected due to the family farmers' risk aversion or their preference not to hire labor.

I theorize that (1) while the maximum level of output on the family farm was determined by the labor constraint set by family labor (because they were risk-averse and chose a level of labor at which, in downturns, labor could be underpaid and paid no cash), (2) cash needs to finance the mortgage provided a strong incentive to approach the maximum level of output that family labor could produce. This incentive operated to help avert the risk of no cash to pay the mortgage in the downturn.

The farm household allocated the labor of the household between work and leisure in order to maximize its utility. The labor allocated to work on output for the market led to money income, which the farm family used, in part, to finance the ownership of the farm. The labor allocated to work on output for on-farm use provided conventional utility via consumption.[7] The farm household desired to be self-sufficient in food. The farm household also produced housing, clothing, and other non-food consumption goods and services. Families had to trade off preferences between the utility derived from work and leisure (non-market work). We assume that farm families wanted as much utility as they could obtain.

The small family farm was a utility maximizer and this farm family allocated enough labor to non-market work to produce food and non-food self-sufficiency. This is a simplification because self-sufficiency was not absolute, exchanges were made in the local rural community and even from markets further away. At certain point, the marginal utility of leisure (non-market work providing self-sufficiency in food and non-food) was equal to the marginal disutility of laboring for the market. The amount of unpaid effort and the amount of work for the market was thus determined. This was no pressure to mechanize for the following reason: The goal of the small family farm was to own the present farm they were operating. The amount marketed depended on the surplus above food (and non-food) self-sufficiency, with given techniques. As long as that surplus, when marketed, was enough to pay the mortgage, then the goals of self-sufficiency (consumption) and the benefits of farm ownership would not lead to mechanization. If that initial marketed surplus was not enough to pay the mortgage, that would have put pressure on the small family farmer to mechanize. My claim is that this pressure did not exist on the small family farm.

There was pressure to mechanize for a utility-maximizing medium-sized family farm. This farm is allocating family labor to the same "leisure" time activity, work for on-farm use to produce self-sufficiency, as the small family farm. However, the family on the medium-sized family farm worked more than the small family farm because they obtained positive utility from increasing the quantity of land owned beyond a farm providing self-sufficiency plus surplus enough to pay the mortgage.[8] The pressure to mechanize for a utility maximizer whose utility is a function of the benefits of owning a medium-sized family farm is the need to produce more cash crops than the labor force of his family can accomplish in order to finance the ownership of the farm.

A farm is more than land. An additional pressure to mechanize comes from the need to have livestock and farm implements and machinery to operate the land on the farm. This farm household works more on output to market because they obtain utility from it which outweighs the disutility of laboring for the market involved. Assume that this medium-sized family farm has increased its debt for livestock or implements and machines as well as for the farm land. This increases the risk that, if the harvest fails or prices drop radically, the surplus will not be enough to cover the mortgage plus the debt for livestock and machines. Fear of this risk could put pressure on the farm to mechanize or mechanize further. The marginal utility of the product of the extra work is equal to the marginal disutility of that working for the market.

A third pressure to mechanize was the positive utility obtained from increasing the level of family consumption beyond food self-sufficiency. While the farm household retained the goal of food self-sufficiency, it soon dropped the goal of producing its own household goods and clothing. By working for the market, the farm household could purchase quality textiles, clothing, footwear, and lumber on the market. This meant a reallocation of the labor in the farm household. Family labor is no longer allocated to making non-food self-sufficiency such as clothing and footwear; it is allocated to work for the market.

The pressure to mechanize on large business farms is as described by David in his profit scale threshold model (see Chapter 2) and by Fleisig in his market labor-constraint model (see Chapter 3).

To illustrate these cases, we look at computer-generated farms from the manuscript census sample. First, we look at the lack of pressure to mechanize on the small family farm. The goal of a small family farm was to own a 40-acre farm, enough to support the family and enough surplus to pay the mortgage. Forty acres cost $50 at government prices. Wheat was the main cash crop, especially for farmers without the resources to buy livestock. To illustrate a small family farm in the farm-making stage, I selected from the Bateman-Foust sample a farm with 40 total acres, which was a farm at the twentieth percentile. This farm produced no wheat. The farmer was busy with improving his land and feeding the family. To illustrate the small family farm in the fully developed form, I selected a farm with 40 improved acres, which I found in a farm at the 45.7 percentile. This farmer is producing five acres of wheat, which at 12.2 bushels per acre, and $1.02 a bushel, would give him an annual cash income of $62. I assume that this is enough to finance the ownership of the 40-acre farm and the draft animals and farm implements needed to operate it. This was no pressure to mechanize on the small family farm in either stage of development.

Second, we look for pressure to mechanize on a medium-sized family farm. To illustrate a medium-sized family farm in the farm-making stage, I selected a farm with 160 total acres, which was a farm at the 81.3 percentile. We see the cost of the land is $200 at government prices for 160 acres. This farmer is producing 16 acres of wheat which means an annual revenue of $199. In the case of this particular farm this seems not to be the pressure to mechanize. The pressure came from the need for livestock and farm implements and machinery to operate this 160-acre farm. The value of the livestock was $599 and the value of the farm implements and machinery was $129. Added to the cost of the land, his debt could be as high as $928. The marketed surplus of $199 (wheat revenue) would not be enough to finance this ownership and operation of this farm. In addition, there is the pressure of the family's desire for quality clothing and housing. The head of the farm household made the boots and shoes of the family in the winter. The wife of the head of household made the men's clothing. By allocating their labor away from this and to market activity, they could buy boots and shoes and men's clothing and they could replace their log cabin with lumber from the saw mill. To see this pressure manifested in the fully developed stage of a medium-sized family farm, I selected a farm with 160 improved acres, which I found on the farm at the 95.3 percentile. This medium-sized family farm in its developed stage will show the production of 28 acres of wheat. This generated $348 in marketed surplus and required mechanization. His corn was mechanized also, as 46 acres was beyond the capacity of the labor force of the farm family. This farm is probably practicing mixed farming, that is, production of grains and animal products. The wheat grain was produced for the market; dairy and meat livestock was produced for the market and feed corn produced on the farm.

In sum, for the medium-sized family farm, the pressure to mechanize came from the desire to finance the debt for a medium-sized farm, including land, livestock, and implements to operate the farm. The attainment of ownership of such a working farm gave the utility-maximizing farm household the benefits it had as its goal. When the debt or the need for current cash grew beyond the capacity of the farm family to produce, it mechanized.

The large farm had different pressures to mechanize. To illustrate the large farm in the farm-making stage, I selected a farm with 640 total acres, which was a farm at the 99.3 percentile. The cost of the land at government prices was $800, the value of livestock was $2,025, and the value of the implement was $475. The value of the farm was $136,000. This is a highly capitalized farm and the operator and owner of it must certainly have desired a profit from such an investment. This farmer was producing 66 acres of wheat and 95 acres of corn. This farm had to be using hired labor, as these acreages of land use were beyond the capacity of the labor force of a farm family. As this farm developed, it ran into pressure to mechanize. To illustrate a large farm at the fully developed stage, I selected a farm with 640 improved acres, which I found on a farm at the 99.85 percentile. This profit-maximizing farm has increased its wheat acreage to 105 acres and corn to 177 acres. It is this farm which mechanized because of the rise in the cost of labor over the 1850s and/or due to the increased constraint in the labor market. Recall, however, that there were not many of these farms.

Predominant Wheat Producers

We have two kinds of pressures to mechanize, on one hand, the pressure on farmers with the goal of utility maximization and on the other, pressure on farmers with the goal of profit maximization. We know already that the predominant size of farm is the medium-sized family farm, judged both in numbers and in land used. We now want to test whether or not these medium-sized family farms, with their risk-averse utility-maximizing goals pressuring for mechanization, were the predominant wheat producers, among those that mechanized. Again we want to know if the medium-sized utility-maximizing farm was the predominant wheat producer judged by numbers and judged by proportion of wheat output.

Table 4.4 shows the distribution of reaper-adopting farms by the quantity of acres of wheat produced. In the manuscript census sample, using the criteria developed in Appendix A, I inferred that 268 farms had adopted the reaper. In Chapter 2 we accepted Olmstead's revision of the threshold of profitability as 78 acres of wheat. That is, profit maximization dictated reaper adoption at the scale of 78 acres of wheat. Any farmer who adopted the reaper and produced less than the profit-maximizing scale of 78 acres can be assumed to be a risk-averse utility-maximizing family farmer. As this table shows, 94.8 percent of the farms that adopted the reaper were producing less than 78 acres of wheat. The mean farm produced 40 acres of wheat; the median farm produced 33; and the mode farm, 25, thus all were risk-averse utility-maximizing producers.

Table 4.4 also shows that of the 268 farms that adopted the reaper only 14 (or only 5.2 percent) produced more than 77 acres of wheat and thus could be considered profit maximizers. The 94.8 percent of farms producing

Table 4.4
Predominant Wheat Producers

Range of Wheat Acreage	No. of Reaper Adopters	No. of Acres of Wheat	Percent of Reaper Adopters	Percent of Wheat Produced
20 - 77	254	9,041	94.8	85
more than 77	14	1,548	5.2	15
Total	268	10,589	100.0	100

Source: Fred Bateman and James D. Foust, *Agricultural and Demographic Records for Rural Households in the North, 1860* (Ann Arbor, MI: Inter-University Consortium for Political and Social Research, 1976).

Note: N = 268 reaper adopters by criterion of $200 as a minimum for inferring the adoption of the reaper, see Appendix A.

in the 20 to 77-acre range, produced 85 percent of the mechanized wheat. Not only did more wheat mechanizers do so under utility-maximizing pressures, but the utility maximizers were the dominant producers of mechanically cut wheat.

The argument is that the medium-sized family farm that adopted the reaper and produced between 20 and 78 acres of wheat, accounted for 94.8 percent of the farms that adopted the reaper and more importantly, accounted for 85 percent of all wheat produced by the set of farms that adopted the reaper.

CAPITAL EQUIPMENT AS THE DEPENDENT VARIABLE: MECHANIZATION AND ADOPTION OF THE REAPER

First, I argue that the medium-sized commercial family farm system made for an income distribution that generated a crucial mass market for mass-produced farm machinery. Second, I test to see if this system was the predominant purchaser of capital equipment, among those farms that mechanized.

Income Distribution and the Market for Farm Machinery

Without farm machinery, the food demands of industrialization probably would not have been met. But without the family farm system and its broad, deep, and growing market for farm machinery, the mass production of that machinery probably would not have been taken on. It is the goal of this section to explain this and provide evidence for it.

In neoclassical analysis, resource endowment must be specified before any hypothesis or prediction can be deduced from the theory. Income distribution is taken as given, but affects demand and thus prices. One view on the effect of income distribution is that unequal income distribution leads to development via the economic agents with substantial income being savers and investors. Another view is that if the surplus is significant, then a relatively equal income distribution leads to development via the provision of a broad market for commercially and industrially produced goods and services. If the surplus is small, then equal distribution of income does not lead to development as only a weak market is generated.

Income distribution is determined by factor prices and the initial resource endowments, as well as by how the surplus from market expansion is distributed. How the surplus is distributed is determined, in part, by what the initial resource endowments are and how they are held. For example, if the land is owned by the farmers, then they have control of the surplus, as opposed to the case where the farmers rent and the surplus goes to landowners, or the case where government taxes are so high that all the surplus goes to the government. If the surplus cannot be reinvested in the farm, then the future income does not grow. Favorable income distribution and favorable surplus distribution then provide a favorable structure of demand for market development.

In the case of the Old Northwest in the mid-nineteenth century, the initial resource endowment was abundant and relatively equally distributed. This led to a relatively equal income distribution, given factor prices. Ownership of the land, among other influences, meant that the surplus from expanding markets was under the control of the farmers. Control meant the ability to decide on output, input, technique, and investment decisions. The significant surplus was relatively equally distributed, supporting the relatively equal and abundant income distribution. The outcome was the development of a broad market for farm machinery.

Recall that in Chapter 2, third section, we argued that in explaining the timing of the adoption of the reaper in the mid-1850s, mention should be made of the acceleration of production and sales of mechanical reapers. The McCormick Works in Chicago mass produced reapers starting in 1848 and by 1852 had learned enough by doing that the reaper was a reasonably priced, durable, and reliable machine. In 1855, there was a dramatic acceleration of production and sales. McCormick probably would not have taken on the mass production of the reaper if he had not anticipated the mass market for his machinery. He moved his production from Walnut Grove, Virginia, where slave agriculture did not provide a mass market, to Chicago, in the middle of the family farm system.

Fleisig argued that the labor-constrained farm was smaller than the unconstrained farm because there were economies of scale beyond the market labor-constrained size.[9] An alternative view would be that there were few economies of scale beyond the capacity of the labor force of the family farm because the farm machinery, the basis of economies of scale, was designed for the family farm. Parker writes that farm machinery in the nineteenth century was designed for the labor force of the family farm and for the power unit of the family farm which was the family team of horses.[10] A business farm, larger than a medium-sized family farm, then, would merely have sets of farm machinery, each set capturing the same economies of scale obtained by the medium-sized family farm with its one set.

Fleisig also argued that the labor-constrained farm would have a higher capital-labor ratio, that this was mechanization itself, although this farm would use absolutely less capital than an unconstrained farm. An alternative view is that the high capital-labor ratio on the medium-sized family farm reflected the adaptation of the technology of the industrial revolution, itself highly capital-intensive, to family farm agriculture. Both Bogue and Parker refer to this industrialization of agriculture.[11]

On this view, that the farm machinery was made for family farmers and that the technology was from the industrial revolution, the appropriate representation of mechanization is the decision to purchase capital on the market, given the supply of labor in the farm household. This is an alternative to Fleisig's characterization of mechanization as a high capital-labor ratio, but a low absolute use of capital. Limiting the labor force of the farm to that of the family caused high capital per farm. This is an alternative to Fleisig's market labor constraint (plus some specified conditions of production) causing low capital per farm.

Predominant Capital Equipment Purchasers

If I am correct about the medium-sized family farm providing the crucial mass market for mass-produced farm machinery, then one would expect that the predominant purchaser of farm machinery would be the medium-sized family farm. If we use the value of farm implements and machinery on a farm as a proxy for the amount of capital equipment purchased, then we can test this proposition. The case is the reaper adopters in the Old Northwest in 1860, inferred from the manuscript census sample. Table 4.5 shows the distribution of farms that adopted the reaper by the value of their farm implements and machinery. It is based on a total of 268 farms inferred to have adopted the reaper. The 14 farms identified as profit maximizers, defined by the fact that they produced at the profit-maximizing level of wheat, were examined for the value of their farm implements and machinery. Each was found to have capital equipment worth more than $575. The remaining farms, utility maximizers, had less than $575 in capital equipment. These farms accounted for 94.8 percent of the farms that adopted the reaper. The mean farm had $322, the median $258, and the mode $200. The predominant kind of purchaser in the capital equipment market was the medium-sized commercial family farm that was a utility maximizer.

The important point is not only the number of purchasers in the farm capital equipment market, but the proportion of the market. Table 4.5 also shows that the total value of capital equipment on farms that adopted the reaper was $86,230. Of this $72,230 was owned by utility-maximizing farms, or 84 percent. The 5.2 percent of reaper adopters that were profit maximizers purchased only 16 percent of the capital equipment.

The argument is that the medium-sized family farms that adopted the reaper and produced between 20 and 78 acres of wheat, as risk-averse utility maximizers, accounted for 94.7 percent of the farms that adopted the reaper and, more importantly, accounted for 84 percent of all capital equipment purchased by the set of farms that adopted the reaper.

Table 4.5
Predominant Capital Equipment Purchasers

Range of VOI	No. of Reaper Adopters	Value of Capital Equipment	Percent of Reaper Adopters	Percent of Capital Equipment
less than $575	254	$72,230	94.8	84
more than $575	14	$14,000	5.2	16
Total	268	$86,230	100.0	100

Source: Fred Bateman and James D. Foust, *Agricultural and Demographic Records for Rural Households in the North, 1860* (Ann Arbor, MI: Inter-University Consortium for Political and Social Research, 1976).

Note: N = 268 reaper adopters, by criterion of $200 VOI minimum for inferring the adoption of the reaper, see Appendix A. VOI means value of implements. These 14 farms were those which produced over 78 acres of wheat and possessed more than $575 in farm implements and machinery.

CONCLUSION

The environment in which reaper adoption took place was a farm economy made up of many medium-sized family farms. This was favorable to agricultural revolution because these farm families controlled more land than they could operate with their own labor. Thus when their cash needs pressured them to produce at a scale of production beyond that which could be carried out by the family itself, they were prepared to overcome their traditional risk aversion and purchase capital goods in the market. The evidence of this chapter suggests that the predominant mechanized wheat producers were medium-sized family farms and that the predominant capital good purchasers, among reaper adopters, were medium-sized family farmers, producing below the profit-maximizing scale of wheat output.

The evidence of this chapter suggests that Hypothesis 4 should be retained. The institutional structure of the family farm system was a favorable initial condition for the adoption of farm machinery because it was based on a relatively equal distribution of abundant land which generated many farmers with sufficient surplus and incentive to purchase capital goods.

What was rational for the medium-sized family farm was also rational for the whole U.S. economy. The American Northeast was industrializing and it needed the provision of food and the provision of a market for industrially produced capital goods. The family farm system, predominated by the medium-sized family farms, provided the food and the market for capital goods.

I conclude that the family farm model held up very well on the tests to which it was put. The evidence is consistent with the theorizing on the family farm. In a farm economy made up of predominantly medium-sized family farms, there appears to have existed rational reasons for producing wheat for the market, and rational reasons for purchasing capital goods. Economies in world history have begun to industrialize and thus call for an increase of food production for the market. Without a favorable environment, this call for food goes unanswered. Without favorable agricultural institutions providing a favorable environment, there will be no reaction to price signals. Then there would be no speed up of agricultural revolution when a catalyst such as the Civil War appears on the scene. Rasmussen's catalyst theory presupposes a favorable environment provided by the family farm system. As indicated by his article in *Scientific American* and in conversations with this writer, Rasmussen is well aware of the favorable nature of this family farm system. It is the economists that need to include the main features of the family farm agricultural institutions in their models. Fleisig's model of the family farm as a labor-constrained profit-maximizing firm was a start toward this goal. Wright's analysis took it even further, by including the family farm goals of self-sufficiency in food and the rational desire to own a farm. In my next chapter, I construct two econometric models of the adoption of the reaper which include the main features of the family farm system, as well as purely economic and market forces.

NOTES

1. Wayne D. Rasmussen, "The Civil War: A Catalyst of Agricultural Revolution," *Agricultural History* 39 (October 1965):187-95.

2. Marvin Towne and Wayne Rasmussen, "Farm Gross Product and Gross Investment during the Nineteenth Century," in *Trends in the American Economy*, vol. 24 of *Studies in Income and Wealth* (Princeton: Princeton University Press, 1960), pp. 260-61.

3. Wayne Rasmussen, "The Mechanization of Agriculture," *Scientific American* 247 (September 1987).

4. *Printed Census*, 1860, see Chapter 1.

5. The mean size farm was 124 total acres both in the printed census which includes all farms in the universe and in the manuscript census sample which includes approximately one in 100 farms. This means that the sample is not biased in total acres of land per farm.

6. Clarence Danhof, "Farm-Making Costs and the 'Safety Valve':1850-1860," *Agricultural History* 49 (June 1941):330.

7. See for example, Howard Wachtel, *Labor and the Economy* (New York: Harcourt Brace Jovanovich, 1984), p. 51, for a neoclassical analysis of the household's preferences for income-producing and non-income-producing time.

8. More work was obtained on the medium-sized family farm by having family members work longer hours, work more intensely, and more carefully (higher quality labor). They were presumably more ambitious and more industrious.

9. Heywood Fleisig, "Slavery, the Supply of Agricultural Labor and the Industrialization of the South," *Journal of Economic History* 36 (September 1976):578.

10. Parker, "Agriculture," in Lance Davis et al. (Eds.), *American Economic Growth* (New York: Harper and Row, 1972), pp. 393-396.

11. Allan Bogue, *From Prairie to Corn Belt* (Chicago: University of Chicago Press, 1963), p. 148; Parker, "Agriculture," pp. 379-89.

5
ECONOMETRIC ANALYSIS
OF REAPER ADOPTION

The purpose of the econometric analysis is to demonstrate the important role of agricultural institutions in the adoption of the reaper in the Old Northwest as of 1860. Two econometric models were developed. One model states that the probability of reaper adoption depended upon certain economic and institutional characteristics of the farm. The other model states that the probability of reaper adoption depended upon certain economic and institutional characteristics of the township.

The plan of this chapter is as follows. First, I describe the logit probability technique. Second, I describe the manuscript census sample used to estimate the logit models. Third, I describe the concepts and measurement of the variables in the models and relate them to the four hypotheses of the family farm thesis. In the fourth section, I specify the farm model and the township model. This is followed by a section which reports the results. The final section offers an interpretation of the results which relates them to the four hypotheses of the family farm thesis.

THE LOGIT TECHNIQUE

Models of qualitative choice have been developed for analyzing behavioral responses that are qualitative. The dependent variable in this model is discontinuous and is characterized by two or more qualitative choices.

Binary-choice models are used when the dependent variable is dichotomous. The choice of adopting the reaper is a yes or no decision. In the conventional regression analysis, dummy variables are used for explanatory variables that are dichotomous. The farm operator owning the farm operated is a yes or no explanatory variable in this study. Normal regression techniques can be used in this latter case. However, when the dependent variable is dichotomous, special techniques must be used.

The Individual Logit Model

Binary-choice models assume that "individuals are faced with a choice between two alternatives and that the choice they make depends on the characteristics of the individuals."[1] If we have information on the attributes and on the choices actually made, then we can estimate an equation that can be used to predict the probability of an individual not in the original sample adopting the reaper. We expect that the degree to which a farmer is specialized in wheat production is an important determinant of the decision to adopt the reaper. That is, highly specialized farmers are more likely to adopt the reaper than slightly specialized farmers, ceteris paribus. We do not have enough information to predict exactly each and every farmer who will adopt the reaper. However, we can predict the likelihood of an individual farmer's adoption of the reaper, given knowledge of how specialized he is.

Because it is the likelihood of individuals making particular choices that is estimated, these models are called probability models. If we assume that the probability of an individual farmer adopting the reaper is a linear function of his degree of specialization, we specify the model as a linear probability model. There are alternative model specifications which are a function of alternative "assumptions about the probabilistic nature of the decision making process."[2] For simplicity we look at the linear probability model first.

The regression form of the linear probability model is:

$$Y_i = a + bX_i + e_i \text{ where} \tag{5.1}$$

- X_i = value of attribute, for example, degree of specialization for the ith farmer
- Y_i = 1 if first option is chosen (adopt the reaper), 0 if second option is chosen (not adopt the reaper)
- e_i = independently distributed random variable with 0 mean.[3]

In order to interpret this equation it is transformed to:

$$P_i = a + bX_i.\text{[4]}$$ (5.2)

This equation describes the probability that a farmer will adopt the reaper given information on his degree of specialization. The slope of the regression line is interpreted as the change in the probability of adopting the reaper given a one-unit change in the degree of specialization for each individual farmer.

The most serious weakness with this linear specification of the probability model is revealed when it is used to predict.[5] Given extreme degrees of specialization or extreme lack of it, the predicted probability of adopting the reaper for an individual farmer might be less than zero or more than one. This does not make sense because probability is defined as being in the interval (0,1). It is possible to constrain the predicted probability to the (0,1) range, but this distorts the estimated parameters and the predicted probabilities. A better solution to the problem will be found in the logit technique, discussed below.

We want to transform the linear probability model so that we can "translate values of attribute X, which may range in value over the entire real line, to a probability which ranges in value from zero to one." It seems appropriate to use some notion of probability to make this transformation. The notion used is that of a cumulative probability function, symbolized as F. The general form of the transformation is:

$$P_i = F(a + bX_i) = F(Z_i).\text{[6]}$$ (5.3)

Z_i is a "theoretical (but not actually measured) index . . . which is determined by an explanatory variable X_i, as in the linear probability model."[7] This is symbolized as:

$$Z_i = a + bX_i$$ (5.4)

From estimating a and b we can determine for each individual whether or not his index Z_i has a high value or a low value. The logit model is designed to estimate a and b plus categorize the individuals as to high and low Z_i.

We can interpret Z_i as the propensity of farmer i to adopt the reaper. Each farmer has a different propensity to adopt the reaper based on his attributes or the attributes of his farm. We infer which farmers adopted the reaper.[8] We assume that the index of the propensity to adopt the reaper is a linear function of the degree of specialization for each farmer.

The technique is to let Y be a dummy variable which equals one if the farmer adopts the reaper and equals zero if he does not. Then for each individual farmer, Z_i^* "represents the critical cut off value which translates the underlying index into a . . . [reaper decision]." The farmer adopts the reaper if his propensity to adopt the reaper (Z_i) is greater than the critical cutoff value (Z_i^*). Next, "we assume that Z_i^*, the probability that Z_i^* is equal to or less than Z_i, can be computed from the cumulative logistic probability function." The cumulative logic function "assigns to a number Z the probability that any arbitrary Z^* will be less than Z_i."[9]

As there are many cumulative probability functions one must be specified. If we use a uniform distribution, we obtain a constrained form of the linear probability model, which we rejected previously. If a normal distribution is specified, the probit model is the result. From a computational point of view, this specification is difficult and thus not used in many cases.[10] If we specify a logistic distribution, the logit model is the result. This is the technique chosen for this study. The cumulative logistic function is written:

$$P_i = F(Z_i) = \frac{1}{1 + e^{-Z}} \tag{5.5}$$

By construction, the variable P_i will lie in the $(0,1)$ interval. We have successfully transformed the linear probability model. An illustration of this is given in Table 5.1 using the manuscript census sample and the reaper adoption model.

The logit model is specified as follows:

$$P_i = F(Z_i) = F(a + bX_i) = \frac{1}{1 + e^{-Z_i}} = \frac{1}{1 + e^{-(a+bX_i)}} \tag{5.6}$$

The base of natural logarithms, e, is approximately 2.718. "P_i is the probability of an individual making a certain choice given knowledge of X_i."[11]

Let us think about the difference between the linear probability model and the logit model. In the linear probability model the relationship between the explanatory variable and the probability of making a positive choice is linear, which is to say that the relationship is the same regardless of the value of the explanatory variable. Some choices may be of this nature. The logit probability model is nonlinear. This means that the relationship between the explanatory variable and the probability of making a positive choice depends upon the value of the explanatory variable. The cumulative logistic distribution has its greatest slope (the geographic representation of the relationship between the explanatory variable and the probability of making a positive choice) when the probability is equal to one-half.

Table 5.1
The Logistic Transformation

Z	F(Z)
-6.9	0.001
-6.7	0.001
-6.3	0.002
-6.1	0.002
-4.6	0.010
-3.6	0.027
-2.4	0.082
-0.8	0.307
0.2	0.560
3.1	0.960
21.5	0.990

Source: Fred Bateman and James D. Foust, *Agricultural and Demographic Records for Rural Households in the North, 1860* (Ann Arbor, MI: Inter-University Consortium for Political and Social Research, 1976).

In terms of the regression model, this implies that changes in the independent variable will have their greatest impact on the probability of choosing a given option at the midpoint of the distribution. The rather low slopes near the end points of the distribution imply that large changes in X are necessary to bring about a small change in probability.[12]

This means that in this study we assume that an increase in specialization will increase the probability of adopting the reaper only slightly for a farmer who is barely specialized and who is unlikely to change his choice under any conditions, and for a highly specialized farmer who is likely to have adopted the reaper already before the increase in specialization. A change in specialization will have a more substantial impact on the probability of adopting the reaper in the middle range of specialization.

Table 5.2 shows a comparison of the linear probability model and the logit model using 1860 Old Northwest data, with n = 4,336 wheat farms. The same variables are statistically significant and have the same signs, but the absolute values of the estimated parameters are substantially smaller, that is, quantitatively less important. They are distorted by the constraint of the need in the linear probability model to keep probability within the (0,1) range.

Because the logit model is nonlinear in the parameters, the maximum likelihood procedure is used to estimate the parameters. Once we estimate

Table 5.2
Comparison of Linear Probability Model and Logit Model

	LOGIT (ML)			LPM (OLS)		
Explanatory Variables	Coefficient	SE	t	Coefficient	SE	t
SPECIAL	3.8387	0.2917	13.2	0.2312	0.0167	13.816
VOF	0.0002	0.00003	6.7	0.00002	0.000002	11.415
IA	0.0099	0.0013	7.6	0.0007	0.0001	8.431
OWN	0.8556	0.2229	3.8	0.0304	0.0100	3.097
Constant	-6.9336	0.3629	-19.1	-0.1601	0.0142	-11.268

Source: Fred Bateman and James D. Foust, *Agricultural and Demographic Records for Rural Households in the North, 1860* (Ann Arbor, MI: Inter-University Consortium for Political and Social Research, 1976).

Note: Statistically significant at the 5 percent level when t = or > 1.960.

the parameters of the logit model, we can determine which of the independent variables are statistically significant by comparing the parameters to the standard errors of estimation, as in the standard t-tests of conventional regression analysis. The parameters are then used to predict probabilities of reaper adoptions for economic agents not in the original sample. The formula is:

$$\text{Prob}_i = \frac{1}{1 + e^{-Z}_i}. \tag{5.7}$$

To determine the absolute quantitative importance of the statistically significant variables, the slope of the variable with respect to the probability of reaper adoption is calculated with Equation (5.8). Since the slope differs across the distribution, the responsiveness of various economic agents across that distribution can be differentiated.

$$\text{slope}_i = \frac{d\text{Prob}_i}{dX_{1i}} = \frac{b_1 \, e^z}{(e^z + 1)^2}. \tag{5.8}$$

To determine the relative quantitative importance of the statistically significant variables, we calculate the elasticity of each variable with respect to change in the predicted probability with the Equation (5.9). Elasticity varies across the distribution and thus we can examine, in percentage terms, the differential responsiveness of economic agents across that distribution.

$$\text{elasticity}_i = \frac{b_1 \, e^z}{(e^z + 1)^2} \ast \frac{X_{1i}}{\text{Prob}_i} \tag{5.9}$$

The Group Logit Model

In this model the dependent variable is constructed by grouping the data of a dichotomous nature as in the individual logit. For example, in my farm model, I infer the farms that adopted the reaper and assign them the value of one and those inferred to have not adopted the reaper are assigned the value of zero. These data are grouped into townships and the dependent variable is the proportion of farms in the township inferred to have adopted the reaper. The model will now predict the probability of an individual farmer adopting the reaper given the characteristics of the township he farms in. This variable ranges from zero to one. This grouping of data requires a change in the logit technique.

The probability of a farmer adopting a reaper in township i will be approximated by utilizing the observed frequency of farmers adopting the reaper in each township. Equation (5.10) states that we can approximate the probability of reaper adoption in a township by using the observed (in my case inferred) frequency of reaper adoption and dividing the number of observed reaper adopters by the number of farms in the township.

$$P_i = \frac{r_i}{n_i} \quad \text{where} \tag{5.10}$$

- P = probability of reaper adoption
- r_i = number of farms who adopt the reaper
- n_i = number of farms in the township.

The group logit model is specified in Equation (5.11). Z is now the log of the odds of reaper adoption.

$$\log \frac{P_i}{1 - P_i} = Z_i = a + bX_i \qquad (5.11)$$

The form for estimating the group logit is:

$$\log \frac{r_i}{n_i - r_i} = a + bX_i + e_i \qquad (5.12)$$

Notice that in the group form, the regression equation is linear in the parameters and we can use the ordinary least squares technique to estimate the parameters.

One final technical point is in order. Notice in Equation (5.12) we are taking the log of the odds of the farmer adopting the reaper. "If P_i happens to equal either zero or one, the odds, $P_i/(1-P_i)$, will equal zero or infinity and the logarithm of the odds will be undefined."[13] Thus the following adjustment is made:

$$\log \frac{r_i + 1/2}{n_i - r_i + 1/2} = a + bX_i \qquad (5.13)$$

There are several weaknesses in the group technique used in this study. They all have to do with assumptions required for the use of the ordinary least squares procedure of estimating parameters of the model.[14] The most severe weakness is that the error term in the logit model is heteroscedastic, that is, the variance of the error term is not constant for all observations.[15] This causes a loss of efficiency.[16] The correction for this is worse than the problem. It just has to be accepted as a weakness in the model. It does not affect the farm model which is estimated with the maximum likelihood technique. It is a weakness in the township group model because it is estimated with the ordinary least squares procedure which assumes that the error term is homoscedastic, that is, the variance of the error term is constant for all observations.

A second, related problem is that the distribution of the error term is not normal. This is an assumption of the ordinary least squares procedure and thus effects only the township model.[17] This is a problem in the use of t-tests. This means that we must be careful in making claims about the statistical significance of the explanatory variables.

A third problem arises in the group logit model. In order to approximate probability from observed frequency, sufficient repetitions need to occur in each group. The rule of thumb requires n_i to be at least five. One of my 46 townships had less than five farms. When r_i/n_i approaches either zero or one, the expression for V_i (the variance of the error term) gets arbitrarily large.[18] This could lead to inaccurate parameter estimates. In my township sample, no r_i/n_i approaches one. However, I do have 14 townships (out of 46) where r_i/n_i approaches zero. This is because 30 percent of the townships had no reaper adoptions. These weaknesses of the group logit model must be kept in mind in interpreting the results.

THE MANUSCRIPT CENSUS SAMPLE

"The only comprehensive source of nineteenth-century micro-economic data, the manuscript returns of the federal censuses, exist only for 1850 through 1880."[19] In 1840 the Bureau of the Census took its first agricultural census and the data were collected on a county basis, and thus are not micro-data. These documents were moved to the National Archives in 1934. In 1850, 1860, 1870, and 1880, the Bureau of Census took an agricultural census by visiting every farm in the country. In 1918 when the bureau moved to a new building they distributed these manuscripts to the individual states.[20] One problem with these censuses is that farmers were suspicious of the federal government and perhaps feared eventual taxation on the basis of their evaluation of their farms, output, etc. Here is a note I found in the 1840 manuscript census returns for Carroll County, Ohio:

I would here remark, on making return of ten townships, within Carroll, allocated to me, opposition of the principal leaders of the federal 'coonskin hard cider party, rendered it utterly impossible to procure statistical information contemplated by the law. In short, one fourth of the federal party would answer no other questions than those that related alone to the number and ages of their families, pre-emptorally [*sic*] to answer any of the others.[21]

This is a weakness of this study, but it is the only micro-data available.

Because the manuscripts are scattered all over the country in individual state depositories, they are difficult to use. The National Science Foundation financed the taking of a sample of the 1860 manuscript returns, first for the southern states, and then for the northern states.[22] Because this 1860 sample is the only one we have as of this date, we have had to make do with the 1860 cross-section to infer change over time. This is a weakness of this study. It is hoped that, in time, a sample will be taken of the 1850 manuscripts.

The sample used in this study is a subset of the Bateman-Foust sample of the Census Manuscripts of 1860 for the northern states. The full sample contained 21,118 rural households in the American North. I created a subset by taking only those households which were located in the five states of the Old Northwest: Ohio, Indiana, Illinois, Michigan, and Wisconsin; a total of 9,494 rural households. Of these 9,494 rural households, 5,756 were farms. Table 5.3 gives the names of the 46 townships where these 5,756 farms were located.

Regional Representativeness

The sample contains 0.96 percent of farms in the population. One would expect the outputs and inputs of these farms to represent approximately 0.96 percent of the outputs and inputs of the population. If we use 0.96 percent as a standard, then characteristics of the sample with values substantially greater than 0.96 show upward bias, and those substantially smaller than 0.96 show downward bias. See Table 5.4. How well does the sample represent the region of the Old Northwest? The sample is representative in terms of the total number of acres in farms, measured in total acres (TA). However, judged in terms of land in cultivation, the sample has a downward bias, having less improved acres than one would expect from the population total of improved acres. We could say the sample farms were slightly less developed, however, the potential was there to have the same size farms (TA). The sample is slightly biased toward a corn and livestock (VOLS) economy and slightly biased away from a wheat economy. The sample is slightly biased toward less valuable farms with less valuable implements (VOI).

Farm Representativeness

To test the representativeness of the average farm in the sample, tests were carried out to see if the sample means of various characteristics of farms were similar to population means for these farm attributes. Population means are available from the Printed Census. T-statistics were calculated with the formula:

$$t = \frac{\bar{x} - u}{s \sqrt{n}}$$

X is the sample mean, u is the population mean, s is the standard deviation of the sample, and n is the number of observations in the sample. If t is less than 1.96, then the sample was held to be representative. If t is greater than 1.96, then the sample was held to be biased in this characteristic. How representative is the sample in terms of characteristics of the average or mean farm? See Table 5.5. The average farm in the sample is biased in

Table 5.3
Townships in the Manuscript Census Sample, Old Northwest, 1860

State	County	Township	No. of Farms
Illinois	1. Knox	Penifer	76
	2. Livingston	Nevada	22
	3. Brown	Ripley	17
	4. Bureau	Fairfield	55
	5. Dewitt	Barnett	84
	6. Kendall	Seward	137
	7. McDonough	Macomb	85
	8. Macoupin	T10,R6	80
	9. Massac	T16,R5	30
	10. Whiteside	Union Grove	109
	11. Williamson	T10,R4	146
	12. Adams	Honey Creek	96
Indiana	13. Clinton	Perry	175
	14. Franklin	Highland	212
	15. Fulton	Aubbeenaubee	107
	16. Knox	Washington	135
	17. LaGrange	Newbury	112
	18. Morgan	Gregg	162
	19. Posey	Harmony	161
	20. Putnam	Mill Creek	52
	21. Shelby	Moral	209
	22. Switzerland	Cotton	165
	23. Wabash	La Gro	479
	24. Tippecanoe	Wea	134
	25. Warren		101
	26. Warwick	Boone	347
	27. Washington		336
	28. Wells	Harrison	163
	29. Gibson	Johnson	265
Michigan	30. Cheboygan	Inverness	13
	31. Emmett	La Croix	39
	32. Huron	Rubicon	12
	33. Monroe	Summerfield	103
	34. Siawassee	Fairfield	30
	35. Washtenaw	Augusta	138
	36. Ottawa	Holland	134
	37. Clinton	Bingham	107
	38. Van Buren	Waverly	47
Ohio	39. Harrison	North	79
	40. Licking	St. Albans	194
	41. Morrow	Perry	109
	42. Noble	Beaver	136
Wisconsin	43. Douglas	Nemadjo	3
	44. Iowa	Waldwich	180
	45. Juneau	Clearfield	11
	46. Waukesha	Ocono	1692
The Old Northwest			5,756

Table 5.4
Regional Representativeness

Characteristic	Sample	Universe	Percent	Bias
UI	341,409	31,510,429	1.08	upward
Corn (bu)	2,850,667	280,268,862	1.02	upward
TA	711,097	72,696,843	0.98	upward
VOLS	2,287,257	236,263,729	0.97	upward
Number of farms	5,756	596,717	0.96	standard
VOI($)	517,169	56,810,980	0.91	downward
IA	369,625	41,186,414	0.90	downward
Wheat (bu)	2,850,667	280,268,862	0.86	downward
VOF($)	14,237,489	1,735,742,858	0.82	downward

Source: Fred Bateman and James D. Foust, *Agricultural and Demographic Records for Rural Households in the North, 1860* (Ann Arbor, MI: Inter-University Consortium for Political and Social Research, 1976) and *Printed Census, 1860*, Old Northwest.

Note: UI is unimproved acres; TA is total acres; VOLS is value of livestock; VOI is value of implements; IA is improved acres; VOF is value of the farm.

Table 5.5
Farm Representativeness

Characteristic	Sample Mean	Universe Mean	Standard Deviation	t	bias
UI	59	54	154	2.46	upward
Corn (bu)	495	477	1129	1.21	no bias
TA (acres)	124	124	183	0	no bias
VOLS ($)	397	402	384	- 0.98	no bias
VOI ($)	90	97	102	- 5.15	downward
IA	64	70	67	- 6.82	downward
Wheat (bu)	120	136	164	- 7.31	downward
VOF ($)	2474	2957	2668	-13.58	downward

Source: Fred Bateman and James D. Foust, *Agricultural and Demographic Records for Rural Households in the North, 1860* (Ann Arbor, MI: Inter-University Consortium for Political and Social Research, 1976) and *Printed Census, 1860*, Old Northwest.

Note: UI is unimproved acres; TA is total acres; VOLS is value of livestock; VOI is value of implements; IA is improved acres; VOF is value of the farm.

exactly the same ways as the aggregate characteristics of the region were. This time we have statistical tests and can say that there is no bias in total acres, corn, or in the value of livestock for the average farm. There is an upward bias in unimproved land (UI) and a downward bias in improved land (IA). The average farm in the sample was the same size as the average farm in the population, but it was less developed. There is a downward bias in wheat production, in the value of implements, and in the value of farms.

Distributional Representativeness

To test the representativeness of the sample in terms of size distribution, the X^2 test was carried out. X^2 is defined as:

$$X^2 = \frac{\Sigma \ (E_i - O_i)}{\Sigma \ (E_i)}$$

where O_i is observed frequency in the sample and E_i is expected frequency in the sample. A X^2 less than 12.592 means that the sample is representative at 5 percent level of significance. See Table 5.6. The size distribution of the sample as a whole is not representative. There are far too many small farms in the 100- to 499-acre range to be considered representative. We had already discovered that the sample farms are less developed. Looking closely at the size categories, we can see that the main problem is too many farms in the 20 to 49 acres (IA) range. A slight problem is also that there were too few farms in the 100- to 499-range in the sample.

The econometric analysis of farms used a sample of 4,336 wheat farms rather than the full 5,756 farms in the sample. If we compare the sample means on improved acres and on the value of the farm with the universe mean on these characteristics, we find that the improved acres on a wheat farm are not biased but that the value of the farm is still biased downward. See Table 5.7.

Explaining The Bias

The most important source of bias lies in the intentional selection of rural townships by Bateman and Foust. It was their purpose to take a sample of rural households. I shall now describe the procedure they used to obtain rural households in order to see in detail the source of the bias we have found in the sample.

Table 5.6
Distributional Representativeness

Size Categories	Universe		Expected Number in Sample	Observed in Sample		$(O_i-E_i)^2$
(IA)	Number	Percent		Number	Percent	E_i
3-9	11,416	2.00	113	131	2	.87
10-19	41,747	7.00	394	458	8	10.40
20-49	196,358	34.00	1913	2267	40	65.50
50-99	194,955	34.00	1913	1853	33	1.88
100-499	127,044	22.00	1238	1071	19	22.50
500-999	1,876	0.30	0	12	0	
1000-over	394	0.07	0	4	0	
						$X^2=103.15$

Source: Fred Bateman and James D. Foust, *Agricultural and Demographic Records for Rural Households in the North, 1860* (Ann Arbor, MI: Inter-University Consortium for Political and Social Research, 1976) and *Printed Census, 1860, Old Northwest*.

Note: IA is improved acres, % is percent; see text for O, E, and X.

Table 5.7
Representativeness of Wheat Farms

Characteristic	Sample Mean	Universe Mean	Standard Deviation	t-Statistic
IA	70.5	70	67.5	+0.5
VOF	$2722	$2957	2748	-5.6

Source: Fred Bateman and James D. Foust, *Agricultural and Demographic Records for Rural Households in the North, 1860* (Ann Arbor, MI: Inter-University Consortium for Political and Social Research, 1976) and *Printed Census, 1860, Old Northwest*.

Note: IA is improved acres; VOF is value of the farm.

First, they took a random sample of counties in the northern United States. If a county had at least 90 percent of its population residing within the largest city, this county was excluded from the sample. Second, they took at random one township from each county selected in the first round. If a township had at least 90 percent of its population engaged in non-farming occupations, this township was excluded from the sample. All of the households in these rural townships were used for the sample. This is a cluster, rather than random, sample of households.

If we assume that farms in rural counties and in rural townships were less developed than farms near towns and cities, then we have an explanation of the bias that we have found. The farms measured in total acres were just as large near or far from cities, but they appear to have been less developed. Furthermore, farms in rural areas may have been less likely to produce wheat for the market, although they seem to produce as much corn and livestock. Finally, it appears that farms in rural areas were less valuable and had less capital invested in farm implements.

A second source of bias in the sample may be due to errors in the Printed Census which we are using for the population statistics. When Bateman and Foust adjusted the population statistics by 10 percent and by 15 percent, many more t-tests showed no bias.[23]

How the Bias Affects the Analysis

First, let us look at the effect of the rural bias on the farm model. The dependent variable is the adoption of the reaper which is inferred from the value of farm implements being at least $150, the quantity of wheat produced being at least 20 acres, and on the number of horses being at least two. For all farms in the sample, the value of implements and the wheat output are less than those values in the population. This will cause an underestimation of the farms that adopted the reaper. The independent variable of specialization is also based on wheat output, so this will be underestimated as well. The independent variable of the value of the farm will be underestimated because the sample is biased downward on this attribute. The precise sample used in this farm model is 4,336 wheat farms and they were found to be representative of the population farms in terms of the number of improved acres. Thus the values of this variable should not be biased. Underestimation of the above-mentioned variables should not affect the analysis because they refer to variables that are not debated. The one variable that I use to differentiate the family farm thesis from the profit-maximizing models of David and Fleisig is based upon the interpretation of the results on the variable of improved acres and on this there seems to be no rural bias.

Slightly more serious is the effect of the rural bias on the township model. All farms are included in the grouping of the individual datum, unlike the farm model that uses just wheat farms. Because the full 5,756 farms in the sample showed a downward bias in wheat production and the value of implements, two of the three criteria for inferring the adoption of the reaper, then less farms (in a township) will be inferred to have adopted the reaper. The dependent variable will be underestimated. The specialization measure will be underestimated for the same two reasons given above, the downward bias against wheat and the upward bias toward corn. The land equality variable is the proportion of farms in a township that are 40 or less total acres. In the regional bias calculation, the sample showed more total acres than would be expected from the population data. However, the mean farm was not biased in total acres. Thus the proportion of small farms in a township may be overestimated. The land concentration variable is the proportion of land in improved acres that is operated by the top 10 percent of the farms in a township. Analyzing the representativeness of the size distribution of farms in the sample showed a bias toward small farms in the 20- to forty-nine-acre range, and a slight bias away from large farms of the 100- to 499-acre range. Thus, this variable may be underestimated. These are serious biases, but this is the only sample we have. The interpretation of the results of the econometric analysis must be cautious.

In addition to the problems of the manuscript censuses themselves and the bias of the sample, there is one other serious problem. In Chapter 4 we discussed the inadequacy of the measurement of the farm employees available per farm operator. This is due to the fact that the 1860 census was the first census that attempted to differentiate between farmers and farm laborers. Atack writes that, "A large fraction of the population listed its occupation as 'laborer.' Recent work by Tom Weiss suggests that accepting these as agricultural laborers may be a serious error."[24] Until further work can be done on adequate measurement of farm labor, we must cautiously use the measures that we have developed in Chapter 3.

A final word on the effect of the rural bias on the analyses of Chapter 2, 3, and 4 of this text. The inferred extent of the adoption of the reaper should be considered a lower bound due to the bias of the sample toward less valuable farm implements and less wheat output. More critical is the bias toward less wheat output for the claim made that there were not enough farms producing near the threshold of profitability to account for reaper adoption, made in Chapter 2. The sample biases the results toward my claim. However, the bias is small compared to the distance between the profit-maximizing scale of wheat production and the actual level scale.

The mean farm in the sample produced 120 bushels of wheat, or 9.8 acres using the yield of 12.2 bushels per acre. The mean farm in the population produced 136 bushels or 11.1 acres. David argued that the reaper was adopted in conjunction with the attainment of the threshold of profitability, which, using Olmstead's revisions, was 78 acres of small grains. In Chapter 2 I argued that the threshold should be measured in wheat. If these arguments are accepted, then only 5.2 percent of the farms that adopted the reaper were producing 78 acres of wheat. The bias of the sample, judged by the 9.8 acres of the mean farm in the sample, compared to the 11.1 acres of the mean farm in the population, is not large. The sample value is 0.88 of the population value. This is small compared to the difference between David's threshold of profitability of 78 acres of wheat, and the sample finding that 94.8 percent of the farms that adopted the reaper produced less than 78 acres of wheat. In Chapter 2 we found that the mean farm that adopted the reaper produced 40 acres of wheat, the median farm, 33 acres, and the mode farm only 25.

As with the analysis of Chapter 3, we must be cautious in interpreting the results because of the downward bias of the sample on the value of implements and the improved acres on the farm. They were found to be less than Fleisig would have us expect. Especially problematic is the measurement of the farm employees available per farm operator.

Also in Chapter 3, the variable on the proportion of farms in the township that are in the medium-sized family farm range would be underestimated due to the rural bias of the sample, the bias to underestimate the improved acres on a farm. A further problem arises due to conflict over how much a family could operate. Atack writes that, "Surely 110 acres is a farm greater than a family could farm in the mid-nineteenth century without hired labor."[25]

THE VARIABLES

The Variables in the Farm Model

Adoption of the Reaper (AR) (0 or 1)

In order to construct the dependent variable, the adoption of the reaper had to be inferred. Data do not exist for establishing this as fact. As described in Appendix A, the adoption of the reaper was inferred on the basis of a threefold criteria: The farmer reported to the census enumerator: (1) at least 20 acres of wheat, the physical limit to what the farm operator could harvest himself by hand; (2) at least two horses to pull the machinery; and (3) at least $150 of farm implements and machinery. The value of this variable is either one if we infer that the farmer adopted the reaper, or zero if we infer that he did not adopt the reaper. To test sensitivity of results to the choice of $150, a second set of estimates were made using $200 as the criterion. Once the model is estimated we can calculate predicted probabilities of reaper adoption for hypothetical farms. Thus we will be able to see if the probability of reaper adoption varies significantly for small family farms, medium-sized family farms, and large business farms. Atack and Bateman have used a similar method to infer the adoption of the reaper. They use the value of farm implements and small grain acreage.[26]

Specialization (SPECIAL) (0 to 1)

This variable represents the major economic force behind reaper adoption. This independent variable was estimated by constructing the ratio of the value of wheat produced on a farm compared to the sum of the value of wheat and corn produced. Corn and wheat output are given in the agricultural census. The prices are from Towne and Rasmussen. The index is $1.02 times the bushels of wheat divided by the sum of $1.02 times the bushels of wheat and $0.46 times the bushels of corn. This variable is a rough proxy for wheat output. It was felt that since the dependent variable contained the information that the farm had at least 20 acres of wheat, that the wheat output of a farm should not be used as an independent variable. This variable represents the necessary, but not sufficient cause of reaper adoption which all three models would include. This variable thus does not discriminate between the three models. It stands for the fact that the American Northeast was industrializing and increasing its demand for food. This caused the price of wheat to rise and the farmer to increase his specialization in wheat. We can use this variable to test for differential responsiveness of the three kinds of farms. Were medium-sized family farms more responsive to reaper adoption when they increased their specialization in wheat? If so then this would support Hypotheses 1 and 4. Hypothesis 1: Risk-averse utility-maximizing family farms rationally adopted the reaper in the 1850s at a scale of production below the threshold at which profit maximization would have dictated the adoption of the reaper. Hypothesis 4: The institutional structure of the family farm system was a favorable initial condition for the adoption of farm machinery because it was based on a relatively equal distribution of abundant land which generated many farmers with a sufficient surplus and incentive to purchase capital goods.

Improved Acres (IA)

Improved acres on a farm is directly reported in the agricultural census. This variable is the most important independent variable because on the basis of it we can observe the behavior of small, medium, and large farms. We can also infer from the size, in improved acres, whether or not the farm was a family farm. We can thus observe the behavior of a small family farm, for example, a 35 acre farm, approximately enough to support a family, given soil fertility; a medium-sized family farm, for example, a 55- to 165-

improved-acre farm, approximately enough to occupy the labor force of a farm family, given the technology of the day; and a large business farm, for example, a 300-acre farm, more land than a family could operate, given the technology of the day. We can compare the probability of adopting a reaper on the three farms, the responsiveness of the three kinds of farms in increased probability of reaper adoption with respect to increases in the extent of specialization, the value of the farm, and in the improved acres on the farm. It is here that we can differentiate between the view of Paul David on large farms adopting the reaper and the family farm model on medium-sized family farms adopting the reaper. Hypotheses 1 and 4 are tested with the analysis of this variable.

Value of the Farm (VOF)

The value of the farm is directly reported in the agricultural census. The variable stands for the pressure to mechanize via the need to finance the owned farm: the more valuable the farm, the more likely a farmer would have to mechanize in order to grow the wheat in order to get the cash to pay off the mortgage. In addition, it stands for the equity-risk principle: the more valuable the farm, the less the risk of purchasing productive capital in the market, such as the reaper. Moreover, it stands for credit worthiness with the machine suppliers, such as McCormick who sold his reapers on credit. Additionally, this variable can be used as a rough proxy for resource endowment.

Ownership of the Farm by Farm Operator (OWN) (0 or 1)

This information is not directly given by the census. The variable was constructed by assigning the value one (meaning owned) if the value of real estate reported by the farm head of household was equal to or greater than the value of the farm operated and assigning the value zero if not (meaning not owned). It should be noted that the value of real estate owned by the farm operator was reported in the population census, whereas the value of the farm is reported in the agricultural census. Bateman and Foust matched the two censuses by the name of the head of the farm household, thus making the construction of this variable possible. Atack and Bateman have "estimated tenancy on the basis of a comparison between the agricultural schedules and real estate reported on the population schedules."[27] This variable tests for the family farm model claim that the kind of land-holding and tenure is an important aspect of what makes some agricultural systems favorable to agricultural improvement, that is, Hypothesis 3. The institutional structure of the family farm system was a favorable initial condition for the adoption of farm machinery because it made ownership possible for many farmers through the purchase of land. Owning a farm, it is claimed, makes a farmer more likely to adopt improvements, such as the reaper. As such, this variable represents institutional cause of reaper adoption. It will be compared to specialization, as the major economic cause to determine relative importance of the two types of causes.

The Variables in the Township Model

Proportion of Farms Adopting the Reaper in the Township (AR/1 - AR) (0 to 1)

Once adoption of the reaper has been inferred on an individual farm basis, these inferences can be aggregated at the township level. The ratio of the number of farms inferred to have adopted the reaper to the number of farms inferred to have not adopted the reaper is the index of the proportion of farms adopting the reaper in each township. The construction of this dependent variable allows for the exploration of characteristics of the farm economy which promoted or held back reaper adoption. Once the parameters of this model are estimated, we can calculate the probability of a farmer adopting a reaper in a given township with certain land distributions and other economic characteristics.

Specialization (SPECIAL) (0 to 1)

This variable was constructed in the same manner as described in the section above on farm variables. Here the index was calculated for the whole township. It is a measure of how specialized in wheat relative to corn in value terms a township was. It represents the necessary, but not sufficient cause of the adoption of the reaper for all three models. It is the major economic variable in the township model and will be used to compare its quantitative importance with respect to the institutional variable of land equality.

Farm Employees per Farm Operator (FEFO)

This variable was constructed from occupational data from the population census. Bateman and Foust took a cluster sample of all households in the rural township in order to capture the potential supply of agricultural labor. Some farm employees lived in rural non-farm households. To form this variable I calculated the number of people in the township who reported a farming occupation. I subtracted the number of farms in a township to remove farm operators and to be left with farmers without farms, as potential hired labor. I divided this by the number of farms to obtain the number of farm employees available per farm operator. This measure is roughly the number of employees per farm and is a proxy for a labor constraint. Note that this variable (FEFO) as a measure of labor available is the opposite of labor constraint, as in Fleisig. This variable was suggested by Fleisig, who claimed that labor constraints on individual farms caused the mechanization of agriculture in the North. I have argued that very little of the labor on the family farm was hired labor and that for various reasons family farmers preferred not to hire labor. Since the system was largely made up of these family farmers, I do not expect the labor available in a township to be a significant predictor of reaper adoption. If this variable is not statistically significant, then we have reason to support Hypothesis 2: Risk-averse utility-maximizing family farms rationally adopted the reaper in the 1850s when they wanted to produce more wheat than they could with family labor.

Land Concentration (DC) (0 to 1)

This variable is the proportion of land, measured in improved acres, that the top 10 percent of farms in a township operated. This variable was constructed as one of three measures of the land distribution, the measure of concentration at the top of the distribution. Land equality, discussed below, is the measure of the equality at the bottom of the distribution. The third measure, that of the middle of the distribution, is tested in Chapters 3 and 4. Together, these three explanatory variables are to be used to test Hypothesis 4 on the favorable land distribution as a cause of the adoption of farm machinery. This variable is to test the idea that unequal distribution of income (using unequal distribution of land as its proxy) is better for development via the effect on saving and investment of high income, wealth, and landholders. On this view, the adoption of the reaper should be at a higher rate in townships with high degree of land concentration. The family farm thesis claims that the family farm system of many medium-sized family farms was a better agricultural system than one with a high concentration of land because it provided a potential wide market for industrially produced farm machinery. On this view, land concentration is not expected to be a significant variable.

Land Equality (DE) (0 to 1)

This variable is the proportion of farms in a township that are 40 total acres or less. It is a measure of the proportion of small farms in the township. In the family farm model a distinction is made between small and medium-sized family farms. Small family farms are not expected to adopt the reaper, whereas medium-sized family farms are expected to have a high probability of adopting the reaper. On this view this variable should be negative and statistically significant. This variable also shows the distinction between equal distribution with and without surplus farm production. A system with many small family farms probably does not generate much of a surplus output beyond food self-sufficiency and thus is not favorable to agricultural improvement. This variable is the major institutional variable in the township model and will be used to compare the importance of institutional influences with economic forces, represented in the variable of specialization.

SPECIFICATION OF THE ECONOMETRIC MODELS

The Farm Model

N = 4336 wheat farms in Old Northwest in 1860.
Estimated with maximum likelihood procedure.

$$P_i = \frac{1}{1 + e^{-Z_i}} \quad \text{where } Z_i =$$

$$a + b_1 \text{ SPECIAL}_i + b_2 \text{ IA}_i + b_3 \text{ VOF}_i + b_4 \text{ OWN}_i + u_i \quad (i = 1,...n)$$

where

- P = probability of adopting the reaper, 0 if do not adopt, 1 if adopt the reaper, (minimum of \$150 value of implements);
- SPECIAL = degree of specialization in wheat relative to corn, in value terms (\$);
- IA = improved acres on the farm (IA);
- VOF = value of the farm (\$);
- OWN = 1 if own farm, 0 if do not own; inferred from the value of the farm relative to value of real estate held by farm head of household.

The Township Model

N = 46 townships in the Old Northwest in 1860.
Estimated with ordinary least squares procedure.

$$\log \frac{P_i + 1/2}{1 - P_i + 1/2} = a + b_1 \text{ SPECIAL}_i - b_2 \text{ DE}_i$$

$$+ b_3 \text{ DC}_i - b_4 \text{ FEFO}_i + u_i \quad (i = 1,...n)$$

where

- P = probability of adopting the reaper in a township, number of farms inferred to have adopted the reaper (minimum of \$200 value of implements);
- SPECIAL = degree of specialization in wheat, relative to corn, in value terms;
- DE = land equality, proportion of farms having less than 40 total acres in land in township;
- DC = land concentration, proportion of land (in improved acres) held by the top 10 percent of farms in township;
- FEFO = farm employees available per farm operator.

THE RESULTS OF THE ECONOMETRIC ANALYSIS

Farm Results

All four of the explanatory variables were found to be statistically significant, having the right signs, and being quantitatively important. The model was found to be a good predictor: the rank correlation between the predicted probabilities of the model and the inferred responses in the sample was 0.77. The predicted probability of reaper adoption ranged from 0.0001 to 99 percent. It was inferred that 357 of the 4,336 wheat farms adopted the reaper or 8.2 percent of all farms that grew some wheat, using the $150 minimum criterion of the value of farm implements for inferring adoption.

The Estimated Parameters for the Farm Model

The maximum likelihood parameter estimates are:

$$P_i = \frac{1}{1 + e^{-Z_i}} \quad \text{where}$$

$$Z_i = -6.9336^* + 3.8387^* \text{SPECIAL}_i + 0.0099^* \text{IA}_i + 0.0002^* \text{VOF}_i$$
$$\quad (0.3629) \quad (0.2917) \qquad\qquad (0.0013) \qquad (0.00003)$$
$$\quad (-19.1) \quad (13.2) \qquad\qquad\quad (7.6) \qquad\quad (6.7)$$

$$\quad + 0.8556^* \text{OWN}_i$$
$$\quad (0.2229)$$
$$\quad (3.8)$$

Standard errors are given in parentheses below the estimated parameters. Below these are the t-statistics. The asterisks show which variables are statistically significant at 5 percent level, that is, when t is at least 1.96.

All four variables were statistically significant and bore the correct positive sign. The farmer operating a more specialized wheat farm had a greater chance of adopting the reaper than a less specialized farmer. The larger the farm in improved acres of land and the more valuable the farm, the more likely the farm operator would adopt the reaper. Owner operators were more likely to adopt the reaper than tenants.

Predicted Probabilities for Farms

In Table 5.8 the predicted probability of adopting the reaper has been calculated with the above estimated parameters for selected farms. The

Table 5.8
Predicted Probabilities for Selected Farms

Percentile	OWN	SPECIAL	IA	VOF	Prob
0	·	.002	2	0	.001
1	0	.030	10	200	0.001
5	0	.090	16	500	0.002
10	0	0.130	20	700	0.002
25	1	0.240	35	1000	0.010
50	1	0.400	55	2000	0.030
75	1	0.570	80	3435	0.080
90	1	0.750	130	5500	0.310
95	1	0.850	165	7014	0.560
99	1	0.950	300	13,000	0.960
100	1	0.990	1500	44,400	0.990
Mean	0.81	0.420	71	$2,722	0.030

Source: Fred Bateman and James D. Foust, *Agricultural and Demographic Records for Rural Households in the North, 1860* (Ann Arbor, MI: Inter-University Consortium for Political and Social Research, 1976).

Note: N = 4,336 wheat producing farms; VOI criterion of $150. Prob is predicted probability of reaper adoption; IA is improved acres, VOF is value of the farm ($).

most significant result is the difference in the probability of reaper adoption for small, medium, and large farms. First, the small family farm, if defined as a 35-acre farm, had a 1 percent chance of adopting the reaper. This farm was owned, 24 percent specialized in wheat, and worth $1,000. Second, the medium-sized family farm, if defined as a 165-acre farm, had an 8 percent chance of adopting the reaper. This farm was owned, 57 percent specialized in wheat, and worth $3,435. Note that this eight percent chance of reaper adoption is typical in that, of all 4,336 wheat farms in the sample, 8 percent adopted the reaper. Third, the large business farm, if defined as a 300-acre farm, had a 96 percent chance of reaper adoption. This farm was owned, 95 percent specialized in wheat, and worth $13,000. While this business farm was more likely to adopt the reaper than the medium-sized family farm, there were very few of them, they accounted for only a small proportion of farms that adopted the reaper and a small part of overall market for reapers.

Slopes of the Farm Variables

Each statistically significant variable in the logit model has a slope with respect to the predicted probability of reaper adoption. The slope of the specialization variable, for example, represents the change in the predicted probability of reaper adoption, given a one unit change in the specialization index. The slope will vary according to where the farm is located in the distribution. Normally, the slopes are evaluated for the mean, but in this study the mean farm did not adopt the reaper. The slope of any explanatory variable will be greatest where probability of a positive choice is near 0.5. For this reason, we evaluate the slopes for the farm with a probability of adopting the reaper of 0.56, the farm at the 95th percentile.

Table 5.9 gives the slopes for the three continuous variables. Ownership is evaluated separately because it is a dummy variable; see below. The specialization slope of this farm (at the 95th percentile) is 0.948, the improved acres slope is 0.002445, and the value of the farm slope is 0.0000494. Beginning with the specialization slope, it means that if this farm

Table 5.9
Slopes of the Farm Variables

	Slopes		
Percentile	Special	Improved Acres	Value of Farm
0	.004	.000010	.0000002
1	.005	.000012	.0000003
5	.007	.000018	.0000004
10	.009	.000022	.0000004
25	.037	.000097	.0000020
50	.100	.000257	.0000052
75	.290	.000748	.0000151
90	.817	.002108	.0000426
95	.948	.002445	.0000494
99	.153	.000394	.0000080
100	1.852e-9	4.78e-12	9.65e-14
Mean	.122	.000314	.0000064

Source: Fred Bateman and James D. Foust, *Agricultural and Demographic Records for Rural Households in the North, 1860* (Ann Arbor, MI: Inter-University Consortium for Political and Social Research, 1976).

Note: N = 4,336 wheat producing farms.

increases its specialization by one unit (0.01 in the specialization index) from 0.75 to 0.76, then the probability of reaper adoption is increased by 0.948 units (0.01 in the probability index) from 0.56 to 0.56948. That is to say, a one unit increase in specialization leads to nearly a one unit increase in the probability of reaper adoption. The slope for the improved acres variable and for the value of the farm variable are interpreted similarly. Because the units of improved acres range from two to 1500, and the units of the value of the farm range from zero to $44,400 and the units of probability range from zero to one, slope is a noncompelling way to see the quantitative importance of these variables. Below elasticities are used to get around this problem, by expressing all variables in percents.

But first, note that the slope varies across the distribution. This means that we can identify differential responsiveness across farm sizes. A unit change in specialization, improved acreage, or value of the farm has a quantitatively different impact depending upon the size of the farm. The medium-sized family farms are more responsive than either the small family farm or the large business farm. Consider first, a unit change in specialization. The small family farm of 35 acres at the 25th percentile increases its probability of reaper adoption by a 0.04 of a percentage point, the medium-sized family farm of 165 acres at the 95th percentile increases its probability of reaper adoption by a 0.95 of a percentage point, and the large business farm of 300 acres at the 99th percentile increases its probability of reaper adoption by only a 0.15 of a percentage point. Likewise with a unit change in the number of acres in cultivation, the small family farm increases its probability of reaper adoption by 0.01 percentage point, the medium-sized family farm by 0.24 percentage point, and the large business farm by only 0.04 percentage point. Third, with a unit change in the value of the farm, the increase in the probability of reaper adoption for a small family farm is 0.0002, for a medium-sized family farm is 0.0049, and for a large business farm is 0.0008. The responsiveness of the medium-sized family farm in adopting the reaper in association with increases in specialization, land in cultivation, and value of farm is greater than the responsiveness of the small family farm and greater than that of the large business farm.

The logit model is designed to have the slope steepest at the probability of a positive choice near one-half. The point is that the data fit this model. It turns out that the medium-sized family farm at the larger end of its range, has this near half chance of reaper adoption. It is the most responsive farm, that is, it is more likely to adopt the reaper in response to an increase in its degree of specialization, to an increase in its land in cultivation, and to an increase in farm value. This is precisely the point of the family farm thesis on the causes of reaper adoption.

Elasticities of the Farm Variables

The elasticity of the probability of reaper adoption with respect to each of the explanatory variables is similar to the slope except it is expressed in percentages, not units. The elasticity of the predicted probability of reaper adoption with respect to a change in specialization, for example, means that for a 1 percent increase in the degree of specialization, the numeric value of the elasticity tells the percent change in the predicted probability. The elasticity of the probability of reaper adoption with respect to changes in the farm variables varies across the distribution. To interpret the meaning of elasticity, let us take a medium-sized family farm of 165 acres at the 95th percentile, see Table 5.10. This farm has a 56 percent chance of reaper adoption. If the operator of this farm increased his extent of specialization by 1 percent, the probability of his adopting the reaper is increased by 1.45 percent. If the land in cultivation is increased by 1 percent, the probability of reaper adoption increased 0.73 percent. If the value of this farm increased 1 percent, the effect on the probability of reaper adoption is to

Table 5.10
Elasticities of the Farm Variables

	Elasticities		
Percentile	Special	Improved Acres	Value of Farm
0	.01	.020	.000
1	.12	.099	.048
5	.34	.158	.112
10	.50	.198	.125
25	.91	.343	.203
50	1.49	.530	.390
75	2.01	.727	.630
90	1.99	.891	.762
95	1.45	.727	.624
99	.15	.123	.109
100	1.852e-9	7.242e-9	4.328e-9
Mean	1.56	.680	.530

Source: Fred Bateman and James D. Foust, *Agricultural and Demographic Records for Rural Households in the North, 1860* (Ann Arbor, MI.: Inter-University Consortium for Political and Social Research, 1976).

Note: N = 4,336 wheat farms; VOI criterion of $150.

increase it by 0.62 percent. The elasticity of the probability of adoption the reaper with respect to a change in the extent of specialization is greater than unity elasticity. The elasticity with respect to a change in the land in cultivation and the value of the farm is positive, but not quite unity.

Just as we found the slope the steepest for medium-sized family farms above, the elasticity is greater for medium-sized family farms than for small family farms and large business farms. This is true for a 1 percent change in specialization, land in cultivation, and the value of the farm. First, let us look at the specialization elasticities. All the medium-sized family farms, at the 50th, 75th, 90th, and 95th percentiles and the mean farm have unit elasticity or greater, 1.49, 2.01, 1.99, 1.45, and 1.56 respectively. The small farm at the 25th percentile had elasticity of 0.91 and the large business farm had elasticity of 0.15. Similarly for elasticities for changes in land in cultivation, the elasticities for the medium-sized family farm are larger than those of the small and large farms. The range of elasticities for the medium farms is from 0.73 to 0.68, whereas for the small farm the elasticity is 0.34 and for the large farm it is 0.12. Again for the elasticities for changes in the value of the farm, they are greater for the medium-sized family farms than for the small or large farms. The range of elasticities for the medium farm is 0.63 to 0.53, whereas the elasticity for a small farm is 0.20 and for the large farm it is 0.11. These results are the same as the results on the slopes, the only difference is that the slope is calculated in units and the elasticity is calculated in percents.

To compare the relative quantitative importance of ownership with respect to the other three explanatory variables, we can look at the mean farm that has a ownership value of 0.81. The mean farm had 71 improved acres of land, a medium-sized family farm. The predicted probability of this farm adopting the reaper was 0.03. The elasticity of the four variables are: specialization 1.7, improved acres of land on the farm 0.75, value of the farm 0.58, and ownership 0.73. Roughly then, we can say that ownership was as important as the number of improved acres on the farm, more important than the value of the farm, but not as important as the extent of specialization in wheat, when it comes to increasing the probability of adopting the reaper.

Ownership Evaluated Separately

Because ownership is a dummy variable, it does not make sense to calculate the slope and elasticity of ownership with respect to predicted probability. In Table 5.11 the probability of adopting the reaper for selected farms is calculated separately for owned and non-owned farms. The place where it makes the most difference quantitatively is at the 90th percentile. A non-owned farm at the 90th percentile had a 16 percent chance of adopting the reaper, whereas an owned farm had a 31 percent chance. This

Table 5.11
Probability Evaluated Separately for Owned and Non-Owned Farms

Percentile Farm	Size in Improved Acres	Probability of Adopting the Reaper	
		Own	Non-Owned
0	2	0.2	0.1
1	10	0.3	0.1
5	16	0.4	0.2
10	20	0.5	0.2
25	35	1.0	0.4
50	55	3.0	1.0
75	80	8.0	4.0
90	130	31.0	16.0
95	165	55.0	52.0
99	300	96.0	91.0
100	1500	99+	99+

Source: Fred Bateman and James D. Foust, *Agricultural and Demographic Records for Rural Households in the North, 1860* (Ann Arbor, MI: Inter-University Consortium for Political and Social Research, 1976).

Note: N = 4,336 wheat farms; VOI criterion is $150.

is nearly double, but more importantly it is an absolute increase of 15 percentage points. Note that this farm was 130 acres, a medium-sized family farm. The probability of adopting the reaper is also doubled on the 80-acre farm but only from 0.04 to 0.08. Ownership did not make much difference on the large farm; the 300-acre farm that was owned increased the probability of reaper adoption from a 91 percent chance to a 96 percent chance. Owning a small farm increased the probability of reaper adoption from 0.4 to a 1 percent chance, absolutely a very small change.

Township Results

Two of the four explanatory variables were found to be statistically significant and quantitatively important. The R^2 for the township model was 0.2380. The smallness of this value "suggests that a good deal of variance in the model is still unexplained. Nonetheless one can still use the results of the model to study several . . . factors which do correlate highly with "[reaper adoption]."[28] The range of predicted probability of reaper adoption was from 0.004 to 14 percent, using the minimum of $200 in farm implements as the criterion for inferring adoption.

The Estimated Parameters for the Township Model

The ordinary least squares parameter estimates are:

$$\log \frac{P_i + 1/2}{1 - P_i + 1/2} = \underset{\substack{(0.3653) \\ (-9.719)}}{-3.5503^*} + \underset{\substack{(0.6940) \\ (2.654)}}{1.8419^* \text{SPECIAL}_i} - \underset{\substack{(0.1351) \\ (-2.768)}}{0.0374^* \text{DE}_i}.$$

Standard errors are given in parentheses below the estimated parameters. Below these are the t-statistics. The asterisks show which variables are statistically significant at the 5 percent level, that is, when t is at least 1.96.

Both independent variables were found to be statistically significant. The signs are as expected by the family farm model: specialization is positive and land equality is negative. The more specialized in wheat a township was, the more likely it was that a farmer in that township would adopt the reaper. The less equality of land distribution in a township, or the less small farms in a township, the more likely a farmer there would adopt a reaper.

A second estimated model is now presented to show the lack of statistical significance of two critical variables. The ordinary least squares parameter estimates are:

$$\log \frac{P_i + 1/2}{1 - P_i + 1/2} = \underset{\substack{(3.0549) \\ (-0.596)}}{-5.1270} + \underset{\substack{(1.0040) \\ (2.9)}}{2.9940^* \text{SPECIAL}_i} - \underset{\substack{(0.4031) \\ (-0.934)}}{0.3764 \text{FEFO}_i}$$

$$+ \underset{\substack{(0.0208) \\ (0.096)}}{0.0020 \text{DC}_i}.$$

The farm employees available per farm operator in a township was not statistically significant. The t-statistic is -0.934 which is substantially below the needed 1.96 for 5 percent level confidence in its significance.

Land concentration in a township was not statistically significant. The t-statistic is 0.096 which is substantially below the needed 1.96 for 5 percent level confidence in its signicance.

Predicted Probabilities for Townships

In Table 5.12 the probability of a farmer adopting the reaper in selected townships has been calculated with the estimated parameters. A farm in the township at the 99th percentile, which was 93 percent specialized and had no farms 40 acres or less (DE), had a 14 percent chance of adopting the reaper. At the other extreme, a farm in the township at the first percentile, which was zero specialized in wheat and had 49.3 percent of its farms 40 acres or less, had a 0.4 percent chance of adopting the reaper. A farm in the mean township, which was 37 percent specialized and had 16.8 percent of its farms 40 total acres or less, had a 3 percent chance of adopting the reaper.

Elasticities of the Township Variables

Elasticity varies in the logit model with the range of values involved. Table 5.13 can be used to locate where the elasticity of response is strong, that is, greater than unity elasticity. The impact of specialization on the probability of adopting the reaper is greatest at the 99th percentile township where elasticity is 1.45. There, a 1 percent increase in specialization "causes" a 1.45 percent increase in the probability of adopting the reaper. Elasticity is greater than unity in the range of farms in the 90th- to 99th-percentile townships, which are 69 to 93 percent specialized and have only zero to 0.8 percent of the farms 40 acres or less. In this range, a 1 percent increase in specialization results in an increase in the probability of adopting the reaper of 1.16 to 1.45 percent. The importance of specialization as a cause of adopting the reaper then is primarily at the higher range of specialization.

The impact of land equality (prevalence of small farms) on the probability of adopting the reaper is greatest at the first percentile. There a 1 percent increase in the degree of land equality (prevalence of small farms) "causes" a 2.07 percent decrease in the probability of adopting the reaper. Elasticity is greater than unity in the range of farms in the first to tenth percentile townships, townships which are zero to 12 percent specialized and have 31 to 49.3 percent of their farms 40 acres or less. In this range, a 1 percent increase in land equality results in a decrease in the probability of adopting the reaper of 0.97 to 2.07 percent. The importance of land equality (prevalence of small farms) as an obstacle to adopting the reaper is primarily at the higher range of land equality.

To access the relative importance of the two explanatory variables at the township level, we calculate the elasticity of probability with respect to the two variables for the mean township. The table on township elasticities shows that at the mean township level a 1 percent increase in specialization is associated with a 0.65 percent increase in the probability of a farm adopting the reaper in that township. A 1 percent increase in land equality

Table 5.12
Predicted Probabilities for Selected Townships

Percentile	Special	Land Equality (DE)	Prob
1	0.00	49.3	0.004
5	0.03	42.7	0.010
10	0.12	31.0	0.010
25	0.20	23.5	0.020
50	0.34	16.7	0.030
75	0.54	5.8	0.060
90	0.69	0.8	0.090
95	0.89	0.0	0.130
99	0.93	0.0	0.140
Mean	0.37	16.8	0.030

Source: Fred Bateman and James D. Foust, *Agricultural and Demographic Records for Rural Households in the North, 1860* (Ann Arbor, MI: Inter-University Consortium for Political and Social Research, 1976).

Note: N = 46 townships; Prob = predicted probability of adopting the reaper. VOI criterion is $200.

Table 5.13
Elasticities of Township Variables

	Elasticities	
Percentile	Specialization	Land Equality (DE)
1	0.00	2.07
5	0.03	0.97
10	0.24	1.27
25	0.31	0.74
50	0.57	0.57
75	0.92	0.20
90	1.16	0.03
95	1.41	0.00
99	1.45	0.00
Mean	0.65	0.60

Source: Fred Bateman and James D. Foust, *Agricultural and Demographic Records for Rural Households in the North, 1860* (Ann Arbor, MI: Inter-University Consortium for Political and Social Research, 1976).

Note: N = 46 townships; Percentile refers to percentile rank of the township; VOI criterion is $200.

in this mean township is associated with a 0.60 percent decrease in the probability of a farm adopting the reaper. Given measurement error, this is not a big difference, 0.65 for specialization, and 0.60 for land equality. This suggests that economic and institutional factors were of equal weight in determining reaper adoption.

By looking at the elasticities of the township variable of land equality, we can see how it varies across the range of townships. The township with the most land equality had 49 percent of its farms of a small size, 40 or fewer total acres. If this township had 1 percent more small farms, the probability of a farmer in this township adopting the reaper would be decreased by 2.07 percent. At the 25th-percentile township with 31 percent small farms, if this were increased 1 percent, the effect on the probability of reaper adoption is a 1.27 percent decrease. However, at the median township with only 17 percent small farms, an increase of 1 percent in small farms has the effect of decreasing reaper adoption only by 0.57 percent. That is to say, the problem with small farms is having a system made up of too many of them.

Three Tests of Robustness of the Results

Robustness of the Farm Results as to the Criterion of the Value of the Implements

In this chapter I reported the results of the logit model run on the criterion of a minimum of $150 of farm implements to infer reaper adoption. To test the robustness of these results, I changed the criteria to $200. In Table 5.14 the logit model results are given for two criteria. The ability of the model to predict reaper adoption changes from 0.77 to 0.79 with the change from $150 to $200. Considering measurement errors this is not significant. The number of wheat farms inferred to have adopted the reaper changes from 357 to 262 with the change from $150 to $200, or from 8.2 percent of wheat farms to 6.0 wheat farms. The same variables are statistically significant in both cases. I conclude that the farm results are robust. Specification of the criteria for inferring adopting the reaper with the value of the implements at $150 or more is not the cause of the results. See Appendix A for determination of the criterion of $150 versus $200.

Robustness of the Farm Results as to Choice of Sample

In this chapter I reported the results of the logit model run on wheat farms, that is, farms that grew some wheat. To test the robustness of the results, I ran the logit model on all farms that grew either wheat and/or corn. The predictive ability of the model was virtually the same, 0.77 with wheat farms and 0.78 with grain farms. Of wheat farms, 357 adopted the

Table 5.14
Robustness of Farm Results on Criterion of Implements

Explanatory Variable	Adopt the Reaper ($150)			Adopt the Reaper ($200)		
	Coefficient	SE	t	Coefficient	SE	t
Special	3.8387	0.2917	13.2	3.5161	0.4193	8.4
VOF	0.0002	0.00003	6.7	0.0002	0.00003	6.7
IA	0.0099	0.0013	7.6	0.0114	0.0114	8.1
OWN	0.8556	0.2229	3.8	0.6460	0.2442	2.6
Constant	-6.9336	0.3629	19.1	-7.0904	0.4193	16.9

Source: Fred Bateman and James D. Foust, *Agricultural and Demographic Records for Rural Households in the North, 1860* (Ann Arbor, MI: Inter-University Consortium for Political and Social Research, 1976).

Note: T = 1.960 statistically significant at 5 percent level; n = 4,336 wheat farms.

reaper or 8.2 percent. Of grain farms, 370 adopted the reaper or 6.7 percent. Table 5.15 shows that the same variables are statistically significant whether one uses wheat farms or grain farms. The results are robust and do not depend upon the specification of the sample. The idea had been that we wanted the structural parameters of wheat farmers because if a farmer did not grow wheat, he was not likely to adopt a reaper.

Robustness of the Township Results as to the Criterion on the Value of Implements

Table 5.16 shows the group logit results using the criterion of $150 minimum for the value of farm implements, for inferring reaper adoption. In the same table, we see the results using the criterion of $200 minimum to infer reaper adoption. Using the criterion of $200, the number of farms inferred to have adopted the reaper is reduced from 369 to 268, or from 6.4 percent to 4.7 percent. The R^2 is reduced from 0.4176 to 0.3655. The variables are statistically significant for both criteria. I conclude that the township results are robust, that the specification of the criteria for inferring adopting the reaper with the value of the implements at $200 or more is not the cause of the results.

Table 5.15
Robustness of Farm Results with Respect to Choice of Sample

Explanatory Variation	Wheat Farms			Grain Farms (corn and/or wheat)		
	Coefficient	SE	t	Coefficient	SE	t
Special	3.8387	0.2917	13.2	3.5342	0.3784	14.8
VOF	0.0002	0.00003	6.7	0.0003	0.00004	7.5
IA	0.0099	0.0013	7.6	0.0078	0.0017	4.6
OWN	0.8556	0.2229	3.8	0.9586	0.2169	4.4
Constant	-6.9336	0.3629	19.1	-6.6610	0.3784	17.6

Source: Fred Bateman and James D. Foust, *Agricultural and Demographic Records for Rural Households in the North, 1860* (Ann Arbor, MI: Inter-University Consortium for Political and Social Research, 1976).

Table 5.16
Robustness of Township Results

Explanatory Variables	Adopt the Reaper ($150)			Adopt the Reaper ($200)		
	Coefficient	SE	t	Coefficient	SE	t
LEFO	-0.3764	0.4031	0.9	0.5985	0.3494	1.7
Special	2.9440	1.0040	2.9	2.6410	0.9040	2.9
DC	0.0020	0.0208	0.1	0.0025	0.0157	0.2
Constant	-5.1270	3.0549	-1.7	-5.2422	2.0922	-2.5

Source: Fred Bateman and James D. Foust, *Agricultural and Demographic Records for Rural Households in the North, 1860* (Ann Arbor, MI: Inter-University Consortium for Political and Social Research, 1976).

Note: Statistically significant at 5 percent level when t = or > 1.960.

Three Tests of Multicollinearity in the Farm Model

On the basis of the following three tests, I judge the extent of multi-collinearity in the farm model not harmful. The degree of multicollinearity is harmful if, when one removes one explanatory variable of the model's ability to predict does not change. On basis of calculations in Table 5.17, I judge multicollinearity is not harmful.

Multicollinearity is harmful if one explanatory variable can be predicted by the others. See Table 5.18. Specialization is not predicted with improved acres or value of the farm. However, the value of the farm (VOF) does depend upon the number of improved acres (IA) and vice versa. Obviously the value of a farm depends on how many acres in the farm. In my judgment, this multicollinearity is not harmful.

Multicollinearity is harmful if estimates of regression coefficients are correlated. See Table 5.19. Only the value of the farm (VOF) and improved acres (IA) are correlated. In my judgement, this multicollinearity is not harmful.

INTERPRETATION OF THE RESULTS

Farm Results Interpreted

Some of the results of the farm model are consistent with David's rising wage model and with the family farm model. As both models would have us expect, the more specialized in wheat, the larger the farm in improved

Table 5.17
Test 1 on Multicollinearity

	Rank Correlation of Predicted Probabilities and Observed Response
All four variables	0.793
Exclude OWN	0.784
Exclude VOF	0.779
Exclude Special	0.750
Exclude IA	0.718

Source: Fred Bateman and James D. Foust, *Agricultural and Demographic Records for Rural Households in the North, 1860* (Ann Arbor, MI: Inter-University Consortium for Political and Social Research, 1976).

Table 5.18

Test 2 on Multicollinearity

	R^2
Special = f (IA, VOF, OWN)	0.02
VOF= f (Special, IA, OWN)	0.56
IA= f (Special, VOF, OWN)	0.57

Source: Fred Bateman and James D. Foust, *Agricultural and Demographic Records for Rural Households in the North, 1860* (Ann Arbor, MI: Inter-University Consortium for Political and Social Research, 1976).

acres, and the greater the value of the farm, the more probable the operator of this farm would adopt the reaper. However, this does not prove much. While it is true that the farm at the 99th and 100th percentile have the highest probability of reaper adoption, there were not very many of these large farms and they accounted for a small proportion of reaper adopters and a small proportion of the market for farm machinery. On the other hand, the responsiveness of farmers across the distribution of farms varies, and it was found that medium-sized family farms were the most responsive, followed by the small family farms and the large business farms. This is in the nature of the logit model, but the data fits the model. I take this as evidence consistent with the claim that the medium-sized family farms were the most responsive to their own changes in specialization, land in cultivation, and farm values by adopting the reaper.

Specialization in wheat was quantitatively the most important variable. The range of specialization was from 0.2 percent to 99 percent, with a mean

Table 5.19

Test 3 on Multicollinearity

	Special	IA	OWN	VOF
Special	1.00			
IA	0.20	1.00		
OWN	0.02	0.02	1.00	
VOF	0.10	0.67	0.06	1.00

Source: Fred Bateman and James D. Foust, *Agricultural and Demographic Records for Rural Households in the North, 1860* (Ann Arbor, MI: Inter-University Consortium for Political and Social Research, 1976).

value of 42 percent. The predicted probability of adopting the reaper ranged from 0.1 percent to 99 percent, with a mean value of 3 percent. This result puts the various theories in perspective because if the American Northeast had not been industrializing and increasing its demand for food, farmers would not have increased their wheat production. If farmers had not increased their wheat production they would not have mechanized and this is true for all the theories. My argument is that many countries have industrialized and their agricultural systems have not responded to market signals by producing food for this market. The family farm thesis is that the system of many medium-sized family farms was a responsive agricultural system made up of risk-averse utility maximizers that wanted to finance the ownership of their farms and also to increase the level of family consumption above food self-sufficiency provided on the farm. David and Fleisig assume that the farm economy is responsive and made up of profit maximizers, who when faced with a rising price of labor with respect to the price of capital, adopted the reaper and/or who when faced with a labor constraint, mechanized.

More important in interpretation and discriminating between the theories is the variable of the number of improved acres on the farm. It tells not only size but kind of farm, assuming that size is related to how much land is needed to support a family and how much land a family can operate. If we take the 35-improved-acre farm as a small family farm, the 55- to 165-improved-acre farm as a medium-sized family farm, and a 300-acre farm as a large business farm, then we can argue that the most response farm was the medium-sized family farm. This is judged by fact that the slope and elasticity of all three variables, improved acres, specialization, and value of the farm, were greatest for the medium-sized family farm. This variable can be interpreted as explaining the location of the adoption of the reaper. We might argue that it occurred in the Old Northwest because it was made up of medium-sized family farms. It did not occur in the American South because large slave farms were predominant, with small family farms second in importance. The adoption of the reaper occurred in the United States because of the medium-sized family farm system there. It did not occur in France because of the small family farm system. In time the reaper was adopted in Britain which had a system of large farms that purchased labor in the market. Since this kind of agricultural system did not exist in the United States, we can say that a cause, or initial condition, of reaper adoption was the responsive medium-sized family farm system there.

The value of the farm was part of the causal mechanism of reaper adoption for various reasons. It was risky for the family farmer to purchase capital in the market, and as land values rose and as he developed his farm, he became more wealthy. This reduced the risk relative to his assets. This variable can also be interpreted as representing initial resource endowment.

The fact that ownership was a significant variable is support for the view that land tenure and holding is an importance aspect of an agricultural system. The possibility of owning a farm gave the risk-averse utility-maximizing farmer the incentive to produce for the market and to mechanize when he needed to produce more than the capacity of the labor force of his farm family. As an owner operator he was in charge of output, input, and investment decisions and was in control of the surplus obtained from producing for the market. His surplus did not go to rent. Also it did not go to taxes as was the case in many European countries.

The results can be interpreted to explain the timing of the adoption of the reaper, if we infer from this cross-section analysis to change over time. From 1850 to 1860, the farmers of the Old Northwest increased their specialization in wheat, increased their acreage in cultivation through farm-making, and the value of their farms rose, due to farm-making and the increase in land values. Increasing specialization brought the family farmer up to the physical limit of wheat harvesting and the profit maximizers up to the threshold of profitability in reaper adoption. The rise in improved acres per farm is similarly a cause of the timing of the adoption of the reaper; the more improved acres, the more wheat that could be grown. The rise in farms' values caused the adoption of reaper by raising the wealth of farmers and reducing the relative risk.

To illustrate this point, consider the farm at the 90th percentile. Assume that this farm in 1860 represents the condition of another farm in 1850. Table 5.20 shows the characteristics of this farm and the changes in it over time. It was worth $5500, was 0.75 specialized, and had 130 improved acres. It had a 31 percent chance of adopting the reaper. The growth rates in the Old Northwest for the 1850s were an increase of 62 percent in the value of the mean farm, 26 percent in the degree of specialization of the mean farm, and 13 percent in the value of the mean farm. If we assume that the above specified farm grew at these rates over the 1850s, the resulting new farm would be worth $8,910, be 0.95 specialized, and have 147 improved acres. Using the elasticities obtained in the logit model, each of the changes alone would increase the probability of reaper adoption to 78, 83, and 43 respectively and ceteris paribus. This is in comparison with a probability of 31 percent in 1850.

This analysis gives a different quantitative evaluation of the explanatory variables. While the elasticity of response is stronger for improved acres, 0.891, than for the value of the farm, 0.762, in fact, the growth rate of the value of farms in this period is so great that it had a greater impact on increasing the probability of adopting the reaper, to 78 percent, than the increase in improved acreage, to 43 percent. The increase in improved acres led the medium-sized family farm up against its capacity to operate the farm, but it still had the problem of risk. Risk was diminished by the increasing value of the farm.

Table 5.20
The Timing of Reaper Adoption

	1850 Farm	1850s Growth Rates	1860 Farm	Elasticities	New Probabilities (ceteris paribus)
VOF	$5500	62	$8910	0.762	0.78
SPECIAL	0.75	26	0.95	1.990	0.83
IA	130	13	147	0.891	0.43

Source: Fred Bateman and James D. Foust, *Agricultural and Demographic Records for Rural Households in the North, 1860* (Ann Arbor, MI: Inter-University Consortium for Political and Social Research, 1976) and the *Printed Census, 1850 and 1860*.

Note: Original probability of reaper adoption was 31 percent. All values and elasticities are given for the farm at the 90th percentile of all wheat farms.

In conclusion, the results of the farm model support my definition of the family farm and the idea that there is a small family farm that behaves differently than the medium-sized family farm and differently than a large business farm.

Township Results Interpreted

Specialization, again, is quantitatively the most important variable. The range of specialization in the townships was from zero to 93 percent, with a mean value of 37 percent. The range of predicted probabilities was from zero to 14 percent, with a mean value of 3 percent. I interpret this township result in the same way as the farm result on specialization. That is to say, that without the American Northeast industrializing, there would have been no reaper adoption.

The ratio of farm employees per farm operator in a township had no effect on the rate of reaper adoption in the econometric model. The range was from 0.07 to 2.27, with a mean value of 0.65. The mode was 0.1. This suggests that Fleisig was incorrect and that Hypothesis 2 is correct. That is to say, family farmers adopted the reaper because they wanted to produce more wheat than could be cut by the family and because they preferred not to hire labor, not because that labor was scarce and expensive.

We found that townships with more small farms were less likely to adopt the reaper. The range of small farms in a township was from zero to 49 percent, with a mean value of 16.8 percent. If we infer from this township analysis to a regional or country basis, we could argue that a region or country that is made up of many small farms will not be likely to adopt the reaper, mechanize, or form capital with new farm technology. This is because there is less likelihood of a surplus on small farms and many small farms are not a wide market for industrially produced farm machinery.

The degree of land concentration in a township had no effect on the rate of reaper adoption. The range was from 26 to 86 percent of land operated by the top 10 percent of farms, with a mean value of 37 percent. Again if infer from the township analysis to regions or countries, we could argue that it is not necessary to have unequal income distribution, wealth distribution, and/or land distribution, as long as there is a reasonable surplus in the farm economy, for that economy to develop production and productivity. Conversely, given a potential surplus in the system, a relatively equal distribution of land is favorable to agricultural improvements via the provision of a potential wide market for industrially produced farm machinery. These two sets of results support Hypothesis 4.

CONCLUSION

The major conclusion of this chapter is that agricultural institutions were important in causing the adoption of the reaper.

The results of the farm model suggest that medium-sized commercial family farms were more responsive to changes than were small family farms and large business farms. I take this as partial confirming evidence for Hypothesis 1: Risk-averse utility-maximizing family farmers rationally adopted the reaper in the 1850s at a scale of production below the threshold at which profit maximizing would have dictated the adoption of the reaper. Also in the farm model, the agricultural institutional variable of ownership was statistically significant and quantitatively important. I take this as indirect evidence for Hypothesis 3: The institutional structure of the family farm system was a favorable initial condition for the adoption of farm machinery because it made ownership possible for many farmers through the purchase of land.

In the township model, the labor available variable was found to be not statistically significant. This supports Hypothesis 2: Risk-averse utility-maximizing family farmers rationally adopted the reaper in the 1850s when they wanted to produce more wheat than the family would harvest. Also in the township model, the agricultural institutional variable of land equality was statistically significant, negative, and quantitatively important. I take this as indirect partial evidence for Hypothesis 4: The institutional structure of the family farm system was a favorable initial condition for the adoption of farm machinery because it was based on a relatively equal distribution of abundant land which generated many farmers with a sufficient surplus and incentive to purchase capital goods.

In the concluding chapter, evidence and arguments from Chapters 2 through 5 are integrated to determine how well David's model, Fleisig's model, and the family farm model held up to testing.

NOTES

1. Robert S. Pindyck and Daniel L. Rubinfeld, "Models of Qualitative Choice," in *Econometric Models, Economic Forecasts* (New York: McGraw Hill, 1981), p. 274.

2. Ibid., p. 274.

3. Ibid., p. 275.

4. Ibid., p. 275.

5. Ibid., p. 277.

6. Ibid., p. 280.

7. Ibid., p. 281.

8. This is a potential weakness of my analysis, that of measurement error. Normally observations on the dependent variable are used. In my case I had to infer reaper adoption.

9. Pindyck and Rubinfeld, "Models of Qualitative Choice," p. 281.

10. Ibid., p. 287.

11. Ibid., p. 287.

12. Ibid., p. 289.

13. Ibid., p. 289.

14. See for example, Subodh C. Mathur, "Econometric Methods and Applications" (manuscript, Washington, D.C., November 1984, to locate contact this author or Dr. Mathur at the World Bank), chapter on "Formulation of Econometric Models," section on disturbance terms.

15. Ibid., p. 276.

16. Efficiency is a property of an estimator concerned with the distances of the values of an estimator from the value of the parameter. In a sampling distribution, it is desirable to have the smallest variance possible. See for example, Jan Kmenta, *Elements of Econometrics* (New York: Macmillan, 1971), p. 12.

17. Pindyck and Rubinfeld, "Models of Qualitative Choice," pp. 276-77.

18. Ibid., p. 293.

19. William Parker, "Agriculture," in Lance Davis et al. (Eds.), *American Economic Growth* (New York: Harper and Row, 1972), p. 369.

20. See Carroll D. Wright, *The History and Growth of the U.S. Census* (Washington, D.C.: Government Printing Office, 1900).

21. *Manuscript Census, 1840*, Carroll County, Ohio. National Archives, Washington, D.C.

22. Southern sample taken by Robert E. Gallman and William Parker, with direct responsibility in selecting the sample by Nancy Shriner. Northern sample taken by Fred Bateman and James D. Foust, and put on computer tape by Jeremy Atack. See Fred Bateman and James D. Foust, "A Sample of Rural Households Selected From the 1860 Manuscript Censuses," *Agricultural History* 48, 1 (1974): 75-93.

23. Bateman and Foust, "A Sample," p. 92.

24. Written correspondence with Jeremy Atack, May 5, 1983.

25. Written correspondence with Jeremy Atack, May 5, 1983.

26. Written correspondence, Jeremy Atack, May 5, 1983 and Fred Bateman, June 23, 1983.

27. Written correspondence with Jeremy Atack, May 5, 1983.

28. Pindyck and Rubinfeld, "Models of Qualitative Choice," pp. 279-28.

6
CONCLUSION

The empirical evidence presented in Chapters 2 through 5 support the general thesis of the book:

Family farm agricultural institutions were a favorable initial condition for the adoption of farm machinery in the American Midwest in the nineteenth century because they were based on a relatively equal distribution of abundant land which generated many farmers with sufficient surplus and incentive to purchase capital goods. Without the farm machinery the food needs of U.S. industrialization probably would not have been met. But without the family farm system, the mass production of that machinery probably would not have been taken on. Agricultural institutions were crucial in the tremendous agricultural expansion and concurrent industrialization of the United States in the nineteenth century.

By family farm agricultural institutions, I mean a system of medium-sized family farms where there was enough land to support the family but not more than could be worked by the labor force of the farm family. The basis of this system was the fact of relative abundance of agricultural resources (land relative to population) and the federal policy of a relatively egalitarian distribution of that land. It was the medium-sized family farm, not the small family farm, that had the surplus sufficient to purchase capital goods. Farmers on both sizes of family farms had the incentive to own their own farm, but the incentive to own a medium-sized family farm (a more ambitious goal) led to the purchase of capital goods.

The family with the medium-sized family farm was engaged in general farming, that is, they had not specialized in a cash crop. Moreover, in the 1850s, this family was engaged in farm-making. Once their farm-making was complete and once the market was signaling them to specialize in wheat, the medium-sized family farm could no longer harvest—with its own labor—the amount of wheat that they wanted to sell in the market. They wanted to take advantage of the opportunity to produce for the market in order to speed up and complete the financing of their mortgaged farm. They preferred not to hire wage labor and thus, when farm machinery came on the market, they adopted it.

In the first section of this final chapter, I draw together the evidence presented in Chapters 2 through 5 as they support the family farm thesis in the form of the four hypotheses on the relationship between farm machinery adoption and the family farm system. In the second section, I present a political economy of the family farm system as it existed in the American Midwest in the mid-nineteenth century, its connections with the American Northeast, and its contrast with the American South. I conclude with some policy implications for the Third World today.

EVIDENCE FOR THE FOUR HYPOTHESES

In the 1850s in the Old Northwest farmers began to adopt the horse-drawn mechanical reaper. This was the beginning of the first American agricultural revolution in which a whole set of horse-drawn machinery would be adopted and then dramatically increase the productivity of labor in grain production. Four hypotheses were tested on an Old Northwest subset of the Bateman-Foust sample of manuscript censuses of 1860.

There are three reasons to retain Hypothesis 1: Risk-averse utility-maximizing family farmers rationally adopted the reaper at a scale of production below the threshold at which profit maximization would have dictated adoption. (1) In Chapter 2, we found that most of the farmers who adopted the reaper were producing at less than 78 acres of wheat, the level at which profit maximizing would have dictated adoption. They were precocious. This is a reason to reject David's explanation of reaper adoption. (2) In Chapter 4, we found that among the farmers who adopted the reaper, the dominant proportion of the wheat output was produced by medium-sized family farms, not the large business farms. The medium-sized family farm is the risk-averse utility maximizer and the large business farm is the profit maximizer. The former were the food producers for U.S. industrialization. (3) In Chapter 5, we found that farms in the medium-sized family farm range were more responsive than large business farms to increases in farm size, farm value, and degree of specialization, in that these changes led to a greater increase in the probability of reaper adoption. They were responsive.

There are two reasons to retain Hypothesis 2: Risk-averse utility-maximizing family farmers rationally adopted the reaper at a scale of production above the threshold at which the family could no longer harvest the crop by hand with their own labor. This hypothesis should be retained because the only plausible alternative hypothesis was found lacking: (1) In Chapter 3, we found that there was no statistically significant linear correlation between the labor available in a township and reaper adoption rates. Furthermore, labor available in a township was not associated with other economic behaviors of the family farm system: wheat output per farm, capital per farm, or land per farm. We also found that, in this farm system in the Old Northwest in the 1850s, most of the labor on the farm was provided by the farm operator. A family farm is a "one-man farm." This is one reason to reject Fleisig's labor-constraint explanation of northern mechanization. (2) In Chapter 5, we found that the labor available in a township was not a significant variable in the econometric model of reaper adoption. This is a second reason to reject Fleisig's model.

My strongest result provides a persuasive reason to retain Hypothesis 3: The institutional structure of the family farm system was a favorable initial condition for the adoption of farm machinery because it made farm ownership possible for many farmers. (1) In Chapter 5, we found that the probability of reaper adoption was substantially increased when the farmer owned the farm that he operated. Moreover, the significance of ownership was greater for the medium-sized family farms than for small family farms or large business farms. The farmers increased their production for the market to earn cash to pay off the mortgages on their farms.

There are four reasons to retain Hypothesis 4: The institutional structure of the family farm system was a favorable initial condition for the adoption of farm machinery because it was based on a relatively equal distribution of abundant land which generated many farmers with a sufficient surplus and an incentive to purchase capital goods. (1) In Chapter 3, we found that townships with a high proportion of medium-sized family farms (our proxy for moderately equal land distribution) were townships with high capital per farm. (2) In Chapter 4, we found that among farmers who had adopted the reaper, most of the farm implements and machinery were held by medium-sized family farms, not large business farms. (3) In Chapter 5, we found that townships with large degrees of land concentration were not the townships with high rates of reaper adoption. (4) Also in Chapter 5, we found that townships with high proportions of small family farms (our proxy for extreme land equality) were townships with low rates of reaper adoption. With all these reasons to retain the four hypotheses, I believe that the family farm thesis should be retained as a crucial part of the explanation of reaper adoption.

A BRIEF POLITICAL ECONOMY OF THE FAMILY FARM SYSTEM AND THE AMERICAN ROAD TO CAPITALISM

The structure of family farm agricultural institutions in the Old Northwest in 1860 can be specified by three major traits: (1) how the land was held: as private property, (2) how its abundance was distributed: relatively equally, and (3) what kind of labor system resulted: family labor, not slave labor or wage labor. These traits are related to the following aspects of the family farm system's economic behavior: (1) the production of food for the industrializing American Northeast, (2) the purchase of industrially produced capital goods, and (3) the adoption of the reaper, the first step in the industrialization of agriculture. This was a crucial aspect of the American road to capitalism.

Private Property

I estimate that four in five farms were held in freehold tenure.[1] This form of unencumbered ownership gave the family control over their resources, the choice of output, and the method of production. The desire to own land is related to the republican belief that one can assure one's own liberty by obtaining ownership of productive property, here land. This idea was given classical expression by John Locke in his *Second Treatise on Government*. Locke claimed that people had a natural right to property based on the mixing of their own labor with the land. This right was qualified by two conditions: (1) there must be enough land for others and this land must be of the same quality; and (2) people must not take more land than they can use without waste, that is, that they can productively use. In nineteenth-century Ohio, there was an attempt to limit the size of land-holdings to 160 acres, the amount that a family could work. It is probably not possible to justify land ownership this way today: but in the nineteenth century in the northern United States, I believe that a plausible case could be made that the family farmers did have a natural right to their farms, in Locke's terms.[2]

Ownership was obtained by purchase of public domain land from the federal government. Land markets in the United States were highly developed by world-historical standards; family-scale landholdings were available on the market, unlike land markets in the countries where only very large holdings were available, such as England. The desire to own land and the need to purchase land drove family farmers into production for the market. Financial capital from the American Northeast (and from Britain) flowed into mortgage companies to allow farmers to purchase land on credit.[3] Thus, a leading feature of family farm agricultural institutions is family scale of ownership. This trait translated into many farmers with sufficient incentive to buy capital goods.

Relatively Equal Income Distribution

Egalitarian federal land policy, among other influences, caused moderate equality of land distribution and thus a farm system of many, medium-sized family farms. Income distribution at this time and in this place was largely determined by land distribution. The predominant land-holders in the farm economy held medium-sized farms, defined as more land than they needed to support the family but not more than could be worked by the family, that is, between 41 to 160 acres. Fifty percent of the farms in the Old Northwest in 1860 were in this medium-sized family farm range and these farmers operated 62 percent of the improved land. Only 5 percent of all farms were large business farms (over 160 acres) and they operated 20 percent of the land. Forty-six percent of the farms were small family farms or smaller (40 acres or less) and they operated 18 percent of the land in cultivation.[4] Thus a second leading trait of family farm agricultural institutions was family scale of production. Egalitarian federal land policy, given the relative abundance of agricultural resources, generated a system of farms in which families were producing a marketable surplus sufficient to purchase capital goods.[5] The reverse case has been made to explain why the southern region of the United States did not develop in the nineteenth century. There the income distribution was so unequal that no domestic markets could develop.[6]

Family Labor System

On average, there were 1.46 farm workers per farm in the Old Northwest in 1860. One worker on the farm was the farm operator and head of the farm household. The remaining 0.46 worker per farm was accounted for by an unpaid son, a paid son of a neighbor, or a young farmer in need of off-farm income. Eleven percent of farms in the Old Northwest in 1860 were 40 acres or less, measured in total acres that include improved and unimproved land. These farm households may have allocated family labor to wage employment off their own farms because they did not have enough land to support the family. Nineteen percent of farms in the Old Northwest in 1860 were larger than 160 total acres. If a family can operate 160 total acres when engaged in general farming and in the farm-making stage, then the demand for hired labor probably came from farms larger than 160 total acres. Thus we can see that there was only a small supply of hired wage labor available, but also that there was only a small demand for hired wage labor. The predominant kind of labor system was the family labor system, which accounted for at least 71 percent of the labor on the farms. Thus a third leading trait of family farm agricultural institutions was the family labor system. Labor per farm was not determined by market forces alone. It was determined, in large part, by the institutional structure of the family farm system. This trait was a cause of the pressure to adopt the reaper before the farm had reached a scale beyond which profit maximization would have dictated reaper adoption.

Recall that at this time in the southern United States there was slave labor agriculture. Also at this time, in the North, both in the Northeast and the (Old) Northwest, the process of industrialization was causing the development of a wage-labor system. The family farms were in a transition. Prior to the economic opportunities of the nineteenth century, family farms were unwilling to bid for wage labor.[7] Historians made no mistakes about the nature of these family farms.[8] But in the nineteenth century, these farms increasingly participated in markets and economists were tempted to analyze them as profit-maximizing firms. This is inappropriate, not because they did not *sell* their entire product in the market, but because they did not *buy* labor in the market. They had to buy land in the market. And they came to buy capital in the market. But even to this day, most U.S. farms do not use wage labor to produce the U.S. food supply.

Agrarian Structure and Economic Development

The above described three traits of the family farm agricultural institutions—family scale of ownership, family scale of production, and family labor—constitute the agrarian structure of the Old Northwest in the mid-nineteenth century. Mogens Boserup has argued that agrarian structure either helps or hinders the take-off into modern economic growth.[9] As discussed in detail in the introductory essay, Robert Brenner has argued that agrarian class structures explain how and why Western Europe pulled ahead of Eastern Europe in the fourteenth century and how and why England pulled ahead of France in the seventeenth century.[10] Jones and Woolf have addressed the historical problems of agrarian change and economic development in Europe.[11] Johnston and Mellor have discussed the role of agriculture in the development of Third World countries today.[12] Parker has written of the role of agriculture in American economic development.[13] This role has three major aspects: the provision of food for industrial labor, the provision of a market for industrially produced consumer and producer goods, and the release of labor. We turn now to a more detailed discussion of these aspects of the relationship of the agrarian structure of the Old Northwest to the industrializing United States.

Production of Food for Industrialization

When economies industrialize, people move from the countryside, where they produced their own food, to the towns and cities where they must purchase food. In the United States, the food was supplied by medium-sized commercial family farms using family labor. This contrasts with Britain where food for industrialization was provided by large business farms, rented by capitalist tenants who relied exclusively on a permanent, year-round, hired labor force.[14] The evidence suggests that the American system was at least as good as the British in providing food for industrialization, with the U.S. system providing cheaper food. Eighty-five percent of the mechanically harvested wheat in the Old Northwest in 1860 was produced by medium-sized family farms and only 15 percent by farmers producing above the estimated profit-maximizing scale. At least 68 percent of the labor time devoted to producing the marketed food output for the North as of 1860 was of family labor. Family labor was capable of supplying the food needed for industrialization. Townships with proportionally more medium-sized family farms produced higher outputs of wheat per farm.

Market for Industrially Produced Capital Goods

Consider now the market for capital goods provided by the family farm system.[15] By 1860, there were over a half a million farms in the Old Northwest. The number of farms had grown 53 percent over the boom decade of the 1850s as more easterners and Europeans immigrated. I estimate that 50 percent of these farms—a quarter of a million—were medium-sized commercial family farms. This was the potential mass market for farm machinery.[16] The actual market in 1860 was comprised of the roughly 26,000 medium-sized commercial family farms that purchased a reaper. By comparison about 1,500 large business farms purchased reapers. This suggests that the family farm system was a wide and growing potential market for farm machinery.

Moreover, of the $85,000 worth of capital goods (the total value of the capital goods owned by reaper adopters in my sample), only $14,000 (16 percent) was on farms that were producing above the estimated profit-max-imizing scale and roughly $72,000 (84 percent) was on farms that were producing below the estimated profit-maximizing scale. The predominant capital goods purchasers were medium-sized family farms, not large business firms.

Other evidence suggests that the family labor constraint did not prevent medium-sized family farms from using an absolutely large quantity of capital goods, that is, even they were able to capture economies of scale. Townships with proportionally more medium-sized family farms purchased more capital goods per farm.

The market for capital goods provided by the family farm system was, in part, the cause of the mass production of farm machinery. Mass production of farm machinery meant an abundant supply of machinery at reasonable prices that led to a large demand for farm machinery. Without the farm machinery, the food needs of industrialization probably would not have been met. But without the family farm system, the mass production of farm machinery probably would not have been taken on. Without the relatively equal distribution of abundant resources to families, the medium-sized commercial family farm system probably would not have existed. It is in this sense that the family farm was a cause of American industrialization.

The American Road to Capitalism

The family farm system purchased capital goods even though they did not hire wage labor. Agriculture was industrialized for the first time in world history in the Old Northwest region of the United States. But the agricultural system there was not capitalist agriculture. This is a distinctive feature of the American road to capitalism. It began with and was aided by a non-capitalist form of agriculture. The British road to capitalism actually began with capitalist agriculture in the seventeenth century. The French peasant system of agriculture was a hindrance to economic development. The slave labor system in the antebellum South and sharecropping in the postbellum South both held back southern development. Taiwan and South Korea have family farms and they have developed broadly, economically, if not politically. The Soviet Union is held back even today by its agrarian structure, the collective farms set up in the late 1920s. The United States, with its medium-sized commercial family farm system, has the most productive agriculture in the world today.

POLICY IMPLICATIONS FOR THE THIRD WORLD

Turning now to present problems of Third World developing countries, my findings suggest ways in which agricultural policy could be designed to encourage the development of agricultural institutions that are responsive and favorable to the spread of markets and agricultural improvement. Most importantly, my study suggests that large scale farming based on hired labor and profit maximization are not necessary for development, and that the medium-sized family farming would be preferable due to its responsiveness and proven productivity.[17] Obviously, many Third World countries do not have the abundant agricultural resources that the United States had in the nineteenth century, but this need not preclude the adoption of some form of family farm system. If there was not an abundance of good agricultural land, a limited number of families could be selected (even by lottery) to operate the number of medium-sized family farms that could be created on the given supply of good land. The idea is not that every family should have a medium-sized farm, but that the farms should be medium-sized family farms. This insures a large set of farmers with sufficient surplus and incentive to purchase the capital goods needed for the agricultural improvements for development. It is the responsiveness of the family farm that is its key asset.[18]

For example, compare the Philippines to Taiwan. Taiwan had land reform resulting in large numbers of medium-sized family farms and is developing rapidly. In the Philippines, by contrast, land ownership is highly concentrated, resulting in large estates and servile labor. Development in the Philippines has been slow, if not negative, in the recent world economic conditions. With the new democratically elected government, there is some hope, but progress on land reform is quite slow.

Another example is the case of sub-Saharan Africa. Early on, after independence, many African countries set up marketing boards. Essentially what they did was to buy food from African family farmers at low prices and deliver it to the cities. There, government policies subsidized the cost of food. The surplus was taken from farmers and used to subsidize urban development. It has not worked. The standard of living in Africa is lower than it was 20 years ago and there is more inequality in income distribution. Only now is it realized, by some, that without rural and agricultural development, there is not much development at all. Marketing boards are being dismantled now in some African countries and the African family farmers are receiving much higher prices for their food crops. This should help with the development effort.

In Central America, economic development is at a low level and not increasing much. However, the one country in this region that is doing better than the others is the one with a family farm system, Costa Rica.[19]

Is it necessary that income distribution worsens before it gets better in the course of modern economic growth? Brazil has grown rapidly and has worsened its income distribution. Other countries such as Sri Lanka have grown some and have improved their income distribution. Explicit policies for income distribution can prevent the worsening of income distribution in the course of development. The case of the Old Northwest region of the United States demonstrates that relatively equal income distributions are beneficial to economic development.

In conclusion, we have found that neoclassical economics of the profit-maximizing firm is not capable of explaining the behavior of family farmers in the Old Northwest in the 1850s when they were the first popular adopters of the horse-drawn mechanical reaper. It is more appropriate to treat the family farm as a utility-maximizing household concerned with the benefits of farm ownership more than with maximizing the level of consumption.

Given a relative abundance of agricultural resources, a policy of relative egalitarian distribution of that land is beneficial for economic development via industrialization in the nineteenth century. Not only did federal land policy work in setting up a relatively egalitarian society, this was supportive of modern economic growth.

NOTES

1. Using the Bateman-Foust sample, I compared the value of the farm in the agricultural census with the value of real estate owned by the head of the household in the demographic census to infer ownership. Jonathan Hughes, *The Governmental Habit: Economic Controls from Colonial Times to the Present* (New York: Basic Books, 1977). See pp. 20-21, 51-53 on the Northwest Ordinances which established the form of tenure. See pp. 15-18 and 165-66 on land tenure in fee simple, and see pp. 13-14, and 18-19 for land tenure in free and common socage.

2. John Locke, *Two Treatises of Government* (London: Dent, 1975). See also Gary Comstock (Ed.), *Is There A Moral Obligation to Save the Family Farm?* (Ames: Iowa State University Press, 1987).

3. Jane Knodell, "Innovation and Integration in Interregional Finance: The Old Northwest, 1810-1845," San Francisco, paper presented at annual meeting of the Economic History Association, September 17-20, 1987.

4. Normally we would be concerned about the potential poverty of those families with less than enough land to support themselves. But in this case of abundance, relatively equally distributed, the families that reported less than 40 acres of improved land were, in fact, families with more land, although much of it unimproved. Thus in time they would report enough acres of land to support themselves.

5. On the role of income distribution and economic development, see Gary Fields, *Poverty, Inequality, and Development* (New York: Cambridge University Press, 1980); Irma Adelman and Sherman Robinson, *Income Distribution Policy in Developing Countries: A Case Study of Korea* (Stanford: Stanford University Press, 1978); John C. H. Fei, Gustav Ranis, and Shirley W. Y. Kuo, *Growth with Equity: The Taiwan Case* (New York: Oxford University Press, 1979). On economic equality, see Amartya Sen, *On Economic Inequality* (Oxford: Oxford University Press, 1973).

6. For institutional analyses of the southern region of the U.S., see Eugene D. Genovese, *The Political Economy of Slavery: Studies on the Economy and Society of the Slave South* (New York: Random House, 1965); Fred Bateman and Thomas Weiss, *A Deplorable Scarcity* (Chapel Hill: University of North Carolina Press, 1981); Roger Ransom and Richard Sutch, *One Kind of Freedom: The Economic Consequences of Emancipation* (New York: Cambridge University Press, 1977); Gavin Wright, *The Political Economy of the Cotton South: Households, Markets, and Wealth in the Nineteenth Century* (New York: W. W. Norton, 1978); and Gavin Wright, *Old*

South, New South: Revolutions in the Southern Economy Since the Civil War (New York: Basic Books, 1986).

7. See James Henretta, "Families and Farms: Mentalité in Pre-industrial America," *William and Mary Quarterly* 35, 3rd series (1978):3-32, on the unwillingness of family farmers to bid for wage labor.

8. For what family farming was like in the colonial period before the economic opportunities of the nineteenth century, see John J. McCusker and Russell R. Menard, *The Economy of British America, 1607-1789* (Chapel Hill: University of North Carolina Press, 1985).

9. Mogens Boserup, "Agrarian Structure and Take-Off," in W. W. Rostow (Ed.), *The Economics of Take-Off into Sustained Growth* (London: Macmillan, 1963).

10. Robert Brenner, "Agrarian Class Structure and Economic Development in Pre-Industrial Europe," *Past and Present* 1976.

11. E. L. Jones and S. J. Woolf (Eds.), *Agrarian Change and Economic Development: The Historical Problems* (London: Methuen, 1969).

12. Bruce F. Johnston and John W. Mellor, "The Role of Agriculture in Economic Development," *American Economic Review* 1961.

13. William Parker, "Agriculture," in Lance Davis et al. (Eds.), *American Economic Growth* (New York: Harper and Row, 1972).

14. For institutional analyses of European economic development, see T. H. Aston and C. H. E. Philpin (Eds.), *The Brenner Debate: Agrarian Class Structure and Economic Development in Pre-Industrial Europe* (New York: Cambridge University Press, 1985) and John W. Shaffer, *Family and Farm: Agrarian Change and Household Organization in the Loire Valley, 1500-1900* (Albany: State University of New York Press, 1982); Maurice Dobb, *Studies in the Development of Capitalism* (London: Routledge and Kegan Paul, 1963); Rodney Hilton (Ed.), *The Transition from Feudalism to Capitalism* (London: New Left Books, 1978); John Weeks, *Capital and Exploitation* (Princeton: Princeton University Press, 1981); and Aidan Foster-Carter, "The Modes of Production Controversy," *New Left Review* 107 (January/February 1978). For an institutional analysis of American economic development, see Charles Post, "The American Road to Capitalism," *New Left Review* 133 (May/June 1982) and Kevin D. Kelly, "The Independent Mode of Production," *Review of Radical Political Economy* 11 (Spring 1979).

15. On the importance of capital goods in the process of industrialization, see W. G. Hoffman, *The Growth of Industrial Economies* (New York: Oceana, 1958) and Karl Marx, *Capital*, 3 vols. (New York: International Publishers, 1975).

16. Nathan Rosenberg, *The American System of Manufacturing* (Edinburgh: University of Edinburgh Press, 1969).

17. On land reform see Subrata Ghatak and Ken Ingersent, *Agriculture and Economic Development* (Baltimore: Johns Hopkins University Press, 1984), pp. 217-51.

18. On the problems of nonresponsive agricultural institutions in the Third World today, see Inderjit Singh, Lyn Squire, and John Strauss (Eds.), *Agricultural Household Models* (Baltimore: Johns Hopkins University Press, 1986); W. Arthur Lewis, *The Evolution of the International Economic Order* (Princeton: Princeton University Press, 1978); Gerald M. Meier, *Emerging from Poverty: The Economics That Really Matters* (New York: Oxford University Press, 1984). On the problem of problematic agricultural institutions in the Soviet Union, see Paul R. Gregory and

Robert C. Stuart, *Soviet Economic Structure and Performance* (New York: Harper and Row, 1986).

19. John Weeks, *The Economies of Central America* (New York: Holmes and Meier, 1985).

APPENDIX A:
ESTIMATIONS OF THE EXTENT
OF REAPER ADOPTION

The objective of this appendix is to make estimates of the extent of the adoption of the reaper in the Old Northwest in 1859. First, I make a macro-estimate based on the production of reapers. In order to achieve this, a time series of reaper production is constructed. An estimate of the adoption of the reaper as of 1849 is made for comparison. Second, a micro-estimate of the extent of reaper adoption in 1859 is made based on the manuscript census sample, inferring individual adopters.

MACRO-ESTIMATE FOR HARVEST OF 1859

Leo Rogin estimated the proportion of the wheat harvested west of the Alleghenies in the late 1850s which was cut mechanically.[1] Paul David corrects certain errors that Rogin made.[2] There are certain corrections to be made on David's estimate, thus after surveying these two estimates, I offer my own estimate.

Rogin established the procedure of comparing the wheat actually harvested with how much wheat could have been harvested given the stock of reapers available. As to the wheat actually harvested, Rogin used the 1859 Census figure of 119 million bushels of wheat produced west of the Alleghenies (out of 173 million in the United States) in 1859. Converting bushels to acres, Rogin used a yield of 12 bushels of wheat per acre to transform western production to about 10 million acres. As to the amount of wheat that could have been cut mechanically, Rogin starts from a reaper stock of 73,200. Assuming that each reaper had a capacity of cutting ten acres a day and that the harvest season was ten working days, then the seasonal capacity of a mechanical reaper was 100 acres. Taking the product of the number of reapers and the capacity of each, one obtains 7.32 million acres of wheat that could have been cut by the reaper stock. This assumes that all reapers were used to full capacity. Comparing 7.32 million acres of wheat that could have been cut to the ten million acres that were actually cut regardless of the method used, one obtains about 70 percent of wheat harvested that was mechanically cut west of the Alleghenies.

David criticized Rogin for the use of the figure of 73,200 as the stock of reapers available in the late 1850s.[3] This figure refers to the number of reapers produced between 1845 and 1858, not the stock actually available in the late 1850s. Not all of these reapers would be available for use in 1858. David, working under the assumption that the useful life of the reaper was ten years, argued that to calculate the reapers available for the 1858 harvest, one must calculate the stock net of replacement. Any reaper produced prior to 1848 would not have been available for the 1858 harvest. This lowered the figure to 72,300 reapers. Further, David pointed out that we want the stock net of depreciation. David assumed continuous straight line decay of machines at 0.1 per annum. Also to make this calculation, it was necessary to assume that McCormick sales, of which we have records, was representative of all reaper sales in the time distribution of sales. This reduced the figure to 43,400 in 1858. However, this needed to be adjusted upward because the time distribution of McCormick production was less weighted toward the later half of the period 1848-58 than was the time distribution of aggregate reaper production in the country. On this basis, David estimated that in 1858 there were 50,000 full-capacity reapers in the United States.

A second problem with Rogin's use of this figure was that he assumed that all the reapers were used west of the Alleghenies. David corrected for this by calculating the proportion of the wheat production cut mechanically for the whole United States, not just for west of the Alleghenies. This change of focus required an adjustment of the yield which was lower for the whole United States, down to 11.4 bushels of wheat per acre. In 1859 American wheat production was 173 million bushels or 15 million acres. If there were 50,000 reapers with a capacity of 100 acres each,[4] then five million acres could have been cut mechanically, one-third of what was actually cut (five of 15 million acres).

David also calculates the western proportion, by admittedly falsely assuming all reapers available in the United States were used west of the Alleghenies. Using the net stock then, 50 percent of the western harvest could have been cut mechanically (five of ten million acres).

Four improvements will be made on David's estimate. First, I change the depreciation rate from 0.1 to 0.2., on the basis of Olmstead's criticism (see first section of Chapter 2). The useful life of the reaper in the 1850s was five years, not ten as David had used. This effects the gross stock and the stock net of depreciation.

Second, wheat production is given by the census for the year of 1859, not for 1858 as in Rogin and David's calculation of the reaper stock. The figure for reaper production covered the period of 1845 to 1858, thus production of 1859 was ignored by David and Rogin. Thus, I shall estimate production of reapers in 1859. In addition there is the complication that the harvest is in late June or early July, and consequently only the first half of the year's production was available for that harvest. Likewise at the beginning of the time series relevant to the 1859 harvest, the production in the second half of the year after the harvest of 1854 would likewise be available. The production of these half-years will be added to the net stock.

Third, there is the problem of having aggregate reaper production data for the United States and not knowing its distribution. Rogin used western wheat and American reapers. David corrected this by using American wheat and American reapers. He also estimates western mechanization by assuming that all reapers were used in the West, an assumption which he admits is false. It is known from the historical record that a greater proportion of reapers were adopted in the West than in other parts of the country. In fact, the initial wave of adoption seems to have centered upon the states of the Old Northwest region. It is here that knowing the extent of the adoption of the reaper would be representative of the process. For that reason I calculate the extent of reaper adoption in the Old Northwest, which produced 46 percent (79.8/173 million bushels) of American wheat in the year 1859. To be conservative, I assume that 46 percent of the American reaper stock were used in this region. I assume that the reapers were distributed proportionately with the wheat across the United States.

Fourth, I will drop the assumption of full-capacity use. There are several reasons why this assumption biases the results. Wayne Rasmussen argues that the frequency of breakdowns of the machines in the 1850s were quantitatively so important that the aggregate capacity of the reaper stock would be lowered.[5] Clarence Danhof stated that "by 1857, ten thousand machines were claimed to be in use, enough, if properly distributed, to cut most of the wheat grown in the state [of Ohio]."[6] Parker also states that farm machinery was not used to full capacity.[7] I infer from this that the distribution of reapers was such that they were not used to full capacity. A more conservative assumption would be that a farmer would use his reaper at the threshold of profitability (78 acres, see Chapter 2 for this estimate) not the full capacity (100 acres).

To obtain a new estimate we need to calculate the net reaper stock in 1859. I shall proceed as follows: First I present the facts on reaper production as we have them from Rogin, still the definitive source although the monograph dates from 1931. These are presented in Table A.1. Notice that the page numbers in the table refer to pages in Rogin. Only one correction has been made in Rogin's numbers, the error pointed out by David, on the interpretation of the figure of 73,200. Second, I present the time series of reaper production that I constructed in Table A.2. I had to make nine assumptions to construct the time series and each assumption is coded as an uppercase letter in the time series table and explained below. Third, the time series is used to calculate anew the stock of reapers that was available in the United States in 1859. Fourth, I calculate the stock of reapers that was available in the Old Northwest in 1859.

These are the assumptions used to move from the known facts on reaper production in Table A.1 to the time series of American reaper production in Table A.2:

Assumption A. Rogin reports that by 1839, 45 Hussey reapers had been produced. We know Hussey produced one in 1833. To obtain production for each year between 1834 and 1839 I assume that the production was equally distributed over these five years. I had to assign the year 1839 nine reapers to remove fractional production per year.

Assumption B. A total of 300 New Yorkers were produced in 1849 and 1850. I assume that an equal number were produced in each of the two years.

Assumption C. Rogin reports that 358 Husseys were produced in the 1840s. I assume they were equally distributed in each year. To remove fractions, I assigned the last year of the decade 34 instead of 36 reapers.

Assumption D. The problem was to estimate McCormick production for the year 1850. Rogin claims that by the end of the harvest in 1850 that 4,500 McCormick reapers had been produced. I assume that this claim is compatible with the individual facts that Rogin records on McCormick production for each year in the 1840s. On that assumption, I merely summed the production in the 1840s and subtracted this total from the cumulative claim to obtain the production in the year 1850: (4500 - 3372 = 1128).

Assumption E. Same assumption as in D, except applied now to Hussey production. According to Rogin, by 1850, 500 Husseys had been sold. To obtain production for the year 1850 then, previous production was subtracted from this cumulative total: (500-403 = 97, where 403 is sum of 45 + 358).

Assumption F. Assuming equal distribution across a four-year period allows us to transform the claim that between 1851 and 1854 1,100 Husseys were produced into a yearly series of 275 reapers a year for four years.

Assumption G. Equal distribution is assumed again for the 4,600 McCormick reapers that Rogin reported to have been produced in the 1851-54 period, yielding 1,150 a year. This assumption is confirmed by

Table A.1
Known Facts on Reaper Production in the United States

Date	No.	Kind	Page	Where produced
1833	1	Hussey	73	
By 1839	45	Hussey	73	
1840	2	McCormick	74	Virginia
1842	6	McCormick	74	Virginia
1843	39	McCormick	74	Virginia
1844	50	McCormick	74	Virginia
1845	50	McCormick		Virginia
	150	McCormick	74	Ohio
1846	75	McCormick		Virginia
	200	McCormick	75	New York
1847	500	McCormick	75	Chicago
1848	500	McCormick	75	Chicago
	300	McCormick	75	Illinois
				Ohio
				New York
1849	1,500	McCormick		Chicago
1849-				
1850	300	New Yorker	77	New York
1840s	358	Hussey		
By end				
harvest				
1850	4,500	McCormick		
By 1850	500	Hussey		
1851-				
1854	4,600	McCormick	76	
	1,100	Hussey	76	
1851	500	New Yorker	77	
1854	1,100	Manny	77	Illinois
1855	2,500	McCormick	78	
	2,500	Manny	78	
	1,200	Atkins	78	
	2,500	reapers		New York
	2,500	reapers		Ohio
By 1855	12,000	McCormick	78	
1845-				
1858	73,200	reapers	78	

Source: Leo Rogin, *Introduction of Farm Machinery* (Berkeley: University of California Press, 1931), except for 1845-58 figure, which is from Paul David, "Mechanization."

Note: Page refers to page in Rogin.

Table A.2
Time Series of American Reaper Production

Year	Hussey	McCormick	New Yorker	Manny	Atkins	Non-McCormick	Total
1833	1						1
1834	A7						7
1835	7						7
1836	7						7
1837	7						7
1838	7						7
1839	9						9
1840	C36	2					38
1841	36						36
1842	36	6					42
1843	36	39					75
1844	36	50					86
1845	36	200					236
1846	36	275					311
1847	36	500					536
1848	36	800					836
1849	34	1,500	B150				1,684
1850	E97	D1,128	B150				1,375
1851	F275	G1,150	500				1,925
1852	275	1,150					1,425
1853	275	1,150					1,425
1854	275	1,150		1,100			2,525
1855		2,500		2,500	1,200	5,000	11,200
1856		H3,932				I12,642	16,574
1857		3,932				12,642	16,574
1858		3,932				12,642	16,574
1859		3,932				12,642	16,574
Total	1,600	2,732	800	3,600	1,200	55,568	90,096

Source: Based on Rogin, 1931. See Appendix A for how facts from Rogin were used to construct this time series.

another fact, that by 1855 12,000 McCormick reapers had been sold. In the time series constructed up to this point, I obtain a cumulative production of McCormicks of 11,600 which must have been rounded off to 12,000 for the statement of this fact.

Assumption H. Three assumptions are made here in order to obtain yearly production of McCormick reapers for the years 1855 through 1859. First, we must assume that the cumulative claims are consistent with the individual facts reported. We have the figure, accepted by the Supreme Court of the United States, that between 1845 and 1858 23,299 McCormick reapers were produced. In the time series so far, my cumulative count is 11,503 McCormick reapers from 1845 up to 1855 (23,299 - 11,503 = 11,796). If we assume that production was equally distributed over the three-year period (1856, 1857, and 1858), then we estimate that each year's production was 3,932. The third assumption is required to obtain a figure for the year 1859, and we merely assume that production of that year was similar to the three previous years, and assign it 3,932 reapers.

Assumption I. Here we want a time series 1856 through 1859 for non-McCormick reaper production. We have the Supreme Court accepted figure of 73,200 reapers produced between 1845 and 1858, of which 49,901 were not McCormicks. To obtain the production of non-McCormick reapers, we must assume that this global claim is consistent with the individual facts we have. Then we sum up the production of all non-- McCormick reaper production from 1845 to 1855, from the time series as constructed so far (1,375 Husseys + 800 New Yorkers + 3,600 Mannys + 1,200 Atkins + 5,000 other = 11,975). We subtract this from the cumulative claim (49,901 - 11,975 = 37,926). We obtain the estimate that in the years of 1856, 1857, and 1858 that 37,926 non-McCormick reapers were produced. Assuming equal time distribution, that makes for 12,642 non-McCormick reapers produced in each of the three years. A final assumption of continuity and equal time distribution allows us to assign the year 1859 with 12,642 non-McCormick reapers produced.

In order to estimate the extent of the adoption of the reaper in 1859 we need to calculate the net reaper stock from the time series of reaper production. Procedures used to construct Table A.3 are given below.

Gross production was taken from the time series. Each year was divided into two halves, because the harvest comes in the middle of the reaper production year. I assume that half of the year's production is sold in time for the harvest of a given year, and hence, depreciated from use in that year's harvest. The reaper production after the harvest, assumed to be the second half of the annual production, is not used for that year's harvest and thus is not depreciated.

Reapers produced before the harvest of 1854 are disregarded on the assumption that the useful life of a reaper in this era was five years. Notice that none of the reapers produced in pre-harvest 1854 (nor any of those prior to that) were available for the harvest of 1859; they would have been used in five harvests and dropped out of use after their last harvest of 1858.

Assuming continuous straight line depreciation, as David did, each year one-fifth of the reapers would fall out of use. The depreciation rate is 0.2.

Table A.3
Estimate of the Net Stock of Reapers for the 1859 Harvest

Vintage	Gross Production	Proportion Left	Net Stock
I. Five years old:			
pre-harvest 1854	1,263	0.0	0
II. Four years old:			
post-harvest 1854	1,263	0.2	253
pre-harvest 1855	5,600	0.2	1,120
III. Three years old:			
post-harvest 1855	5,600	0.4	2,240
pre-harvest 1856	8,287	0.4	3,315
IV. Two years old:			
post-harvest 1856	8,287	0.6	4,972
pre-harvest 1857	8,287	0.6	4,972
V. One year old:			
post-harvest 1857	8,287	0.8	6,630
pre-harvest 1858	8,287	0.8	6,630
VI. New:			
post-harvest 1858	8,287	1.0	8,287
pre-harvest 1859	8,287	1.0	8,287
Total	71,735		46,706

Working backwards for a moment, reapers produced in the second half of 1858 and the first half of 1859 would be fresh reapers, never used before. All of them are in the stock of reapers available for the 1859 harvest. Reapers produced in the second half of 1857 and the first half of 1858 would have been used in one harvest, that of 1858. The stock net of depreciation of this vintage would be 0.8 of the production.

The four-year-old vintage reapers would lose 0.2 reapers a year, and thus only 0.2 of them would be left for the harvest of 1859. The three-year-old vintage reapers, losing 0.2 of their numbers each year, would provide 0.4 of their original machines. The two-year-old vintage reapers would have lost 0.2 of their numbers twice, thus 0.6 of them would be available for the 1859 harvest.

I estimate a gross stock of reapers (net of replacement) at 71,735 and a net stock (net of depreciation) at 46,706 full-capacity reapers. Rogin only used a gross stock and simply used the figure of 73,200. David's estimate of gross stock was 72,300 and a net stock of 50,000. My estimate reduced the stock of reapers even further than David did. Although the reduction is not large, the process I used for estimation, I believe, is more precise and representative of the circumstances.

Next we have to adjust this stock of reapers available for the American harvest, to that available for the Old Northwest. The proportion of the American wheat harvest produced in the Old Northwest was 0.46 (79.8/173 million bushels of wheat). We allot them reapers in the same proportion, to obtain a lower bound estimate (46,706 [0.46] = 21,485 reapers).

The estimate of the extent of the adoption of the reaper judged by numbers is as follows. In the Old Northwest in 1859 there were 586,800 farms. Thus the net stock of reapers could have been distributed to nearly 4 percent of the farmers (21,485/586,800 = 0.0366).

The estimate of the extent of the adoption of the reaper judged in proportion of acres of the wheat harvest mechanically cut is as follows. The actual amount of wheat harvested (by hand and machine) in the Old Northwest in 1859 was 79,798,163. Using a yield of 12.2 bushels per acres, that is 6,540,833 acres of wheat. Using the capacity of a reaper at 100 acres a season, the 21,485 reapers could have cut 2,148,500 acres of wheat, which is 32.8 percent of the total. That is, the extent of the adoption of the reaper was one-third of the wheat crop.

This is much less than Rogin's estimate of 70 percent west of the Alleghenies and David's 50 percent west of the Alleghenies, but I believe it is a more accurate estimate. The historical literature locates the 1850s adoption of the reaper in the region of the Old Northwest. Rogin and David's estimates are for a larger region that mine, the West included land west of the Mississippi and the boundary of the Old Northwest stops at the Mississippi.

If we drop the assumption of full-capacity use of the reaper stock and assume only that the reaper was used to the threshold of 78 acres instead of 100 acres full capacity, then the proportion of wheat mechanically cut is 26 percent. This was calculated by taking the product of 21,485 reapers and 78 acres harvested per reaper which is 1,675,830 acres that could have been mechanically harvested, assuming that each reaper on average was used to the threshold scale of 78 acres; 1,675,830 acres is 25.6 percent of 6,540,833 acres of wheat which was harvested (by all methods) in the Old Northwest in 1859. My best estimate is that one-quarter of the wheat harvest was cut mechanically by 4 percent of the farmers.

MACRO-ESTIMATE FOR HARVEST OF 1849

This calculation is made in order to compare before and after the first wave of popular acceptance of the reaper. We obtain the gross reaper stock from the production time series and divide it into the two half-years. Before 1848 the useful life was two years. The machines that were two years old in

1849 are therefore not included in the net stock. From 1848 the useful life was five years.[8] Reapers produced in 1848 and 1849 will be included.

As to the stock, net of depreciations, one-year-old reapers produced after the 1847 harvest, would have been used in the harvest of 1848, and since the depreciation rate prior to 1848 was 0.5, we have to discount half of these reapers. One-year-old reapers produced before the 1848 harvest would have been used one year, but their depreciation rate is 0.2 a year, thus 0.8 of them would be available for the 1849 harvest. New reapers, produced after the 1848 harvest and before the 1849 harvest, would be totally available for the 1849 harvest.

Thus there were 2,178 reapers available for the harvest in 1849. The net stock in 1859 of 46,706 represents more than a twentyfold increase. See calculations in Table A.4.

Given the reaper stock of 2,178 available for the whole United States, we take 0.46 of them as available for the Old Northwest because in 1849 39.3 million bushels of wheat of the 85.9 million bushels produced in the United States were produced in the Old Northwest. We obtain 1,002 reapers (0.46 [2,178] available for the 1849 harvest in the Old Northwest).

In 1849 there were 368,177 farms in the region, thus distribution of the 1,002 reapers makes for under 1 percent of the farms that could have had reapers.

Assuming full-capacity use, the 1,002 reapers could have cut 100,200 acres of wheat; 39.3 million bushels were harvested, which at 12.2 bushels an acres, makes 3,221,311 acres. Therefore, 100,200/3.2 million is 3 percent of the wheat harvested that could have been cut mechanically.

Table A.4
Estimate of the Net Stock of Reapers for the 1849 Harvest

Vintage	Gross Production	Proportion Left	Net Stock
Two year old:			
post-harvest 1846		0	
pre-harvest 1847		0	
One year old:			
post-harvest 1847	268	0.5	134
pre-harvest 1848	418	0.8	334
New			
post-harvest 1848	418	1.0	418
pre-harvest 1849	1,292	1.0	1,292
Total	6,396		2,178

Assuming 0.78 capacity use (using it at the profit threshold level), the 1,002 reapers could have cut 78,156 acres of wheat (78,156/3.2 million is 2.4 percent).

MICRO-ESTIMATE OF THE EXTENT OF REAPER ADOPTION, HARVEST 1859

The objective of this section of the appendix is to make a micro-estimate of the extent of reaper adoption in the Old Northwest in 1859. Micro means an estimate of the individual farms that adopted the reaper. This method makes use of manuscript census sample. The census did not ask if the farmer had a reaper, but it did ask how much wheat was produced, what the value of the farm implements and machinery was, and how many horses there were.

A threefold criteria will be used to infer that the farmer had adopted the reaper: first, the farm must report $200 or more as the value of its farm implements and machinery; second, the farm must report 20 or more acres of wheat; and third, the farm must report two or more horses. All three criteria must be fulfilled. A second estimate will be made on the basis of the value of farm implements being reported as $150 or more, to give us an upper bound estimate, and thus a range, rather than a point estimate. I arrived at this criteria by the following line of reasoning.

First, what value of implements must a farmer have reported to the census enumerator, for us to safely infer that he owned a reaper. We need two preliminary estimates: on one hand, the value of farm implements other than the reaper expected to be on a farm, and on the other hand, the value of a mechanical reaper on the farm. Together these two form a threshold value of implements and machinery for inferring reaper ownership.

As to the value of farm implements without a reaper, there is a literature on the costs of farm-making associated with the debate on the safety-valve theory put forward by the students of F. J. Turner. Danhof estimated that it took $1,000 to make a farm in the 1850s of which $100 was for farm implements.[9] This is cash outlay, not value reported at the time of census, thus it may be too high for our criterion. Furthermore, Rasmussen argues that when asked for the value of his implements and machinery, that the farmer would think only of the big items he had.[10] Discounting the $100 for these two reasons, we assume that the farm implements not including a reaper would be worth under $100.

As to the value of the reaper, David used the figure $138 for the cost of a delivered reaper (from Chicago to Peoria by rail) in 1860. The boom was in the mid-1850s and most of the reapers were bought then. By 1859, the year that the 1860 census asked about, the reaper would be quite depreciated, so let us estimate that it was worth just over $100.

If we add together less than $100 in implements and more than $100 in the reaper, then as an estimate of the value of implements and machinery on a farm needed to infer reaper ownership, we obtain $200. However, to get a range estimate, we make a less stringent criterion of $150 based upon the assumption that farmers may have underestimated the value of their implements and machinery (and other estimates) out of distrust of the federal government.[11] Therefore, $150 would be made up of $75 worth of general farming implements and a reaper valued at $75.

How much wheat needs to have been produced on a farm to conclude that it had adopted a reaper? How much wheat could a farmer harvest by hand himself, not relying on sons or hired labor which was scarce and unreliable? The general opinion was that a man could harvest two acres a day. David uses 2.1 because farming was more extensive in the West. Rasmussen, however, argues that in the states of the Old Northwest the farming was not extensive as it became further west and therefore the two acres a day is the appropriate figure to use. We debated more fully the number of days that the farmer would have to harvest his wheat. Rogin and David use ten working days. Recall that the whole issue of the adoption of the reaper is a bottleneck issue, that there are just so many days in which to harvest or the crop can be lost. On one hand, there was the weather: the possibility of wind that would knock off the grain, as in the case of rain or hailstorms. On the other hand, wheat ripens fast and can shatter when cut too ripe; it falls to the ground and cannot be retrieved. To plan ten days for the harvest of wheat was risky, argues Rasmussen. Yet we can calculate that a farmer could achieve it in ten days. Thus we have ten days at two acres a day making 20 acres of wheat that could be harvested by hand.

The census reported wheat output in bushels. To convert this into acres, we use a yield of 12.2 bushels per acre, based on Parker and Klein. I think it is reasonable to require at least 20 acres of wheat, before inferring that a farmer had adopted a reaper. The criterion then is 244 bushels of wheat or more. The binding constraint is the value of the implements. The acreage of wheat is just to insure that the farmer produced wheat and that the value of the implements includes a reaper.

The inclusion of the horse criteria makes the inference more safe. This was suggested by Rasmussen because the mechanical reaper required two horses to pull it so that it went fast enough for the blades to cut. The ox was not fast enough. This reminds us that the mechanical reaper was not just a machine but also the substitution of animal power for manpower. Bogue's chapter on farm machinery is called learning to farm sitting down.

The results of using this threefold criterion to estimate at the micro-level farms that adopted the reaper are: the lower bound estimate based on the value of implements of $200 or more, is 268 farms (5 percent), which produced 129,191 bushels of wheat (18.7 percent). The upper bound estimate when the value of implements is $150 or more is 370 farms (6 percent), producing 174,840 bushels of wheat (25.2 percent).

NOTES

1. Leo Rogin, *The Introduction of Farm Machinery* (Berkeley: University of California Press, 1931), pp. 78-79.

2. Paul David, "Mechanization of Reaping in the Ante-Bellum Midwest," in Henry Rosovsky (Ed.), *Industrialization in Two Systems: Essays in Honor of Alexander Gershenkron* (New York: John Wiley & Sons, 1966), pp. 10-11.

3. This figure of 73,200 comes from the decision of the Commissioner of Patents in January 1859. It was incorrectly reported in *Country Gentleman*, 1859, as the number of reapers available in 1858. This is the source and interpretation used by Rogin. David correctly designates it as the production of reapers between 1845-1858.

4. David, "Mechanization," p. 11.

5. Wayne Rasmussen, "Mechanization of Agriculture," *Scientific American* 247 (September 1982):76 and personal communication.

6. Clarence Danhof, *Changes in Agriculture* (Cambridge: Harvard University Press, 1969), p. 245.

7. William Parker, "Agriculture," in Lance Davis et al. (Eds.), *American Economic Growth* (New York: Harper and Row, 1972), p. 379.

8. Danhof, *Changes*, pp. 235-36.

9. Clarence Danhof, "Farm-Making Costs," *Journal of Political Economy* 49 (June 1941): 317-59. Also see Robert E. Ankli, "Farm-Making Costs in the 1850s," *Agricultural History* 48 (January 1974): 51-70; and Judith L. V. Klein, "Farm-Making Costs in the 1850's: A Comment," *Agricultural History* 48 (January 1974): 71-74. Both reprinted in James W. Whitaker (Ed.), *Farming in the Midwest, 1840-1900: A Symposium* (Washington D.C.: The Agricultural History Society, 1974).

10. Personal communication.

11. Investigating the manuscript census schedules at the National Archives, I found a message from a census enumerator which said that he could not confirm his figures because the farmers were not very forthcoming in their answers to his queries.

APPENDIX B:
FARM VARIABLES

Observations on the farm variables were taken. Univariate analysis were run and the results are reported in Table B.1. Statistics are based on 5,756 farms.

Table B.1
Observations on Farm Variables

Characteristic	Aggregate	Mean	Median	Mode
Land, improved acres	369,671	64	50	40
Land, total acres	711,117	124	89	80
Wheat (acres)	692,553	10	6	0
Corn (acres)	2,850,667	15	9	9
Specialization		0.36	0.34	
Value of Farm($)	14,237,489	2,474	1,800	2,000
Value of Livestock($)	2,287,257	397	300	300
Value of Implements($)	517,169	90	75	100
Adoption of the Reaper VOI = $200, n = 268				
Wheat (acres)	10,589	40	33	25
VOI ($)	86,230	322	258	200
Adoption of the Reaper VOI = $150, n = 370				
Wheat (acres)	14,331	39	33	25
VOI ($)	101,894	275	200	200

Source: Fred Bateman and James D. Foust, *Agricultural and Demographic Records for Rural Households in the North, 1860* (Ann Arbor, MI: Inter-University Consortium for Political and Social Research, 1976).

Note: VOI means value of implements.

APPENDIX C: TOWNSHIP VARIABLES

Observations were taken at the township level. Statistics were calculated and are reported in Table C.1. Statistics are based on 46 townships.

Table C.1
Observations on Township Variables

Characteristic	Mean	Median	Mode	Max	Min
Adoption of Reaper:					
$150	0.06	0.03	0	0.50	
$200	0.04	0.02	0	0.42	
Land, improved acres	65	57	49	187	11
Land, total acres	135	121	86	398	56
Value of farm ($)	2,340	2,383	238	5,607	238
Value of implements ($)	85	75	68	234	16
Specialization	0.37	0.34	0	0.93	0
Land Equality	0.17	0.17	0	0.49	0
I.A./LF	43	40	5	126	5
FE/FO	0.65	0.55	0.20	2.27	-0.07
Wheat(acres)	9	7	0	30	0
Land Concentration	0.37	0.33	0.30	0.86	0.26

Source: Fred Bateman and James D. Foust, *Agricultural and Demographic Records for Rural Households in the North, 1860* (Ann Arbor, MI: Inter-University Consortium for Political and Social Research, 1976).

Note: Specialization is specialization in wheat compared to corn in value terms; land equality is the proportion of farms in the township that are 40 total acres or less; I.A./LF is improved acres in the township divided by the labor force; FE/FO is farm employees per farm operator; Land Concentration is the proportion of land in improved acres operated by the top 10 percent of farms.

BIBLIOGRAPHY

Adelman, Irma, and Cynthia Taft Morris. "Patterns of Industrialization in the Nineteenth and Early Twentieth Centuries: A Cross-Sectional Quantitative Study." *Research in Economic History* (1980): 1-83.

_____. "Patterns of Market Expansion in the Nineteenth Century: A Quantitative Study." *Research in Economic Anthropology* 1 (1978): 231-324.

Adelman, Irma, and Sherman Robinson. *Income Distribution Policy in Developing Countries: A Case Study of Korea.* Stanford, CA: Stanford University Press, 1978.

Amemiya, Takeshi. "Qualitative Response Models: A Survey." *Journal of Economic Literature* 19 (December 1981): 1,483-1,536.

Anderson, Perry. *Lineages of the Absolutist State.* London: New Left Books, 1974.

_____. *Passages from Antiquity to Feudalism.* London: New Left Books, 1974.

Anderson, Russell H. "Agriculture in Illinois During the Civil War Period." Ph.D. diss., University of Illinois, 1929.

Ankli, Robert E. "Farm-Making Costs in the 1850s." *Agricultural History* 48 (January 1974): 51-70.

Archives Municipales et al. *Nice et la provence orientale à la fin du moyen-age.* Nice: Mairie de Nice, 1989.

Aston, T. H. and C. H. E. Philpin (Eds.). *The Brenner Debate: Agrarian Class Structure and Economic Development in Pre-Industrial Europe.* New York: Cambridge University Press, 1985.

Atack, J. and F. Bateman. "The 'Egalitarian Ideal' and the Distribution of Wealth in the Northern Agricultural Community: A Backward Look." *Review of Economics and Statistics* 63 (February 1981): 124-29.

_____. "Egalitarianism, Inequality and Age: The Rural North in 1860." *Journal of Economic History* 41 (March 1981): 85-93.

_____. "Self-Sufficiency and the Origins of the Marketable Surplus in the Rural North, 1860." Paper presented at the Social Science History Association Meetings, Washington, D.C., Fall, 1983.

_____. *To Their Own Soil: Agriculture in the Antebellum North*. Ames: Iowa State University Press, 1987.

Barkley, Paul W. "A Contemporary Political Economy of Family Farming" *American Journal of Agricultural Economics* 58 (December 1976): 812-19.

Bateman, Fred, and Jeremy Atack. "The Profitability of Northern Agriculture in 1860." *Research in Economic History* 4 (1979): 87-125.

Bateman, Fred, and James D. Foust. *Agricultural and Demographic Records for Rural Households in the North, 1860*. Inter-University Consortium for Political and Social Research. Computer Tape no. 7420. (August 1976) Ann Arbor, Michigan.

_____. "A Sample of Rural Households Selected from the 1860 Manuscript Censuses." *Agricultural History* 48 (1974): 75-93.

Bateman, Fred, and Thomas Weiss. *A Deplorable Scarcity: The Failure of Industrialization in the Slave Economy*. Chapel Hill: University of North Carolina Press, 1981.

Bator, Francis M. "The Simple Analytics of Welfare Maximization." *American Economic Review* (March 1957): 22-59.

Beard, Charles A., and Mary R. Beard. *The Rise of American Civilization*. New York: Macmillan, 1930.

Bernard, Jacques. "Trade and Finance in the Middle Ages, 900-1500." In *The Middle Ages* (Fontana Economic History of Europe) Glasgow: Collins/Fontana, 1972.

Bidwell, Percy W., and John I. Falconer. *History of Agriculture in the Northern United States, 1620-1860*. Washington, D.C.: Carnegie Institute, 1925.

Blalock, Hubert M. *Theory Construction: From Verbal to Mathematical Formulations*. Englewood Cliffs, NJ: Prentice-Hall, 1969.

Bogue, Allan G. *From Prairie to Corn Belt: Farming on the Illinois and Iowa Prairies in the 19th Century*. Chicago: University of Chicago Press, 1963.

Boserup, Mogens. "Agrarian Structure and Take-Off." In *The Economics of Take-Off into Sustained Growth*, pp. 201-24. Edited by W. W. Rostow. London: Macmillan, 1968.

Braudel, Fernand. *The Mediterranean and The Mediterranean World in the Age of Philip II*. 2 vols. Translated from the French by Sian Reynolds. New York: Harper and Row, 1972.

Brenner, Robert. "The Origins of Capitalist Development: a Critique of Neo-Smithian Marxism," *New Left Review* 104 (July/August 1976): 25-92.

Brewster, David E., Wayne D. Rasmussen, and Garth Youngberg. *Farms in Transition: Interdisciplinary Perspectives in Farm Structure*. Ames: Iowa State University Press, 1983.

Buley, R. Carlyle. *The Old Northwest: Pioneer Period, 1815-1840*. Indianapolis: Indiana Historical Society, 1950.

Carter, Harvey L. "Rural Indiana in Transition: 1850-1860." *Agricultural History* 2 (April 1946): 107-21.

Chandler, Alfred D. *The Visible Hand: The Managerial Revolution in American Business*. Boston: Harvard University Press, 1977.

Cobden Club. *Systems of Land Tenure in Various Countries*. London: Macmillan and Co., 1870.

Comstock, Gary (Ed.). *Is There a Moral Obligation to Save the Family Farm?* Ames: Iowa State University Press, 1987.

Curwen, E.C. *Plough and Pasture*. London: Cobbett Press, 1946.

Danhof, Clarence. *Changes in Agriculture: the Northern U.S., 1820-1870*. Cambridge, MA: Harvard University Press, 1969.

_____. "Farm-Making Costs and the 'Safety Valve': 1850-1860." *Journal of Political Economy* 49 (June 1941): 317-59.

David, Paul A. "The Landscape and the Machine: Technical Inter-relatedness, Land Tenure and the Mechanization of the Corn Harvest in Victorian Britain." In *Essays on a Mature Economy: Britain after 1840*. Edited by Donald N. McCloskey. Princeton, NJ: Princeton University Press, 1971.

_____. "Mechanization of Reaping in the Ante-Bellum Midwest." In *Industrialization in Two Systems: Essays in Honor of Alexander Gershenkron*, pp. 3-39. Edited by Henry Rosovsky. New York: John Wiley & Sons, 1966.

Dobb, Maurice. *Studies in the Development of Capitalism*. London: Routledge & Kegan Paul, 1963.

Dorfman, Robert. "Mathematical, or 'Linear,' Programming: A Nonmathematical Exposition." *American Economic Review* (December 1953): 797-825.

Easterlin, Richard A. "Population Change and Farm Settlement in the Northern United States." *Journal of Economic History* 36 (March 1976): 45-83.

Fei, John C. H., Gustav Ranis, and Shirley W. Y. Kuo. *Growth with Equity: The Taiwan Case*. New York: Oxford University Press, 1979.

Fields, Gary S. *Poverty, Inequality, and Development*. New York: Cambridge University Press, 1980.

Fishlow, Albert. *American Railroads and the Transformation of the Antebellum Economy*. Cambridge, MA: Harvard University Press, 1965.

Fleisig, Heywood. "Slavery, the Supply of Agricultural Labor, and the Industrialization of the South." *Journal of Economic History* 36 (September 1976): 572-97.

Fogel, Robert William. *Railroads and American Economic Growth: Essays in Econometric History*. Baltimore: The Johns Hopkins Press, 1964.

Fogel, Robert William and Stanley L. Engerman. *Time on the Cross: The Economics of American Negro Slavery*. Boston: Little, Brown, 1974.

Foner, Eric. *Free Soil, Free Labor, Free Men: The Ideology of the Republican Party Before the Civil War*. New York: Oxford University Press, 1970.

_____. *Reconstruction: the Unfinished Revolution, 1863-1877*. New York: Harper and Row, 1988.

Foster-Carter, Aidan. "The Modes of Production Controversy." *New Left Review* 107 (January/February 1978).

Gates, Paul W. *The Farmer's Age: Agriculture 1815-1860*. Vol. 3 of *The Economic History of the United States*. New York: Harper and Row, 1960.

_____. "The Role of the Land Speculator in Western Development." 165-179. In *Issues in American Economic History: Selected Readings*, 2nd ed. Edited by G. D. Nash. Lexington, Massachusetts: D.C. Heath and Co., 1972.

Genovese, Eugene D. *The Political Economy of Slavery: Studies on the Economy and Society of the Slave South*. New York: Random House, 1965.

Gerschenkron, Alexander. *Continuity in History and Other Essays*. Cambridge: Harvard University Press, 1968.

_____. *Economic Backwardness in Historical Perspective*. Cambridge: Harvard University Press, 1962.

Ghatak, Subrata, and Ken Ingersent. *Agriculture and Economic Development*. Baltimore: Johns Hopkins University Press, 1986.

Green, Rodney. "Urban Industry, Black Resistance, and Racial Restriction in the Antebellum South: A General Model and a Case Study in Urban Virginia." Ph.D. diss. American University, Washington, D.C. 1980.

Gregory, Paul R., and Robert C. Stuart. *Soviet Economic Structure and Performance*. New York: Harper and Row, 1986.

Grigg, David. "The Geography of Farm Size." *Economic Geography* 42 (July 1966): 205-35.

Hacker, Louis M. *The Triumph of American Capitalism: The Development of Forces in American History to the End of the Nineteenth Century*. New York: Columbia University Press, 1947 (originally 1940).

Henretta, James A. "Families and Farms: Mentalité in Pre-industrial America," *William and Mary Quarterly* 35, 3rd series (1978): 3-32.

Hilton, Rodney (Ed.). *The Transition from Feudalism to Capitalism*. London: New Left Books, 1978.

Hirschman, A. O. *The Strategy of Economic Development*. New Haven: Yale University Press, 1958.

Hoffman, W. G. *The Growth of Industrial Economies*. New York: Oceana, 1958.

Hughes, Jonathan. *American Economic History*. 3rd ed. Glenview, IL: Scott, Foresman, 1990.

_____. *The Governmental Habit: Economic Controls from Colonial Times to the Present*. New York: Basic Books, 1977.

_____. *Industrialization and Economic History: Theses and Conjectures*. New York: McGraw-Hill, 1970.

Hutchinson, William T. *Cyrus Hall McCormick: Vol. 1 Seed Time, Vol. 2 Harvest*. New York: D. Appleton Century Co., 1930, 1935.

Johnston, Bruce F., and John W. Mellor. "The Role of Agriculture in Economic Development," *American Economic Review* 1961.

Jones, E. L. and S. J. Woolfe (Eds.). *Agrarian Change and Economic Development: the Historical Problems*. London: Methuen and Co., 1969.

Jones, Lewis R. "'The Mechanization of Reaping and Mowing in American Agriculture, 1833-1870': Comment." *Journal of Economic History* 37 (June 1977): 451-55.

Jones, Ronald W. "The Structure of Simple General Equilibrium Models." *The Journal of Political Economy* 73 (December 1965): 557-72.

Jorgenson, D. W., and Z. Griliches. "The Explanation of Productivity Change." *Review of Economic Studies* 34 (1967): 249-83.

Josephson, Matthew. *The Robber Barons: The Great American Capitalists, 1861-1901*. New York: Harcourt Brace Jovanovich, 1934.

Kellar, Herbert A. "The Reaper as a Factor in the Development of the Agriculture of Illinois, 1834-1865." *Transactions* 34 (1927) Illinois State Historical Society, pp. 105-14.

Kelly, Kevin D. "The Independent Mode of Production," *Review of Radical Political Economy* 11 (Spring 1979).

Kennedy, Gavin. *Invitation to Statistics*. Oxford: Martin Robertson, 1983.

Klein, Judith L. V. "'Farm-Making Costs in the 1850s': A Comment." *Agricultural History* 48 (January 1974): 71-74.

Klingamon, David C. and Vedder, Richard. *Essays in Nineteenth Century Economic History: The Old Northwest*. Athens: Ohio University Press, 1975.

Kmenta, Jan. *Elements of Econometrics*. New York: Macmillan Co., 1971.

Knodell, Jane. "Innovation and Integration in Interregional Finance: The Old Northwest, 1810-1845." Paper presented at the annual meeting of the Economic History Association, San Francisco, September 17-20, 1987.

Kohlmeier, A. L. *The Old Northwest as the Keystone of the Arch of the American Federal Union*. Bloomington, IN: Principia Press, 1938.

Lapasset, M. "Menton sous les Vento," *Bulletin de la Société d'Art d'Histoire du Mentonnais*, no. 54 (Juin 1990).

Lebergott, Stanley. *Manpower in Economic Growth: The American Record Since 1800*. New York: McGraw-Hill Co., 1964.

Le Roy Ladurie, Emmanuel. *The Peasants of Languedoc*. Translated from the French by John Day. Chicago: University of Chicago Press, 1976.

Lewis, W. Arthur. *The Evolution of the International Economic Order*. Princeton: Princeton University Press, 1978.

Locke, John. *Second Treatise of Civil Government*. In *Two Treatises of Government*. London: Everyman's Library, 1924.

Maddala, G. S. *Limited-dependent and Qualitative Variables in Econometrics*. New York: Cambridge University Press, 1983.

Marx, Karl. *Capital*, 3 vols. New York: International Publishers, 1976.

Mathur, Subodh C. "Econometric Methods and Applications." Washington, D.C.: manuscript, 1984 (to locate this manuscript, contact this author or Dr. Mathur at the World Bank).

McCusker, John J., and Russell R. Menard. *The Economy of British America, 1607-1789*. Chapel Hill: University of North Carolina, 1985.

McPherson, James M. *Battle Cry of Freedom: The Civil War Era*. New York: Ballantine Books, 1988.

Meier, Gerald M. *Emerging from Poverty: The Economics That Really Matters*. New York: Oxford University Press, 1984.

Mendels, Franklin. "La Composition du Menage Paysan en France au XIXe siecle: une analyse economique du Mode de Production Domestique." *Annales E.S.C.* 4 (1978): 780-802.

Moore, Barrington, Jr. *Social Origins of Dictatorship and Democracy: Lord and Peasant in the Making of the Modern World*. Boston: Beacon Press, 1966.

Morris, Cynthia Taft, and Irma Adelman. *Comparative Patterns of Economic Development, 1850-1914*. Baltimore: Johns Hopkins University Press, 1988.

Morgan, Dan. *Merchants of Grain*. New York: Penguin Books, 1980.

Newell, William H. "The Agricultural Revolution in Nineteenth-Century France." *Journal of Economic History* 33 (December 1973): 697-731.

Nikolitch, Radoje. "Family Labor and Technological Advance in Farming." *Journal of Farm Economics* 44 (November 1962): 1,061-68.

_____. "Family Operated Farms: Their Compatibility with Technological Advance." *American Journal of Agricultural Economics* 51 (August 1969): 530-45.

North, Douglass C. *Growth and Welfare in the American Past: A New Economic History.* 2nd ed. Englewood Cliffs, NJ: Prentice-Hall, 1974.

North, Douglass C., and R. P. Thomas. "The Rise and Fall of the Manorial System." *Journal of Economic History* 31 (1971).

_____. *The Rise of the Western World.* New York: Cambridge University Press, 1973.

O'Connor, James. "The Twisted Dream." *Monthly Review* 26, 10 (March 1975).

Olmstead, Alan L. "The Diffusion of the Reaper: One More Time!" *Journal of Economic History* 39 (June 1979): 475-76.

_____. "The Mechanization of Reaping and Mowing in American Agriculture, 1833-1870." *Journal of Economic History* 35 (June 1975): 327-52.

Parker, William N. "Agriculture." In *American Economic Growth, an Economist's History of the United States,* p. 369-417. Edited by Lance E. Davis et al. New York: Harper and Row, 1972.

_____. "American Economic Growth: Its Historiography in the Twentieth Century," *Ventures* (Fall 1968): 71-82

Parker, W. N. and Klein, J. L. "Productivity Growth in Grain Production in the U.S., 1840-60 and 1900-10." In *Output, Employment, and Productivity in the U.S. after 1800,* pp. 523-46. Edited by Dorothy S. Brady. *Studies in Income and Wealth* vol. 30. New York: National Bureau of Economic Research, 1966.

Pindyck, Robert S., and Daniel L. Rubinfeld. "Models of Qualitative Choice," pp. 273-315. In *Econometric Models, Economic Forecasts.* New York: McGraw Hill, 1981.

Pomfret, Richard. "The Mechanization of Reaping in Nineteenth-Century Ontario: A Case Study of the Pace and Causes of the Diffusion of Embodied Technical Change." *Journal of Economic History* 36 (June 1976): 399-415.

Post, Charles. "The American Road to Capitalism." *New Left Review* 133 (May/June 1982).

Postan, M.M. "The Chronology of Labor Services." *Transactions of the Royal Historical Society* 20, 4th series (1937).

_____. The Rise of the Money Economy." *Economic History Review* 14 (1944).

Potter, Jim. "Some British Reflections on Turner and the Frontier." *Wisconsin Magazine of History.* 53 (Winter 1969-70): 98-107.

Ransom, Roger. *Conflict and Compromise: The Political Economy of Slavery, Emancipation, and the American Civil War.* New York: Cambridge University Press, 1989.

Ransom, Roger, and Richard Sutch. *One Kind of Freedom: The Economic Consequences of Emancipation.* New York: Cambridge University Press, 1977.

Rasmussen, Wayne D. "The Civil War: A Catalyst of Agricultural Revolution." *Agricultural History* 39 (October 1965): 187-95.

_____. "The Mechanization of Agriculture." *Scientific American* 247 (September 1982): 76-89.

Ricardo, David. "An Essay on the Influence of a Low Price of Corn on the Profits of Stock." In *The Works of David Ricardo* vol. 4, pp. 9-41. Edited by P. Sraffa. Originally 1815.

Rogin, Leo. *The Introduction of Farm Machinery in its Relation to the Productivity of Labor in the Agriculture of the U.S. during the Nineteenth Century*. Berkeley: University of California Press, 1931.

Rosenberg, Nathan. *The American System of Manufacturing*. Edinburgh: University of Edinburgh Press, 1969.

_____. "The Direction of Technological Change: Inducement Mechanisms and Focusing Devices." *Economic Development and Cultural Change* 18 (October 1969): 1-24.

_____. *Technology and American Economic Growth*. White Plains, NY: M. E. Sharpe, Inc., 1972.

Rothstein, Morton. "The Big Farm: Abundance and Scale in American Agriculture." *Agricultural History* 49 (October 1975): 583-97.

Seltzer, Leon E. (Ed.). *The Columbia Lippincott Gazetteer of the World*. New York: Columbia University Press, 1952.

Sen, Amartya. *On Economic Inequality*. Oxford: Oxford University Press, 1973.

Shaffer, John W. *Family and Farm: Agrarian Change and Household Organization in the Loire Valley, 1500-1900*. Albany: State University of New York Press, 1982.

Sherry, Robert. "Comments on O'Connor's Review of *The Twisted Dream*: Independent Commodity Production Versus Petty-Bourgeois Production." *Monthly Review* 28, 1 (May 1976).

Singh, Inderjit, Lyn Squire, and John Strauss (Eds.). *Agricultural Household Models*. Baltimore: Johns Hopkins University Press, 1986.

Social Science Research Council. *The Social Sciences in Historical Study*. A Report on Historiography, Bulletin 64. New York: Social Science Research Council, 1954.

Solow, Robert M. "Technical Change and the Aggregate Production Function." *Review of Economics and Statistics* 39 (1957): 312-20.

Stewart, Robert M. (Ed.) *Readings in Social and Political Philosophy*. New York: Oxford University Press, 1986.

Swan, T. W. "Economic Growth and Capital Accumulation." *The Economic Record* 32 (November 1956): 477-86.

Taylor, George Rogers. *The Transformation Revolution, 1815-1860*. In *The Economic History of the U.S.*, vol 4. New York: Holt, Rinehart and Winston, 1951.

Temin, Peter. *Causal Factors in American Economic Growth in the Nineteenth Century*. In *Studies in Economic History*, vol. 12. London: Macmillian, 1975.

Thompson, E. P. *The Making of the English Working Class*. New York: Random House, 1963.

Towne, Marvin W., and Wayne D. Rasmussen. "Farm Gross Product and Gross Investment During the Nineteenth Century." In *Trends in the American Economy in the 19th Century*, pp. 255-312. *Studies in Income and Wealth*, vol. 24. Princeton: Princeton University Press, 1960.

"Trial of Reapers and Mowers." *Transactions* 2 (1856-1857): 116-124. Springfield, IL: Illinois State Agricultural Society, 1857.

Turner, Frederick Jackson. *The Frontier in American History*. New York: Henry Holt, 1920.

U.S. Census, *Agriculture of the United States in 1860; Compiled from the Original Returns of the Eighth Census*. Washington, D.C., Government Printing Office, 1864.

_____. *The Eighth Census of the United States, 1860, Population*. Washington, D.C.,
        Government Printing Office, 1864.

_____. *Historical Statistics of the U.S., Colonial Times to 1957*. Washington, D.C.:
        Government Printing Office, 1960.

_____. *Manuscript Censuses, 1840*. Washington, D.C.: National Archives.

_____. *The Seventh Census of the United States, 1850, Agriculture*. Washington,
        D.C., Robert Armstrong, 1853.

U.S. Department of Agriculture. *Chronological Landmarks in American Agriculture*.
        Information Bulletin 425 (May 1979).

Wachtel, Howard. *Labor and the Economy*. New York: Harcourt Brace, Jovanovich,
        1984.

Weeks, John. *Capital and Exploitation*. Princeton: Princeton University Press, 1981.

_____. *The Economies of Central America*. New York: Holmes and Meier, 1985.

Weir, David. "Stabilization Regained: A Reappraisal of the U.S. Macroeconomic
        Record, 1890-1980." Paper presented at Washington Area Economic
        History Seminar, August 11, 1985, Washington, D.C.

Whitaker, James W. (Ed.). *Farming in the Midwest 1840-1900*. Washington, D.C.:
        The Agricultural History Society, 1974.

Williamson, J.G. "Greasing the Wheels of Sputtering Export Engines: Midwestern
        Grains and American Growth." *Explorations in Economic History* 17 (July
        1980): 189-217.

_____. *Late Nineteenth Century American Development: a General Equilibrium
        History*. Cambridge: Cambridge University Press, 1974.

_____. "Watersheds and Turning Points: Conjectures on the Long-Term Impact
        of Civil War Financing." *Journal of Economic History* 34, 3 (September
        1974).

Wright, Carroll D. *The History and Growth of the U.S. Census*. Washington, D.C.:
        Government Printing Office, 1900.

Wright, Gavin. *Old South, New South: Revolutions in the Southern Economy Since the
        Civil War*. New York: Basic Books, 1986.

_____. *The Political Economy of the Cotton South: Households, Markets, and Wealth
        in the Nineteenth Century*. New York: W. W. Norton, 1978.

Yang, Donghyu. "Notes on the Wealth Distribution of Farm Households in the
        United States, 1860: A New Look at Two Manuscript Census Samples."
        Explorations in Economic History 21 (January 1984): 88-102.

INDEX

ABOUT THE AUTHOR

SUE HEADLEE is Assistant Professor in the Department of Economics at The American University in Washington, D.C. She teaches economic policy in the Washington Semester Program.